# The Grassroots
of Democracy

# The Grassroots of Democracy

## A Comparative Study of Competition and Its Impact in American Cities in the 1990s

### Norman R. Luttbeg

LEXINGTON BOOKS
*Lanham • Boulder • New York • Oxford*

149311

LEXINGTON BOOKS

Published in the United States of America
by Lexington Books
4720 Boston Way, Lanham, Maryland 20706

12 Hid's Copse Road
Cumnor Hill, Oxford OX2 9JJ, England

British Library Cataloguing in Publication Information Available

**Library of Congress Cataloging-in-Publication Data**

Luttbeg, Norman R.
  The grassroots of democracy  :  a comparative study of competition and its impact
in American cities in the 1990s  /  Norman R. Luttbeg.
    p.    cm.
  Includes bibliographical references and index.
  ISBN 0-7391-0047-5 (cloth  :  alk. paper)
  1. Democracy—United States.  2. Political participation—United States.
3. Municipal government—United States.  4. Cities and towns—United States.
I. Title.
JK1726.L88      1999
320.973'09173'2—dc21                                                    99-43467
                                                                         CIP

Printed in the United States of America

⊖™ The paper used in this publication meets the minimum requirements of American
National Standard for Information Sciences—Permanence of Paper for Printed Library
Materials, ANSI/NISO Z39.48–1992.

This may well be my last book. Like the first, I dedicate it to my father. In his spare time he repaired radios and televisions. I presume that I owe my philosophy of science to his guidance however unintended. Certainly, he was happy when his hypothesis worked out and swore when it did not. I have kept up the tradition even though here I swore more often than I would like. Hopefully my many negative findings will result in further studies that will lead to improvements in our cities.

# Contents

# Preface

City government is "The government closest to the people." I do not know when I first heard this phrase, but it certainly is, in one sense, quite true. We all typically live physically much closer to our local governments. But it was the broader sense that most attracted me, the idea that this government is most responsive and presumably most accountable. Ironically, my career-long interest in questions of representation has, in this monograph, taken me back to studying city governance. My dissertation focused on whether those whose views failed to be reflected in the views of city elites showed they were aware of this lack of representation. I found little to suggest that they did. Here I study competition in municipal elections. Competitive elections are supposed to be the means by which the electorate enforces its sentiments on representatives and thereby policy. One reason I studied cities is that this is supposed to be the most responsive government. Social science is not without critics who say that democracy in at least many cities is nonexistent as elections are manipulated, often by being noncompetitive. At essence, this is my question. Does it matter if elections are competitive in our local governments?

Studying cities, especially 118 randomly chosen cities, has the advantage of having a large sample with some cities being more wealthy southern cities and some poorer northern cities. Moreover, some cities have majority minorities, and some very low taxes and services. While most of the questions I seek to answer in this effort have been answered at the state level, there is always the problem that the South stands out as uncompetitive, nonparticipant, poor, rural, and with few government services. We cannot be certain of the dynamic that interconnects these variables. When we study cities, however, we have greater variations. This is the second reason I studied cities.

While urban America is the center of most of our social problems, such a perspective mainly focuses on core cities rather than the suburbs or autonomous smaller cities. While decline is a major problem in older urban America, I would argue growth is the problem of most American cities. Some would argue that growth cannot or should not be resisted. I often have had the sense, however, that while the pro-growth position is the predominant and most often expressed preference among city council members and candidates for those offices, opposition to growth is the basis of very many challenges to city council incumbents. It is the underlying basis for criticism of most cities' actions. Having lived in too many rapidly growing cities, I continue to be curious why most councils embrace growth.

The study of cities, however, is very inconvenient. No one gathers many of the data on cities that most interest us, meaning that to gather these data one must approach all cities in the study. A large representative sample therefore means many interactions with the number one provider of city data, the city secretary or clerk. While federal law says this information must be publicly available, no money flows to the cities to gather, much less to retain, these data. To study city elections means that you must communicate with the city secretary, that she must take time to gather these data, and that the press of other business in these offices means that the data may be slow in coming. Obviously only through the efforts of these secretaries could these data be gathered. I thank them all even though some grew very short with me as I struggled to understand what I was being told.

American cities certainly have great institutional variations. One city in the sample used all district elections in one election only and abandoned it when many voters had to be escorted out of the polling place where they were not allowed to vote, as their district was not on the ballot at the time. I struggled to understand why turnout was so low for one election. Having not asked if they had ever tried district elections, I was never told they had. Only a follow-up call to the city manager's office revealed what had happened. Such are the difficulties of comparing city elections from all parts of the country. I should say that at first I had hoped to gather comparable information of school districts serving these cities. Here comparable data across the country is even more difficult.

This research has little national appeal, and interest groups in this area may not want to know what the data show. Not surprisingly, it was unfunded. I do need to thank my many research assistants who labored to code these data properly. I thank in order, Megan Goode, Doris McGonagle, Kristin Campbell, Kanishkan Sathasivam, and Andrew Barrett. I am sorry that I excited none of them to study local democracy and hope that the daunting data gathering was not responsible. A mini-grant from Texas A&M University paid for postage and telephone calls. I need also to thank several reviewers of this manuscript. One was critical of studying any but the largest cities, because most social problems centered there and most people, he claimed, lived there. I knew that studying all cities with populations over 25,000 in 1990 could bias the study to smaller cities, but the size of the city only affected the salary city council members received. Because of this reviewer, I did martial my arguments for why he was wrong. Another reviewer strongly suggested that revising the manuscript as a thesis in defense of the research findings would allow the reader to deal with the many findings as they built up to the overall conclusion. I agreed and rewrote the manuscript.

Finally, mea culpa. If we could experimentally induce a random sample of American cities to adopt the city manager form of governance, to use fall rather than spring elections, or to raise council salaries, we could comfortably assess the impact of these reforms as field experiments. However, we have to take what is given. Western cities are far more likely to have to adopt the city manager form, southern cites to use spring elections, and large cities in the northeast to have high salaries. Therefore if some other variable relates to region, we may mistakenly conclude that the use of the city manager or of spring elections affects this variable. Our only recourse is to seek to control factors, such as region, that might also affect variables of interest. This in turn depends on the research to control for what is important and to omit controls that only confuse the reader. This is a delicate effort that I may have not performed adequately. If so, I am sorry; I did my best.

# Chapter 1

# Politics and Competition in American Cities

This is a study of elections in a random sample of modern, American cities. All have 1990 populations of greater than 25,000 people. Conceptually, this study occupies three levels. One is quite specific: What are elections to city councils like in the United States today? Knowing what we know of local elections in our home towns, from various case studies of some cities and from reports submitted by city clerks to occasional articles in the Municipal Yearbook, few would be surprised to learn that only about 25 percent of the electorate vote or that on average city council candidates winning margins are 30 percent. While American cities are supposed to be the level of government closest to the people, in the 1980s and 1990s at least, people seem unlikely to participate and unlikely to have a choice of candidates in competitive elections.

The second level of conceptualization centers on the role of competition in our cities. On nearly any measure of elections, institutions, demography, and policies, cities vary. Some have higher turnouts, some have more candidates seeking each council seat, and some see winners only marginally victorious. This allows a comparative analysis of what types of cities enjoy turnout and competition as well as what the impact of that turnout and competition is on public policy. Such comparative analysis will provide insight into the dynamics of city politics, but relationships may be spurious as some other factor may cause both competition and the policy difference. Although of local politics will be unaffected, these findings should suggest whether pursuing more competition in elections will result in different policy outcomes.

Lastly, this study attempts to deal with the dynamics of democracy at the local level and perhaps more broadly at any level of government. I would hasten to note that these data do not cover all relevant concepts, especially those pertaining to the responsiveness of representatives, the preferences of both the public and its representatives, or the motivations for individuals seeking public office. While these data on competition and turnout, on the ethnicity and gender of council members, and on the institutions used in these cities together with available demographic and policy data permits exploring some aspects of democracy in American cities, certainly there are missing pieces to the puzzle. This is a study of the importance of competition in city elections.

Some will say that finding little competition and the lack of impact of competition on policy is documenting the obvious. They might argue that at very least the middle class is overrepresented on representative institutions at all levels and possibly elections are a nefarious institution intended to make the public think it governs. Others might say that other factors are of higher importance than competition. Recently economists have suggested that economic development is more important than democracy, and certainly the reform movement, as we will discuss below, suggested that efficiency is the main concern in city governance. Even the complexity of modern economies and the resulting time pressure on representatives may preclude much concern with democratic decision-making. City council members, whether in competitive elections or not, may have little time to be responsive, as they struggle to keep their city at the forefront of economic development. Some will say that the "sham" of local democracy must be undone to make local democracy the government, of, by, and for the people. Finally, some would express disinterest in this question, suggesting that urban problems in our big cities, such as juvenile crime, teenage pregnancy, total loss of hope, and other evidence of a breakdown of society, must be resolved regardless of whether it is done democratically or not. All of these ideas notwithstanding, few would discourage competitive elections as an avenue for public involvement. But what if competitive cities enact the same policies as noncompetitive cities?

## Literature on Municipal Politics

This study falls within the context of many literatures of political science, some current and others not. Each will receive attention, beginning at the most specific level and moving ultimately to the more abstract. None of these studies fully assesses the dynamics of politics, elections, and policies; rather, they give only insight into some aspects of these dynamics.

### American Municipal Elections in the 1960s and 1970s

The last nationwide assessment of municipal elections rests on 1975 data. Karnig and Walter (1978) used data from a questionnaire completed by someone in each city. Nearly all cities responded. Without direct access to data in individual cities, this study rests on the accuracy of city secretaries in making the information concerning their cities match the questions. The researchers can only hope that secretaries in cities with at-large by place elections characterized their city's selection as at-large rather than district based. Also, while we know that many cities have staggered terms for their council members, we do not know that the reported information reflects a complete round of elections or just the most recent election.

Nevertheless, these data update our knowledge from an earlier, similar study by Lee (1963). Karnig and Walter mainly focus on trends since this earlier Lee study rather than commenting on the overall character of municipal election in 1975.[1] They note that more incumbents seek reelection, but with little greater success, and that voter participation has fallen. The actual values are probably more important, however. In 1975, 72 percent of incumbents reportedly sought reelection and 78 percent succeeded, meaning that the cities experienced a turnover of 44 percent. They note that this turnover exceeds that for Congress but, despite the "widespread disenchantment with public leaders," local incumbents need not fear their reelection chances. Defeats would seem sufficient to assure accountability, but those seeing the "disadvantages in the defeat of local officials who were doing an effective job" need not fear.[2] They see a balance of enough turnover to assure accountability and incumbents returning to assure effective leadership. They do not and cannot answer the questions of whether this fortuitous balance is achieved in every city or even why it is achieved at all. Most fundamentally, they cannot say if the "balance" makes city governments enact better or less desired public policy.

They argue that turnout rises with the importance of elections as an explanation for low local turnouts. This has unclear implications for the decline in participation they noted between 1962 (33 percent) and 1975 (29 percent). Are local elections becoming less important? They only claim that lower turnout favors incumbents.[3] Overall, the levels reported by both Lee and Karnig and Walter, when compared with U.S. House data, show less incumbency advantage and lower turnout. None of these authors expresses much concern with either fact. Is local turnout low because of the lack of importance of such contests, and how does turnout interact with incumbency advantage? With turnout lower than in congressional elections and with such low turnout advantaging incumbents, should we not find higher rather than lower incumbency advantage in cities as compared with the U.S. House?

While these authors attempt to assess the impact of institutions and there is some consideration of the role of a city's population, other variations are ignored. For example there is no evaluation of whether cities with lower turnout have higher incumbency advantages as posited. The main criticism, however, rests not with the authors' analyses but with the failure to update these data to a period when many—such as Republican national leaders, the news media, and opinion pollsters—see declining confidence in national government and a desire to bring government back to the local level, which means either state or local government.

## Competition at the Local Level

V. O. Key (1949) ignited political scientists' concerns with the level of partisan competition, at least at the state level. Unfortunately, rather than just hypothesizing that competition encourages responsive elected officials, Key sees the level of competition as shaping the scale of government. Follow-up research has largely focused on competition shaping the scale of government. Key argues that when one party dominates elections, that party will appeal only to the "haves" who vote and support candidates and who want limited governmental services and low taxes. With a competitive second party, however, one party will appeal to the "have nots" by recommending an increase in the scale of government to give them more services with taxes paid by those more able to pay. Key stresses the superiority of competition between political parties to that between Democratic party factions within the South in the 1940s, but those studying political parties in the states, citing Key's pioneering work, developed measures of party competition for each state.[4] Like Key, explicitly or implicitly, all advocated greater interparty competition and few questioned whether the measure is unidimensional. Perhaps other variables also influence the policies enacted by the states, such as the wealth of the state or some uniqueness of the South. Furthermore, might competitive elections leading to more responsive representatives in a wealthy state or city not lead to a reduced scale of government?

With 70 percent of American cities having nonpartisan city council elections, the concept of interparty competition obviously cannot apply.[5] It reenters our consideration by way of the community power studies, and those seeking to generate comparative concepts for assessing city politics. The community power studies burst into the literature of social science with the reaction of political scientists to Floyd Hunter's *Community Power Structure*.[6] Hunter included substantial normative reactions to his findings that nonelected individuals manipulated elections and policy in Atlanta; he demanded change and more accountability for those making decisions that influenced Atlantians. Although Hunter sees no accountability in Atlanta through elections and never mentions competition, he clearly calls for greater organization of the poor to communicate their needs.[7] Competition in elections would, as Key argued, afford the "have-nots" the opportunity to communicate their needs by selecting candidates who make certain issue appeals hoping to gain their votes.

The other pole in the clash over the governance of American cities was Robert A. Dahl (1961) in his counterstudy of New Haven in *Who Governs?* Using what he claimed to be superior methods, Dahl finds competition in New Haven. It is a completely different conception of competition than that of Key. If there are sufficient political "skills" among alternative elites who take exception to an unpopular or even unwise decision and also sufficient acceptance of principles of democracy, this elite can take their case to the public and provide alternatives. In turn, the public can "take up the slack" in the system and engage in the unusual act of deciding among elites.[8] Because these elites need not be elected, Dahl's competition is among elites, even the businessmen such as those dominating Atlanta according to Hunter.

A review of the surrounding literature and an accounting for the sharp decline in comparative assessments of municipal politics is beyond my conceptual needs here.[9] Most of the discussion in this literature suggested either open or closed communities, but clearly gradations between where elections settled nothing because incumbents, who do what they are told and face no opponents and defining elections, where the public takes up the slack in the system and makes choices, perhaps reelecting incumbents or perhaps all challengers.[10] Rival candidates in such elections may not have political party labels, but they represent alternative elites' views on community issues. Voters, by way of such competition, have the choice among alternative policies. Hunter did not believe policy in Atlanta favored what the public preferred, while Dahl thought New Haven's did. If there is more competition then, perhaps policies better reflect those preferred by the public, or at least all the public rather than the few who normally bother to vote, namely the well-to-do. While this seems entirely analogous to Key's argument, it need not be limited to the scale of government issues. Non-economic issues may also be biased toward the middle class when there is no competition in a city.

While one could assess a sample of cities to note the incidence of "taking up the slack" elections and noting the resulting differences in policy, there have been no such efforts. Although many are inclined to assume more competition when political parties are present in cities or to assume that all cities having elections must be equally competitive, there have been no studies assessing whether this is true.

## Starting and Encouraging Political Careers

With the premise that democracies need political leadership and that local government can provide the training needed for such leadership, Bledsoe (1993) uses a five-year panel of city council members in selected cities to assess their career paths and ambition.[11] Following up on the ideas of Barber (1965), Bledsoe develops a typology of council members' motives for seeking local elected office. The four types are labeled: Politico, who enjoys politics and aspires for higher office; Community-Regarding, who seeks office for altruistic reasons;[12] Local, who seeks to help real people with their government; and Particularist, who tends to be single-issue oriented and driven by that issue.[13]

Several factors contribute to council members remaining on the council or seeking higher office, both of which Bledsoe views as desirable for democracy. In his study, more professional councils with higher salaries and better support facilities, councils with members with prior experience in office, and councils with partisan elections have council members remaining in office longer. Democracy might be served as well by experienced leaders as by responsive leaders.

Prewitt (1970) and Eulau and Prewitt (1973) studying the San Francisco Bay area city councils also suggest that the absence of ambition for continued or higher office undercuts the responsiveness of local representatives. Bledsoe adds the idea of city councils as training grounds as had previously been encouraged by de Tocqueville. The idea here is simple—experience in office improves leadership and trains officials to lead at higher levels of government. The real question is representation. Experience in office on the council little changes members' desire to represent constituents, but those who endure tend to be attentive to constituents, or at least claim they are.[14] By implication providing leadership on a city council does not imply being unresponsive, rather council members who are disinterested and unambitious soon lose interest in being responsive and in governing. Tenure in office seems to reward those doing a good and responsive job. The presumably unresponsive "volunteers" drop out.

Neither the Prewitt and Eulau Bay area study nor the Bledsoe survey are representative studies of American council members and neither weighs the influences of community factors other than political institutional differences. The exception to this is Prewitt and Eulau's (1969) finding that cities with fewer forced turnovers, or instances where incumbents lost, have leaders who *say* they act on their own rather than consulting community groups (433). Forced turnovers would suggest competitive elections; thus this research would suggest that at least what representatives say is shaped by electoral threat.

This literature nevertheless reveals several uncertainties in our thinking. Do we want leadership or responsiveness from our officials? Do they go together? Presthus (1964) studied four New York communities and suggests that we may have to make the choice.[15] Furthermore, many seek local elective office based on a single interest or impatiently out of civic duty. Both would lack political skills. Can time in office improve this? No doubt we would all prefer city officials to lead, to be responsive, and to want to stay in office. Bledsoe suggests that those who want to stay in office or to seek higher office, as Schlesinger (1966) suggests out of ambition, seem motivated to be responsive and, by staying around, can learn to lead. Is public policy better where elected leaders enjoy longer careers?

Normative considerations certainly continue to divide this research, as it did Hunter and Dahl. There are, however, many dynamics of democracy that are, as yet, unexplored by research or informed only by studies of limited generalizability.

**The Impact of Institutions**

The "reform movement" and the excesses of "machine politics" led to many changes in the institutional form of American cities.[16] We continue to alter institutions confident that doing so will change behavior and policy. Controversy continues to rage as to the costs or benefits, if any, of the movement away from the older format of having checks and balances in municipal government as we have in state and national government. Rather than having a strong mayor able to veto actions by the city council and having his or her veto potentially overridden by the legislative branch, most middle-sized cities have moved to "professional policy-making." A professional city manager, appointed by the representative legislators of the city council, advocates policies based on professional standards. This form of government is nearly identical to that typically of public schools with the professional school superintendent.[17]

There were other institutional changes associated with the reform movement, most notably using at-large seats rather than single member districts, each representing a portion of the city. Commonly, cities with the city manager and council form and using at-large selection are labeled "reformed" cities. Lineberry and Fowler's 1967 study, finding that unreformed cities provided more redistributional services, suggested that these reforms might have the intention of making council members less responsive as well as the avowed purpose of reducing corruption.[18] Liebert (1974) observed that some cities did more than others did and that cities in the Northeast with many functions, including education, were also the "unreformed" cities.[19] Clearly, unreformed cities, with extensive city services required either by the state or tradition, should not be credited for being more responsive in providing those services.

Svara (1990) unabashedly advocates moving to the "reformed" or city manager form of city government, seeing "conflict" within the mayor and council form as harmful to the city, making it perhaps "ungovernable."[20] Examples of the fragmentation evident in the mayor/council form include: council members who act as advocates for neighborhood groups; police chiefs who mobilize those concerned with law and order to resist citizen review of police actions; or mayors who appoint those likely to improve reelection chances.[21] Svara is not alone in his concerns about conflict's harm to cities.[22] He studies six pairs of manager and mayor/council cities with between 120,000 and 650,000 populations matched on demographic and economic characteristics. City members and department heads reported better working relationships and better use of professional staff in his manager cities.[23] There is no assessment of whether manager cities are less responsive to voters or poor voters.

Svara's (1990) survey of a population stratified sample of city council members, however, finds, "It is significant to note that the most frequently mentioned source of frustration—conflict among council members—is as common in council-manager cities (54 percent) as in mayor-council cities (55 percent)."[24] There seems no basis for characterizing mayor/council cities as experiencing more conflict. In this survey, city manager cities' council members complain more about spending long hours than do council members from mayor/council cities. Mayor/council city council members complain about having inadequate staff assistance. Along with too much time away from family, all of these complaints are more common in larger cities. The size of a city may affect how easily it is governed and how easy it is to attract candidates for public offices.

Svara rejects the common literature conclusion that conflict in mayor and council cities contributes to responsiveness while cooperation in council-manager cities enhances the upper stratum's influence.[25] He concludes that once demography and socioeconomic characteristics are controlled, differences between city manager and mayor/council cities in representation of minorities and women vanish. In his study of North Carolina cities as well as in his matched cities, he concludes, "The cooperative pattern, as associated with the council-manager form, is not dependent on unrepresentative official leadership, nor does it produce less responsiveness to racial minority and lower socioeconomic groups than the conflictual pattern (evident in mayor council cities)."[26]

Seeing cooperation as clearly desirable, seeing few differences between city councils' representativeness between forms with the behavior of the mayor largely responsible for differences, and seeing greater conflict coming from more district based council elections, Svara urges more responsible behavior by both mayors and city councils to reduce conflict for the betterment of the community. The interplay among council members and mayors in city manager cities, he argues, can be more constructive, contributing to better public policy, but at no cost to responsiveness.

In part Svara urges mayors and councils in city manager cities to seek more cooperation, but his research conclusion rests on a limited number of matched cities. He predicts that more cooperative effort on the part of council members will result in less conflict in making public policy. He expresses few clear statements to suggest whether he expects elections in mayor/council cities to be more conflictual or to use the more common term, competitive. In fact elections and the public involvement in city governance plays an insignificant role in policy as Svara see it.

While Svara focuses on the impact of municipal government forms, Welch and Bledsoe (1988) consider district rather than at-large election of council members and nonpartisan rather than partisan municipal elections. They study questionnaire responses by individual council members rather than common responses in cities and the interplay between council members as Svara did. Noting that the impact of institutional reforms has been argued since the ancients, they see cities as ideal for analysis, as they vary greatly but are not too socioculturally diverse. Welch and Bledsoe focus on the personal characteristics of those elected, their representational styles and policy predispositions, and how citizens view their local governments. As in this study, concepts of representation integrate their research questions. Like most studies of municipal government, the reform movement between 1890 and 1930 provides the institutional variations that continue as the basis of the impact of institutions argument.[27]

They summarize and cite the still unresolved literature on the impact of single member district versus at-large elections and of nonpartisan versus partisan elections. Reformers saw partisan elections as facilitating straight-ticket voting, balanced slates, and emigrant voting that permitted the urban machine. More recent assessments of cities with partisan versus nonpartisan elections vary between a small negative impact to no impact on African-American representation.[28] Also the movement to nonpartisan elections seemingly helped Republicans, women, and those with high status occupations win municipal office.[29,30,31] Most of the research on the impact of moving to district elections rather than at-large elections, following the federal courts' pressure, is based on the idea that African-American representation would improve were there majority African-American districts to elect African-American candidates. While this will be discussed later, initially at least district elections did encourage African-American representation on city councils.[32] Other impacts have received little attention.[33]

Welch and Bledsoe's sample was intended to sample council members in cities with populations between 50,000 and one million. Of the 1,600 council member sample, 975 returned questionnaires.[34] The typical council member is a 47 year old, white, male lawyer or professional with an income over $45,000 of which $4,400 comes from being a council member. He or she commits 20 hours a week to council duties and has served 3.5 years. African-Americans constitute only 8.5 percent of their respondents, and women 23 percent. Women reportedly work harder as council members and identify themselves as "liberal."[35] Surprisingly, most councils tend to be Democratic, especially those in larger cities, although partisan cleavage reportedly little shows itself, apart from in these larger cities.[36]

Their research suggests that district elections encourage persons of lower education and income to run and win, but that nonpartisan elections modestly increase council members with higher income.[37] Neither structural difference much explains council composition; however, "political structures have a modest impact on the kinds of people elected to office."[38] "Those elected by district are more likely to feel that they represent neighborhoods than do those elected at-large, and those elected at-large are more likely to see themselves as representing the city as a whole."[39]

Finally, they consider the impact of both at-large and partisan elections on representation. They basically support Morgan and Pelissero's (1980) conclusion. Studying eleven cities that adopted two or three reform characteristics, at-large elections, nonpartisan election, and city manager form of government, Morgan and Pelissero found structure little influences policy. Similarly, Welch and Bledsoe endorse Heilig and Mundt's (1984) conclusion that switching from at-large to district elections had no impact on conflict in the council.[40] Sharp cleavages are reported by nearly one half of councils whether at-large, district, partisan, or nonpartisan elections are used, but conflict was much more common in larger cities. This may suggest that Svara's concern with conflict being more heightened in mayor/council cities merely reflects the use of this form in larger cities as well as their having greater conflict.

Some benign researcher or deity has not randomly assigned structural differences among American cities. As a result history and tradition, region, size, and probably even the conservativeness or Republicanness of cities influenced both the adoption of reforms as well as the character of local politics, the policies enacted, and even the breadth of the city's functions. Careful controls for these factors or before-and-after studies of cities making changes, consistently show institutions have little if any effect.

## Minority and Women Representation

No research plums the closeness of the tie between public policy and public opinion at the community level. The jargon of politics speaks reverently of local government being "closer to the people," meaning, one might guess, that the public is more capable of assuring that policy reflects its opinions than is true with more distant and less closely watched governments at the state and national levels. This is not demonstrated, however. Representation or representativeness can be variously assessed, but most of the effort at the local level has been directed to the single question of whether racial minorities and women have accurate or proportional representation on city councils. Like most representative institutions, city councils, as noted by Welch and Bledsoe (1988), misrepresent society. They are too male, too white, too aged, too middle class, too well educated, and probably too interested in politics and too opinionated. Only the first two, gender and race, are captured in available data. Given the racial division of American society and the attention paid to racial bias in legislative bodies by the courts, racial bias attracts the most research attention.

An extensive literature with contradictory findings centers on the relative proportion of African-Americans on city councils and in the publics of American cities. More accurate representation is seen as a priori desirable and some research suggests that better African-American representation, such as a majority black city having a black mayor, increases African-American trust in local government (Abney and Hutcheson 1981; Howell and Fagen 1988; and Bobo and Gilliam 1990). An extensive literature in political science suggests that African-American representation improves with an institutional change from multimember at-large (citywide) to single member, district elections.[41] More recent work, however, suggests a decline of this effect in the 1980s (Welch 1990); nevertheless, she concludes, "Blacks are still most equitably represented by district elections..."(1072). Luttbeg (1995), using data for this book, concludes that the diminishing effects of district elections are lost by the 1990s.[42] This will receive much attention in a later chapter.

Welch includes representation of Hispanics in her 1988 study and concludes that the effects of district rather than at-large selection are "tiny" at best.[43] Although we might expect communities that are responsive to the appeals or demands of African-Americans for representation to also respond to appeals by women and Hispanics, research has not supported such an expectation. While negative relationships between the representation of women and of minorities have been noted, Karnig and Welch (1979) find no relationship in municipal representation and no evidence for "interminority competition."[44]

Many explanations might be offered for differences in the representation achieved by minorities and women. Women are not "residentially segregated" like minorities, allowing a different dynamic for their achieving representation. Since moving to district rather than at-large elections is seen as a device to improve segregated minorities' representation, this might not work for women. Another explanation centers on the absence of a "block vote" by women for women candidates. Moreover, the traditionally dominant white males may yield more easily to women's demands as opposed to minority demands. Finally, without financial encouragement to serve or ambitions to satisfy, women may "volunteer." At any rate a separate literature deals with the success of women in winning seats on city councils.[45]

Obviously women are nearly equally present in all communities while minority populations vary between communities. If the representation of women on city councils closely paralleled that of minorities, we would have a measure applicable in all communities of how demographically representative a council is. The lack of relationship between representation of women and of minorities hardly comes as a surprise to researchers in other areas. Using demographic attributes of state legislators, Luttbeg (1992 and 1998) found ratios of women, blacks, Hispanics, the middle class and other attributes often unrelated or even negatively related.

**The Origins of Episodes of Competition: The Public Taking Up the Slack?**

Abrupt change in politics is uncommon. The riots in our cities in the late 1960s and the change of control in Congress in 1994 are rare events. Not surprisingly, our theories are either steady-state or gradual change theories. Dahl's theory of city politics, however, suggests that the public can on occasionally "take up the slack."[46] Presumably, one of two things can happen in such circumstances. The electorate can "throw the rascals out," or incumbents can be endorsed and reelected. Regardless, the public has its only occasional say; a tie has been made between public opinion and public policy; and democracy has worked, he argues. Is this theory without examples to explain?

Are there episodes of competition where the pubic can have a say?

Certainly, Republicans and mass media pundits acclaim the congressional elections of 1994 as an infrequent example of public clearly stating a preference. In 1994 however, even incumbent Democratic Representatives, against whom the electorate presumably voted, won better than 80 percent of the time. The "rascals" were hardly thrown out, and the Republican "Contract with America" was hardly endorsed overwhelmingly by voters. However, the election results were more consistent than in other recent congressional elections. Congressional elections never see all incumbents challenged and defeated. State legislative elections also show no instances where all "rascals" are defeated or even elections in which all incumbents are closely challenged. As such national and state legislative contests never see either a ringing endorsement of policies enacted nor an electorate that throws those responsible for disliked policies out of public office. City councils, however, on occasion see all incumbents defeated, or at least none up for election returned to the council. This means a turnover of 100 percent. In 1985, many Texas municipal and school board elections showed such turnovers.[47]

Of course, fewer incumbents must seek reelection for a given city's city council than for the U.S. House or state legislatures, thus the odds of all losing are easier. Then again, the odds against all Representatives and legislators winning are also higher, but this does happen often in state legislative contests. Even if it is easier to replace all incumbents at the municipal level, a message may be clearly sent and clearly Dahl had such elections in mind when speaking of the voters "taking up the slack."

Given their smaller number, personal factors may result in many council members choosing to retire voluntarily, leaving the city for employment elsewhere, or even having the misfortune of being the target of ambitious young opponents seeking to begin their careers. Nevertheless, such episodes may represent the true practice of democracy only evident at the local level.

**Political Parties in a Nonpartisan Context**

A few cities retain partisan elections, but partisan activity persists for other local offices, such as U.S. House of Representatives, state upper and lower house representatives, county commissioners and so on. It would be surprising then if partisanship were absent in local elections. It is present. As cited in Bledsoe and Welch (1987), Mayhew (1986) confirms the conventional wisdom that political parties will play an important role in older Northeastern and Midwestern cities that often retain partisan local elections and will be relatively unimportant in the one-party South and in cities of the West with little local partisan experience.[48]

In partisan local elections in Michigan, Eldersveld (1964) noted the impotant role of the parties' strategies. Bledsoe and Welch (1987) confirm this. Their 1982 survey asked three questions to assess party influence even in nonpartisan cities. These were to assess the importance of parties in (1) nominating candidates and running campaign; (2) in contributing money and support to the campaigns; and (3) as a source of cleavage within the city.[49] Larger cities and those outside the South proved more partisan. Partisan elections, not unexpectedly, also increased party impact. Notably, population only proved important in nonpartisan cities. In partisan cities, both at-large elections and being outside the South increased partisan activity.[50] Finally, active parties increased turnout even in nonpartisan cities, outweighing form of government, region, and even whether elections were held simultaneously with state and national elections in increasing turnout. Even informally political parties still contribute to our local politics.

Morlan (1984), studying municipal and national elections cross-nationally, also notes the importance of national political parties in municipal elections. This explains higher local participation abroad.[51] He finds the greatest range of difference between local and national contests in the United States and that in most countries larger cities have lower turnout. This, of course, contradicts the Bledsoe and Welch finding, although Morlan is using courser nationwide data.

The reform movement sought to dampen political parties' importance, at least in municipal elections. But in neglecting the importance of political parties in other local elections, reformers allowed an important means for involving voters, at least as evidenced by turnout, to remain. As judged by answers of council members, partisanship continues in our cities. Bledsoe and Welch show that in more populous cities even nonpartisan elections cannot dampen the role of party organization.

### Economic and Political Factors in Public Policy-Making: The Benefits of Comparison

Peterson (1981) argues that students of local democracy have erroneously presumed that cities had the same latitude of policy action that national governments and thus could be studied using the same concepts. Rather he sees cities immeshed in the federal system that curtailed that latitude. Certainly cities everywhere, whether in a federal or unitary system, have their policy options limited by the national government. This is, of course, not unique to local government, as in a federal system, states too have limitations, and even nation states have limitations imposed by constitutions, treaties, alliances, and the world economy. Unfortunately, we have no cross-national study of municipal governments to assess the impact of limitations imposed by state and national governments on the politics and performance of local government, much less a theory of federalism.[52]

Peterson raises once again the question of whether economic rather than political variables shape municipal public policy (see Dye 1966). He assumes that cities seek to optimize their economic exports, concentrated on factors that contribute to this, and not surprisingly finds economic factors have great influence, with taxation and expenditure policies by the city greatly affecting its "well-being."[53] He suggests that policies can be divided into three categories. Developmental policies enhance the city's economic potential, are based on "user-pay" services, include highways, business parks, and wildlife preserves, and raise the value of surrounding properties. Redistributive policies help the poor and handicapped and hurt economic development by devoting taxes to economically unproductive services. Such policies may reflect compassion but not economic development. Finally, allocational policies, such as fire and police protection, are developmentally neutral. He argues that apart from large cities, the national government provides redistributive services and cities deal with allocational services.

Politics, he says, plays little role in cities' policy-making that, "...they are generally a quiet arena of decision making where political leaders can give reasoned attention to the longer range interests of the city..."[54] With unambitious politicians not interested in establishing connections with constituents, city residents are likely to be frustrated.[55] While he does not use the word, "leadership," clearly he sees city decision-makers advantaged by the absence of politics and the need to respond to the public. Overall, Peterson is satisfied with city politics and sees those politics little affecting city policies. Democracy may not be doing well in cities, but it little matters. While Peterson compares New York City with other central cities, he suggests little variation among cities, with the exception that suburban cities must compete for economic resources with each other and thus may differ from central cities. Such competition would seem to be limited to the level of taxes rather than for citizen support.

Few political scientists embrace his indifference to the quality of democracy and expectation that cities will not vary. Stone (1989 and 1990) also questions the irrelevance of local politics. Peterson, however, does again raises the relative importance of economic variables.[56] He also forces attention to municipalities operating within the limitations imposed by state and national government. Christensen (1995) presents data ranking the states both for local governments' discretionary authority and the degree of the state's dominance in the fiscal partnership with local government that could be used to assess the differences in community politics caused by such independence for local government.[57]

**Large Cities, Economists, the Underclass, and Contemporary Urban Problems**

Large American cities, in particular New York City (Shefter 1989), Chicago (Banfield 1961), and Atlanta (Stone 1989), have attracted continual idiographic analysis focusing on the seriousness of social problems faced, including even federal involvement in their politics. When the mayor of New York merely by winning election as a Republican in a predominantly Democratic city automatically is mentioned as a Republican presidential prospect, we can see that some large cities are on the national stage.

Large cities, which were the concern of the reform movement, were also the most resistant to the imposed reforms. Most, especially in the Northeast and Midwest, retain the older partisan election format and the mayor/council form of municipal government. The economic plight of these cities that experienced substantial white and wealth flight to the suburbs after World War II, the issue of governmentally provided services for the poor underclass rather than to the more likely to vote middle class, the supposed greater diversity of such core cities as compared with the earlier, all white suburbs, and even the greater democracy operating through local level political parties are the hypotheses generated by this core city focus.

Shefter (1989) pessimistically concludes:

American cities fall into one of *two categories*. The first, which is *most typical of the Southwest*, is composed of cities in which local business elites dominate local politics, and their priorities are reflected in the municipal fiscal policy. The second category is composed of cities, such as *New York and other major cities in the Northeast*, in which the local political system possesses a significant autonomy from the hierarchies of civil society and in which politicians and public officials are at times tempted to engage in deficit financing. In such cities fiscal discipline is imposed upon the local government by the municipal bond-rating agencies and the public capital market, and by the threat that if the market closes to the city, political forces allied with local business elites may be able to wage a successful reform campaign and gain control of City Hall. (Italics added; 232)

Based on his New York City case study, he argues that either businessmen dominate the council and impose their values on its policies or in large northeastern cities they force politicians who are responsive to the preferences of the public to bow to business values. Size and region are important to politics, although policies may remain the same.

Peterson (1981) argues another idea derived from the study of large cities and from the perspective of economics in his elaboration of Tiebout (1956). This idea largely focuses on large cities that retain partisan elections. In this logic politicians, assumed to be only interested in reelection and always in competitive elections, are helpless to resist the pressure to reflect the "growth mentality" of constituents (Schneider 1989: 36 also see Cameron 1978). Much of this work fails to support what they view as Key's hypothesis that competition among political parties inevitably leads to an expanded role for government and deficit spending. One party promises to expand services; the other to cut taxes; and inevitably one will promise to do both, initially by making government more efficient. Cameron (1978) finds that while leftist parties matter in governmental growth, competition does not (1253). Moreover, he finds that decentralized, federal governments expand least, meaning that local governments are not the root of this expansion. Finally, Lowery and Berry (1983) assess the impact of competition in American national politics on growth in the national budget and find that competition poorly explains growth.

Schneider, expanding on Tiebout's (1956) idea of strategic decision-making in aggregates, hypothesizes that in the panoply of suburbs surrounding core cities, voters can easily move to the city offering public goods and services of the best quality and quantity at the best price, much as we assume buyers act in choosing among grocery stores. His research, however, suggests that while expenditures can be explained by a city's demography, there is little competition among suburbs in a given metropolitan area and thus "voting with ones feet" entails a move from one metropolitan areas to another rather than a move within a metropolitan area (202-206). I would suspect that this finding would have held had he included core cities along with suburbs.

Ideas derived from economists to account for the growth of government have had most limited success. Furthermore, the assumption that competition results in government growth derived from Key's suggestion that competitive parties will be more responsive to the poorer elements of society, has found very little support at any level and has never been assessed at the local level. It seems unwarranted to see competition between political parties as the best definition of local competition when fewer than one city in five has partisan municipal elections. It is even more questionable to assume competitive local elections when few municipal elections are competitive.

Additionally, a dependence on case studies of large cities results in finding politically independent, large city, public representatives at least struggling to shape municipal policies that the public prefers. This may ultimately find broad support with further study, but Schneider's work with suburbs suggests that economic pressures may not shape the nature of municipal services; that state regulation, traditions, and demographic factors may override economic development as a goal.

Clearly if we wish to assess the impact of competition on public policy, we should at least consider the size of government. Additionally, we should differentiate between suburbs and older core cities, such as Chicago, New York, and Boston. Thus far, however, there has been no assessment of the impact of local city competition on municipal policies, including on the scale of government.

## Democracy in American Cities

Several concepts interweave these disparate literatures. While several concepts, such as leadership, good policy, conflict, the public, representative officials, an unaccountable elite, competitive elections, and governing institutions, appear in most of these literatures, their importance varies. Elections are probably most fundamental, but do they show competition or conflict, apathy or elite control, lack of turnover that allows better public policy or turnover that evidences public control? At the local level no one seems to argue that interest groups or personal interactions replace the role of elections to allow public expression of satisfaction or dissatisfaction. Berry, Portney, and Thomson (1993) do, however, see the benefits of neighborhood organizations to supplement and perhaps sublimate elections.

They study five cities, Birmingham, Dayton, Portland, Oregon, San Antonio, and Saint Paul where such neighborhood organizations have a long standing and recognized role in city policy-making and compare aggregate and public and elite surveys in these cities with matched, comparison communities.[58] They find the benefits of such organizations not reflected in participation, which is "unexceptional,"[59] no greater sharing of issue agendas,[60] and little greater success in stopping local businesses' headlong rush for development.[61] They conclude, "Strong democracy structures (neighborhood groups) channel participants' energies into communal and cooperative activities rather than activities that are fundamentally isolating."[62] They clearly see such neighborhood organizations as empowering and thus encourage them for other communities. Clearly, however, such interests share nothing with the interest groups that operate at state and national levels. Such "havenot" organizations, if only marginally viable in cities, cannot operate at higher levels of government.

Few of these conceptual developments set local democracies apart from state and national democracies. While political economists may suggest that the function of municipalities is to export local business production or to increase its size, political scientists see the same dynamics operating locally that are evident at other levels. Large city politics may reflect the restructuring needs of the poor living in the core city and the wealthy in the suburbs, and cities might be the traditional providers of redistributive governmental services, but the class relatedness of politics corresponds to that in states and the nation. Like other levels of government, cities find white middle-class males, often with business backgrounds, dominating public offices. Such interests also seek to influence the decisions of elected offices. Whose interests then are enacted into public policy?

Marxist ideas thrive in this bias and in the importance of campaign money, private sector contributions of resources for community development from which they benefit, and indeed the entire dynamics of community development. Hunter's concerns for accountability are alive and well.[63] Some see conflict over public policy as evidence that the interests of the elite are meeting productive opposition from those unrepresented or underrepresented on city councils while others see such conflict as dysfunctional and ineffective in improving the city. Competition for public office may be the uncommon result of such conflict and may restore the democracy lost to reforms seeking to remove the corruption and inefficiency of urban machine politics. From this perspective competition restores the public's access to officials and presumably improves public capabilities to vote rationally. It may also improve public satisfaction with government and government officials.

Few city council members could live on their council salaries; thus "volunteers" without ambition may seek council seats and prove unresponsive, although not necessarily because of class-based differences. Cities also differ in that elected officials are always in the community and frequently approachable face-to-face, and local elections, except in the larger cities, cost candidates hundreds of dollars rather than hundreds of thousands of dollars. The representatives and the represented stand less apart at the local level.

Finally, there is a comparative element in these literatures. Cities that differ institutionally are expected to differ in their elections or in their representatives, in the conflict of their politics, and in the policies they enact. Additionally, economic and labor force resources are expected to facilitate governmental actions and even politics. Finally, the competitiveness of local elections should affect policy and perhaps even yield communities where life is more enjoyable, but what improves the likelihood of competitive elections?

## A Simple Model of Local Democracy

Despite research that might argue the relative importance of representation as compared with leadership, development, or minority representation, little in this research adds much to Key's simple model of the importance of competitive elections. This would be the model.

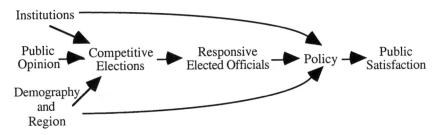

This of course suggests that governmental institutions, including election procedures, public opinion, and demographic attributes, such as minority percentage, population, and suburbanness all affect how competitive elections are. In turn more competitive elections are expected to cause elected officials to be responsive. Public policies enacted by officials should be affected by their representativeness as well as by institutions of government, such as perhaps how well paid they are, and by demography and region, such as how wealthy the city is or how substantial its minority populations are.

Key would go further to suggest that competitive elections would increase the scale of government as the "have nots" opinions would with competitive elections cause elected officials to promise additional services and be pressured to do so. As such he would be focusing on only competitive elections and policy. In the research reported here, several of these concepts are not measured. There are no data on public opinions in these cities, no data on the responsiveness of elected officials, and no data on levels of public satisfaction.

## The Plan of This Book

Chapter 2 describes the sample and institutional variations evident in the sample. Chapter 3 turns to the question of competition noted in these elections and considers the demographic and institutional sources of competition. Chapter 4 considers the impact on policy of many community characteristics, including the level of competition in its elections. The thesis stated at the beginning of this chapter is best defended in Chapters 3 and 4. Chapter 5 turns to explanations for when minorities and women are elected to the city council, and in turn the impact of their better representation on policy. Chapter 6 focuses on episodes of competition evident in these cities. I conclude with a summary of my findings and an effort to see the implications of these research findings. Finally, Appendix B updates information on municipal elections, assesses trends, and considers the variations in such elections. This is not part of the central analysis.

Unfortunately, one vital element has not been captured in my data—public electoral capability. Dahl implies that while the public may lack the skills needed to become a community decision-maker, they clearly possess the capability to choose among alternative elites. Seemingly, they must have the capacity to become informed, to choose among alternative candidates rationally, and to participate at least to the level of casting their informed votes. They need to fulfill the Rational Activist Model.

While we have little research on local electoral behavior, a continuing controversy rages at the congressional and presidential levels. Is public capability in elections sufficient to fulfill democracy? While the partisan commitment so evident among voters may reflect either an early transmission of party identification from parent to child or a "running tally" of actions by one party that satisfy the voter, it lacks relevance when most municipal voters can make no use of this shortcut when casting their vote. Nevertheless, if Dahl is correct a public taking up the slack in the system should reflect more information on the candidates, a rational choice among them, and more participation. If this were true, episodes of competition would reflect the occasional but sufficient capability of the public to monitor its elected officials. If not, elite behavior may explain occasional competition rather than the public taking up the slack.

# Notes

1. Eugene C. Lee, "City Elections: A Statistical Profile," in *The Municipal Year Book 1963* (Chicago: International City Managers' Association, 1963), 74-84.
2. Albert K. Karnig and B. Oliver Walter, "Municipal Elections: Registration, Incumbent Success, and Voter Participation," *Municipal Year Book 1977* (Washington: International City Management Association, 1978), 66.
3. Karnig and Walter, "Municipal Elections," 71.
4. Key himself began these assessments. See V. O. Key, Jr. *American State Politics: An Introduction* (New York: Alfred A. Knopf, 1956), 97-104. Also see: Joseph A. Schlesinger, "A Two-Dimensional Scheme for Classifying the States According to Degree of Inter-Party Competition," *American Political Science Review* (November 1955): 1120-28; Richard E. Dawson and James A. Robinson, "Inter-Party Competition, Economic Variables, and Welfare Policies in the American States," *Journal of Politics* (May 1963): 265-89; Austin Ranney, "Parties in State Politics," in *Politics in the American States: A Comparative Analysis,* Herbert Jacob and Kenneth N. Vines, eds. (Boston: Little, Brown, 1965), 61-99; Thomas R. Dye, "State Legislative Politics," in *Politics in the American States: A Comparative Analysis,* Herbert Jacob and Kenneth N. Vines, eds. (Boston: Little, Brown, 1965), 151-206; Harvey J. Tucker and Ronald E. Weber, "Electoral Change in U.S. States: System Versus Constituency Competition," in *State Legislative Careers,* Gary Moncrief and Joel Thompson, eds. (Ann Arbor: University of Michigan Press, 1992), 35-58; and Norman R. Luttbeg, *Comparing the States and Communities: Politics, Government, and Policy in the United States* (New York: HarperCollins, 1992).
5. Heywood T. Sanders, "The Government of American Cities: Continuity and Change in Structure," in *The Municipal Yearbook 1982* (Washington: International City Management Association, 1982), 181.
6. Floyd Hunter, *Community Power Structure* (Chapel Hill: University of North Carolina Press, 1953), 256-61.
7. Hunter, *Community Power,* 256-61.
8. Robert A. Dahl, *Who Governs?* (New Haven, Conn.: Yale University Press, 1961), 305-25.
9. Good summaries can be found in: Willis D. Hawley and Frederick M. Wirt, eds., *The Search for Community Power* (Englewood Cliffs, N.J.: Prentice-Hall, 1968); Terry N. Clark, ed., *Community Structure and Decision-Making: Comparative Analyses* (San Francisco: Chandler, 1968); and Terry Nichols Clark, *Comparative Community Politics* (New York: John Wiley & Sons, 1974).
10. Such a continuum is suggested in Oliver P. Williams, Harold Herman, Charles S. Liebman, and Thomas R. Dye, *Suburban Differences and Metropolitan Policies: A Philadelphia Story* (Philadelphia: University of Pennsylvania Press, 1965); and Robert E. Agger, Daniel Goldrich, and Bert E. Swanson, *The Rulers and the Ruled: Political Power and Impotence in American Communities* (New York: John Wiley & Sons, 1964).
11. Timothy Bledsoe, *Careers in City Politics: The Case for Urban Democracy* (Pittsburgh: University of Pittsburgh Press, 1993). In all, 215 cities of varying size, region, and primary occupational type and 919 one time council members were included in this study. Just over one-half of those serving in 1982 continued to serve in 1987.

12. These seem the closest counterpart to Prewitt and Eulau's "volunteers."
13. Bledsoe, *Careers,* 67-70.
14. In response to the question assessing representative roles, 32 percent were delegates, 18 percent were either neutral or unresponsive, and just over 50 were trustees. Bledsoe, *Careers,* 92 and 120.
15. Robert Presthus, *Men At the Top* (New York: Oxford University Press, 1964).
16. Charles R. Adrian, "Forms of City Government in American History," *Municipal Year Book 1988* (Washington: International City Management Association, 1988), 3-12.
17. Byron G. Massialas, *Education and the Political System* (Reading, MA: Addison-Wesley, 1969).
18. Robert L. Lineberry and Edmund P. Fowler, "Reformism and Public Policies in American Cities," *American Political Science Review* (September 1967): 701-16.
19. Roland J. Liebert, "Municipal Functions, Structure, and Expenditures," *Social Science Quarterly* (March 1974): 765-83.
20. James H. Svara, *Official Leadership in the City: Patterns of Conflict and Cooperation* (New York: Oxford University Press, 1990).
21. Svara, *Official Leadership,* 40.
22. He cites: Barbara Ferman, *Governing the Ungovernable City: Political Skill, Leadership, and the Modern Mayor* (Philadelphia: Temple University Press, 1985); Douglas Yates, *The Ungovernable City* (Cambridge, MA: MIT Press, 1977); and Frederick M. Wirt, *Power in the City* (Berkeley: University of California Press, 1974).
23. Svara, *Official Leadership,* 54-55.
24. James H. Svara, *A Survey of America's City Councils: Continuity and Change.* (Washington: National League of Cities, 1991), 59.
25. Svara, *A Survey,* 59-60.
26. Svara, *A Survey,* 79.
27. Susan Welch and Timothy Bledsoe, *Urban Reform and Its Consequences: A Study in Representation* (Chicago: University of Chicago Press, 1988), i-17.
28. J. Kramer, "The Election of Blacks to City Councils: A 1970 Status Report and Prolegomenon," *Journal of Black Studies* (June 1971): 443-76; Donald Campbell and Joe Feagin, "Black Politics in the South: A Descriptive Analysis," *Journal of Politics* (February 1975): 12-59; Theodore Robinson and Thomas Dye, "Reforms and Black Representation on City Councils," *Social Science Quarterly* (June 1978): 133-41; Richard Cole, "Citizen Participation in Municipal Politics," *American Journal of Political Science* (November 1975): 761-82; and Albert Karnig and Susan Welch, *Black Representation and Urban Policy* (Chicago: University of Chicago Press, 1981).
29. Eugene Lee, *The Politics of Nonpartisanship* (Berkeley, CA: University of California Press, 1960); Charles Adrian and Oliver Williams, "The Insulation of Local Politics Under the Nonpartisan Ballot," *American Political Science Review* (December 1959): 1052-63; Chester Rogers and Harold Arman, "Nonpartisanship and Election to City Office," *Social Science Quarterly* (March 1971): 941-45; Willis Hawley, *Nonpartisan Elections and the Case for Party Politics* (New York: Wiley, 1973); and Rufus Browning, Dale Rogers Marshall, and David Tabb, *Protest Is Not Enough* (Berkeley: University of California Press, 1984).
30. Albert Karnig and Oliver Walter, "Election of Women to City Councils," *Social Science Quarterly* (March 1976): 605-13; and Susan Welch and Albert

Karnig, "Correlates of Female Office Holding in City Politics," *Journal of Politics* (May 1979): 478-91.

31. Carol Cassel, "Social Background Characteristics of Nonpartisan City Council Members: A Research Note," *Western Political Quarterly* (September 1985): 495-501.

32. Joyce Gelb, "Blacks, Blocs and Ballots," *Polity* 3 (fall): 45-69; Kramer, 443-76; Campbell and Feagin, 12-59; Clinton Jones, "The Impact of Local Election Systems on Black Political Representation," *Urban Affairs Quarterly* (March 1976): 345-54; Albert Karnig, "Black Representation on City Councils," *Urban Affairs Quarterly* (December 1976): 223-42; Delbert Taebel, "Minority Representation on City Councils: The Impact of Structure on Blacks and Hispanics," *Social Science Quarterly* (June 1978): 142-52; Robinson and Dye, "Reforms and Black Representation;" Karnig and Welch, *Black Representation,* 1981; Chandler Davidson and George Korbel, "At Large Elections and Minority Group Representation: A Re-Examination of Historical and Contemporary Evidence," *Journal of Politics* (November 1981): 982-1005; and Peggy Heilig and Robert Mundt, *Your Voice at City Hall* (Albany, N.Y.: State University of New York Press, 1984).

33. On Hispanic representation see: Taebel, "Minority Representation" and Davidson and Korbel, "At Large Elections." On representation of women see: Karnig and Welch, *Black Representation.* On occupational bias see: Heilig and Mundt, *Your Voice*; and Cassell, "Social Background Characteristics."

34. Welch and Bledsoe, *Black Representation,* 19.

35. Welch and Bledsoe, *Black Representation,* 22-30.

36. Welch and Bledsoe, *Black Representation,* 28-30.

37. Welch and Bledsoe, *Black Representation,* 46.

38. Welch and Bledsoe, *Black Representation,* 50.

39. Welch and Bledsoe, *Black Representation,* 67.

40. Welch and Bledsoe, *Black Representation,* 94.

41. Gelb, 45-69; Jones, 345-54; Albert K. Karnig, "Black Representation City Councils: The Impact of District Elections and Socioeconomic Factors," *Urban Affairs Quarterly* 12 (December 1976): 223-42; Delbert Taebel, "Minority Representation on City Councils: The Impact of Structure on Blacks and Hispanics," *Social Science Quarterly* 12 (June 1978): 142-52; Theodore Robinson and Thomas Dye, "Reformism and Representation on City Councils," *Social Science Quarterly* 59 (June 1978): 133-41; Albert Karnig and Susan Welch, "Electoral Structure and Black Representation on City Councils," *Social Science Quarterly* 63 (March 1982): 99-114; Chandler Davidson and George Korbel, "At Large Elections and Minority Group Representation: A Re-Examination of Historical and Contemporary Evidence," *Journal of Politics* 43 (November 1981): 982-1005; Richard Engstrom and Michael McDonald, "The Election of Blacks to City Councils," *American Political Science Review* 75 (June 1981): 344-55; Richard Engstrom and Michael McDonald, "The Underrepresentation of Blacks on City Councils," *Journal of Politics* 44 (November 1982): 1088-1105; Richard Engstrom and Michael McDonald, "The Effect of At-Large Versus District Elections on Racial Representation in U.S. Municipalities," in *Electoral Laws and Their Political Consequences,* Bernard Grofman and Arend Lijphart, eds. (New York: Agathon Press, 1986); and Rufus P. Browning, Dale Rogers Marshall, and David H. Tabb, eds., *Racial Politics in American Cities* (New York: Longman, 1990); and for the opposition point-of-view see: Leonard Cole, *Blacks in Power* (Princeton: Princeton University Press, 1976); Susan MacManus, "City Council Election Procedures and

Minority Representation," *Social Science Quarterly* 59 (June 1978): 153-61; and Susan MacManus, "At Large Elections and Minority Representation: An Adversarial Critique," *Social Science Quarterly* 60 (November 1979): 338-40.

42. Norman R. Luttbeg, "District Versus At-Large City Council Seats: No; Not Again; But Wait, What About Competition?" A paper for presentation at the annual meeting of the Midwest Political Science Association, Palmer House, Chicago, April 6-8 1995.

43. Susan Welch, "The Impact of At-Large Elections on the Representation of Blacks and Hispanics," *Journal of Politics* 52 (November 1990): 1073. Also see: Charles Bullock and Susan MacManus, "Structural Features of Municipalities and the Incidence of Hispanic Council Members," *Social Science Quarterly* (Fall 1990): 75-89.

44. Grace Hall and Alan Saltzstein, "Equal Employment in Urban Governments: The Potential Problem of Interminority Competition," *Public Personnel Management* (November/December 1975): 386-93; Lee Sigelman, "The Curious Case of Women in State and Local Government," *Social Science Quarterly* (June 1976): 250-65; Albert K. Karnig and Susan Welch, "Sex and Ethnic Differences in Municipal Representation," *Social Science Quarterly* (December 1979): 465-81.

45. Albert K. Karnig and Oliver Walter, "Election of Women to City Councils," *Social Science Quarterly* (March 1976): 605-13; Richard Engstrom and Michael McDonald, "The Election of Women to City Councils: Clarifying the Impact of Electoral Arrangements on the Seats/Population Relationship," *American Political Science Review* (February 1981): 344-54; Robert Darcy, Susan Welch, and Janet Clark, *Women, Elections, and Representation* (New York: Longman, 1987); Susan MacManus, "Women on Southern City Councils: A Decade of Change," *Journal of Politics* (February 1989): 32-49; and Nicholas O. Alozie and Lynne I. Manganaro, "Women's Council Representation: Measurement Implications for Public Policy," *Political Research Quarterly* (June 1993): 383-98.

46. Dahl, *Who Governs?*, 305-25.

47. Norman R. Luttbeg, "Multiple Indicators of the Electoral Context of Democratic Responsiveness in Local Government," a paper presented at the annual meeting of the Midwest Political Science Association, 1987.

48. Timothy Bledsoe and Susan Welch, "Patterns of Political Party Activity Among U.S. Cities," *Urban Affairs Quarterly* (December 1987): 249-69; and David R. Mayhew, *Placing Parties in American Politics* (Princeton, N.J.: Princeton University Press, 1986), 197.

49. Bledsoe and Welch, "Patterns of Political Party," 258-59.

50. Bledsoe and Welch, "Patterns of Political Party," 260-63.

51. Robert L. Morlan, "Municipal vs. National Election Voter Turnout: Europe and the United States," *Political Science Quarterly* (Fall 1984): 457-70.

52. Paul E. Peterson, *City Limits* (Chicago: University of Chicago Press, 1981), 13.

53. Peterson, *City Limits*, 32.

54. Peterson, *City Limits*, 109.

55. Peterson, *City Limits*, 127.

56. Peterson cites several other studies of economic influences on municipal expenditures. The published ones include: R. W. Bahl, *Metropolitan City Expenditures: A Comparative Analysis* (Lexington: University of Kentucky Press, 1969); and J. C. Weicher, "Determinants of Central City Expenditures: Some Overlooked Factors and Problems," *National Tax Journal* (1970): 379-96. Others too

have seen stultifying economic and federal limitations on cities. See: Harvey Molotch, "The City as a Growth Machine," *American Journal of Sociology* (1976): 309-31; Mark Gottdiener, *The Decline of Urban Politics* (Newbury Park, CA: Sage, 1987); and Paul Kantor and Stephen David, *The Dependent City* (Glenview, Ill.: Scott, Foresman, 1988).

57. Terry Christensen, *Local Politics: Governing at the Grassroots* (Belmont, CA: Wadsworth, 1995), 89. These data come from the Advisory Commission on Intergovernmental Relation, *Measuring Local Government Discretionary Authority* (Washington: U.S. Government Printing Office, 1981), 59, so they are somewhat dated although changes in this area probably are quite slow.

58. Jeffrey M. Berry, Kent E. Portney, and Ken Thomson, *The Rebirth of Urban Democracy* (Washington: Brookings, 1993), 75.

59. Berry, Portney, and Thomson, *The Rebirth*, 83.

60. Berry, Portney, and Thomson, *The Rebirth*, 125.

61. Berry, Portney, and Thomson, *The Rebirth*, 146.

62. Berry, Portney, and Thomson, *The Rebirth*, 98.

63. See Clarence Stone, "The Politics of Urban Restructuring: A Review Essay," *Western Political Quarterly* (March 1990): 219-31.

# Chapter 2

# A Sample of American Cities

The studies in the previously described literature rest on case studies, national surveys of city secretaries asking for information on their cities, national surveys of city council members, and data contained in the every five year Census of Governments and in directories, especially the Joint Center for Political Studies' *National Rosters of Black Elected Officials*. No national agency gathers information on municipal elections. Even the names of those serving on city councils have been gathered nationally in the National League of Cities' annual *Directory of City Policy Officials* only since 1983. These directories are not archived by the League. Most recently in 1977, the International City/County Management Association's *Municipal Year Book* published reports of election data gathered from the cities, but of course these data are dated as well as of questionable reliability given that city secretaries applied their own definitions when answering.

## The Sample and Data

This study rests on data from a random sample of 121 cities with populations greater than 25,000 as of the Census of 1990.[1] Data gathering began in late 1992 with the erroneous expectation that as many as 20 cities would be uncooperative. Fortunately, most were very cooperative, although surprisingly some complained that they received many such inquiries each month. El Dorado, Arkansas; New Albany, Indiana; and Florence, South Carolina, were alone in never providing information, despite many promises to do so.

Appendix A lists the sample cities. Additionally, the study included all Texas cities with 1990 populations greater than 25,000 not already part of the random sample. This added 57 cities to the 11 Texas cities already in the random sample. Only Victoria failed to provide data, but these data were gathered by other means. Most of the analysis that follows will use the random sample. The Texas cities can provide confirmation of random sample findings with state laws, culture, and politics held constant. This is not to suggest, however, that Texas cities do not vary greatly.

The 1990 Census of Population, the 1992 Census of Governments, the Joint Center for Political Studies' *National Rosters of Black Elected Officials*, and the National League of Cities' annual *Directory of City Policy Officials*, showing membership on city councils each year, provided much information. Additionally, city clerks and secretaries were asked to complete a questionnaire confirming the individuals serving as mayor and on the city councils as well as terms of office and election format, timing of elections, changes in institutional formats over time, salaries, the number of women, Hispanics, and African-Americans serving on their councils, and beginning of service dates on those serving on their city councils in 1983 (the earliest Directory data). Most importantly, they also were the source for election data, such as the number of votes received by each candidate in elections.

The *Directory of City Policy Officials* lists the end of terms for those on city councils. This allowed the estimation for the timing of municipal elections as well as whether council terms overlapped or were staggered. It also indicates the form of government used in each city. Secretaries were asked to confirm the number on their council, the length of term used, the number of staggers used, the form of government, and the dates of their next election, and to provide actual election results for two complete rounds of elections. For example, if the city had four year terms, two staggers, and the next election in 1994, I requested the 1992 and 1988 election results for one stagger and 1990 and 1986 data on the other stagger. In a city with two year terms, no staggers (all council members elected together), and the next election in 1993, only the 1991 and 1989 election results were requested.

Data on two complete rounds of elections counteracts the possibility that one round might be unrepresentative. Since the period captured by two rounds varies from city to city, this handicaps noting patterns of change over a given period, such as between 1985 and 1992. My major concern, however, was to characterize each city's level of competition. Furthermore given record keeping in many cities, getting earlier election data might prove impossible.[2]

## The Data and Achieving Comparability

The great variety of government and election formats used in these cities complicates having comparable measures. Election results included general elections plus runoff and primary election, if used. They provided information on the number of candidates for each seat, the winning margins of the victors, the number of incumbents running and winning, and the total number of ballots cast.

### Elections for Mayor

Since the mayor serves on the council in the city manager form of government, mayoral election results were included in council data for manager cities. Mayoral election data were gathered for mayor/council cities and combined with mayoral election data from manager cities for some analyses.

## Staggered Elections

Since 34 cities (29 %) elect their entire city council each election, for them only two elections constitute two complete rounds. For most of the other cities, the council is divided into two staggers or groupings of council members whose terms overlap. Six cities have three staggers, and one of two commission cities has one of its commissioners elected each year for a five year term. With the exception of this one commission city, averages are for each of the two most recent rounds of elections, with the most recent being called "recent" and the earlier called "prior." The averages for each round were then compared with each election's results for city with no overlapping terms.

## Incumbents

Incumbents were not flagged by any sample city, but directory information permitted identifying them. Three measures were made that involve incumbents.

### Incumbents Running

The percentage of incumbents running is easily calculated. In the case of staggered elections, this was coded as the percentage of incumbents running of those up for reelection in each election. This was then averaged for the round of elections to get a comparable percentage for staggered and unstaggered cities.

### Incumbents Winning

The percentage of incumbents winning was measured as a percentage of those running, thus if 50 percent ran and all won, this was coded as 100 percent. Again, this was averaged for the round to get comparable data.

### Incumbents Returning

The percentage of incumbents returning combines both percentages. If 50 percent ran and 50 percent won, this would mean that only 25 percent returned. The percentage of incumbents returning could be noted from directories but was confirmed with the election data.

## Candidates Per Seat

The number of candidates per seat in cities using primary elections becomes the number of candidates in the primary divided by the number of seats up for election. When cities used runoff elections, the general election provides these data. When election was for the "top three vote getters," the total number of candidates is divided by three. Again a weighted average combines staggered elections into an average for the round.

## Winning Margin

Because many cities use winning plurality rather than simple majority to determine the winner, the winning margin is measured rather than the vote received by the winner. In the case of single member districts, this is the voting percentage difference between the winner and the highest loser. When runoff elections are used, this percentage is from the runoff election. In the case of "top vote getters" elections, each winner's winning margin is that over the top loser. Each winner's winning margin is averaged for the election and a weighted average is used for the round of elections.

## Voting Turnout

The number of registered voters was requested, but this information tends to be unobtainable from past elections. Voting turnout is, therefore, the number of ballots cast divided by the number of voting age citizens in the city.

### Ballots Cast

Since cities typically need only report who won to the state, many keep a count of the number of ballots cast for each candidate, but not the total number of ballot cast or voters in the election. When this was the case, the at-large election with the largest number of votes is taken as an estimate of total votes cast. In district only contests, the highest number of ballots in each district contest was used, multiplied by the appropriate number. If half the districts had an election, the highest number of ballots cast in these contests were multiplied by two. The incomplete data on registered voters required calculating voting turnout of those eligible.

### Citizen Voting Age Population

The 1990 Census provides the number citizens by different ages. This permits enumerating the number of citizens of voting age for each city. In the 1980 Census, however, only the number of citizens in the entire population is reported. The assumption that the percentage of citizens in the entire population holds also for those of voting age allows the calculation of citizen voting age population in 1980. The citizen voting age population (CVAP) is a straight linear projection for each year between 1980 and 1990 and beyond. In some cities the number of citizens of voting age was much lower than the number of people of voting age.

Voting turnout is merely the number of ballots cast divided by the CVAP. Finally, in the case of cities electing only four of seven district council members in a given election, for example, the number of ballots cast was divided by 4/7s of the citizen voting age population for that year.

**Tenure in Office**

Other data were derived from directory information validated where possible with election data. Information on who served on these councils comes primarily from the National League of Cities' *Directory of City Policy Officials.* In 1984, for example, it shows the names of council members and the mayor in 1983. These individuals were followed through more recent directories until they were replaced. The city secretaries provided information on when those serving in 1983 began their service. Two averages were computed from this information. The tenure of those having completed service on the council merely averages the number of years each served. The tenure of those presently on the council is more circumstantial and suspect, being just a present day snapshot of how long those on the council have served. It may, however, reflect change in the community in recent years. Obviously if over time few incumbents run or few win, a community will have very short tenure in office for its council.

# Variety and Representativeness in Institutional Formats

The reforms associated with efforts to reduce the role of political machines have spread broadly across the United States. In this sample, 55.9 percent of the cities are city manager cities as compared with Sanders' (1982) 61.5 percent for cities over 25,000 in population.[3] He also found 34.6 percent to be mayor/council format versus 41.5 percent in this sample and 3.9 percent commission form versus 2.5 percent here. None of the sample cities changed governmental form to mayor/council during the period back to 1982, suggesting that this random sample slightly overrepresents mayor/council cities. One of the sample cities, Mobile, did move from commission to city manager format reflecting the declining popularity of the commission.

Most researchers consider moving to at-large multiple member districts as characteristic of reform efforts, even though more recent efforts by the federal courts have been to move back to district elections to assure minority representation on councils. In these cities 47.5 percent retain at-large districts, 40.7 percent use a variety of at-large and single member districts, and only 11.9 percent use districts exclusively. An International City/County Management Association (1993) voluntary survey of cities over 25,000 population found 49 percent of the responding 818 cities used at-large selection, 12 percent used district selection, and 39 percent used mixed. Cities in this sample appear representative.

The mix of district and at-large councils varies greatly. Only five cities have fewer than half of the council selected from districts and most have better than 60 percent selected from districts. Among city manager cities using some mix of districts and at-large seats, the mayor is the sole at-large council member in eleven cities and one of several at-large members also in eleven cities. Because the impact of moving to more district-based representation on city council is of fundamental concern, later analyses will make great use of the percentage of council seats that are district seats.

Partisan elections were most offensive to reformers, at least for school and municipal governments. Only fourteen cities or 11.9 percent of the sample use partisan elections. In his 1981 data, Sanders (1982) shows 19.0 percent of cities with these populations to have partisan elections, since none of these communities changed from partisan to nonpartisan elections between 1982 and 1992, the sample appears somewhat biased toward nonpartisan cities. Surprisingly, these were not only Northeastern cities.[4] In this sample, cities in thirteen states use partisan elections; eight were in the Northeast if you include three from Ohio. Four were in states west of the Mississippi.

Finally, reformers favored smaller councils. Since the average council includes only 7.8 members, this effort seems successful. Sanders reports an average for cities with these populations of 7.5 members.[5] Only five (4%) cities had councils of fifteen or larger. Two were in the Midwest and three in the Northeast. One third of the councils include five members and nearly 29 percent have seven members. Most, 88.2 percent, have an odd number of members.

Other institutional differences not associated with the reform movement include whether elections are staggered with only a portion of all council members up each election (what Sanders calls overlapping terms), which applies to 71.2 percent of these cities. Sanders reports 78.0 percent.[6] Five of the sample cities (4%) changed to staggered elections between 1982 and 1992, partially explain differences between the sample and Sanders' findings. Seventeen cities (14%) have primary elections. More than half of these primaries are in cities with nonpartisan elections. One California city uses district primaries and at-large general elections, presumably to give only those appealing to the district interests better access to the general election ballot. Nearly 30 percent of these cities (35 cities) use runoff elections, and just over 11 percent have term limits often dating before the Second World War. Term limits are not new to city legislators as they are to their state counterparts.

The average term for these councils is 3.4 years. A four year term is most popular; 66.1 percent (Sanders shows 67.7%). A two year term is second with 27.1 percent of all cities (Sanders shows 26.7%).[7] This is the shortest term. One city uses five year terms. During the period 1982-1992, five cities (4.2%) changed to longer terms of office, and three changed the mayor's term, two from 2 to 4 years and one from 4 to 2 years. In one Kansas city, the term depends on the winning candidates' percentages of the vote. Three of five council members are up for reelection every two years with the top two vote-getters getting four year terms and the third highest getting a two year term. Finally, only fifty-six cities, 47 percent of all cities and 67 percent of city manager cities, use at-large elections exclusively. The two dominant reform features: city manager format and at-large elections, are typically adopted together.

American city governments show a broad range of institution formats. Most of these differences no longer derive from the machinations of the reform movement. Some derive from the pressures on local government to provide better minority representation and some to achieve greater professionalism, but many seem not so much innovative but rather reflect a "why not" mentality. On occasion, one gets the impression that ideas from the past persist. Many Midwest cities use nonpartisan primaries, with the top two candidates going to the general election. On abolishing partisan elections, they merely retained primaries. A nonpartisan primary followed by a general election differs little from the southern preferred general election followed by a runoff election. One difference is that both primary and runoff elections have low turnout, so the primary followed by general election format has more voters participating in the election of council members.

Cities in the sample provide a representative variety of institutional formats.

## Other Attributes of These Cities

The typical city in this sample has a population of just under 84,000 with the smallest having 25,098 people and the largest just over 782,000.[8] The average city population for cities with populations greater than 25,000 in the 1990 Census was 88,022.[9] Just over 45 percent of the cities have populations between 25,000 and 50,000 and 81 percent have populations below 100,000. Comparing the population distributions of the sample and that of all American cities with over 25,000 people in Figure 2.1 suggests a slight underrepresentation of cities below 50,000 and slight overrepresentation of cities with populations between 50,000 and 100,000.[10] The sample appears representative as judged by population. The distribution, however, suggests the gulf between studying America's largest cities and studying typical cities with populations greater than 25,000.

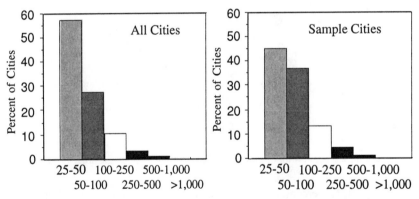

Figure 2.1 Distribution of Populations for All and Sample Cities, 1990

Typically, these cities grew by 15.5 percent between 1980 and 1992, which is representative of the growth of all American cities. All cities with populations greater than 25,000 grew by 22 percent over this period.[11] Population growth of cities within the sample varies greatly. Forty-one (35%) of the cities decline in population, one by better than 20 percent. By contrast, three at least doubled in population, and ten percent grew by more than 50 percent. Clearly the challenge of providing services varies enormously from city to city. African-Americans constitute 12 percent of the populations of these cities; ranging from .1 percent to 58.8 percent. The average is very close to the 11.7 percent average for all cities over 25,000. Similarly, on average Hispanics constitute 9.9 percent of these cities' populations as compared with 10.6 percent of all cities.[12] The percentage Hispanic varies from 0.3 percent to 87.5 percent. Again these cities seem representative of all cities with at least this population.

Racially the cities vary greatly. In 36.5 percent of the cities, all minorities (Hispanic, African-Americans, and Native-Americans) constitute less than 10 percent of the population. By contrast better than 8.7 percent of the cities have at least 50 percent minority populations. At both extremes we might expect few concerns with minority representation, although which minority is to be represented might remain an issue in the case of large percentage minority cities.

This might be expected to be a problem given the total lack of relationship between the percentage African-American and percentage Hispanic shown in figure 2.2.

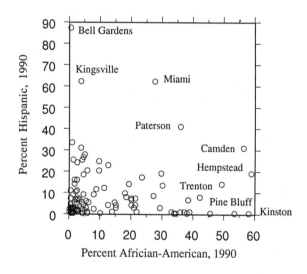

Figure 2.2 Scatterplot of Percent African-American and Hispanic, 1990

The mean, 12 percent, poorly characterizes the data on African-Americans. Nearly 56 percent of these cities are less than 5 percent black, while four (3.5%) have African-American majorities. Similarly, the average percentage Hispanic is 9.9 percent, but fewer than 30 percent of American cities have greater than 10 percent Hispanic populations. Three cities have Hispanic majorities. Many American cities have high African-American or Hispanic percentages, but most have neither. However, ten communities (9%) have white minorities.

The average median age of these cities is 32.4 years, and there is a fairly normal distribution around this age. The mean for all cities is 33.7 percent.[13] Figure 2.3 shows some cities are quite young, with many of school age. Others, while having few young people needing expensive public education, face other citizens' needs for health care and day-to-day living assistance. Similarly, the typical city has 77.7 percent of its public with at least a high school education, and the distribution tends to be close to normal, as shown in figure 2.4.

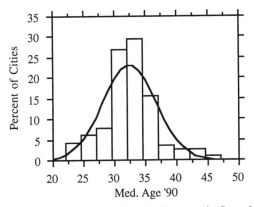

Figure 2.3 Distribution of Median Age in Sample

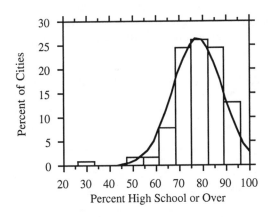

Figure 2.4 Distribution of Percentage With At Least a High School Education in Sample

Median family income across these cities averages just over $37,000, as compared with $37,784 for all cities over 25,000 population. The distribution for the sample, like that for the population, is skewed as shown in figure 2.5. Thirteen percent of the cities have median incomes greater than one standard deviation above the mean for all cities. Typically, 10 percent of the populations in these cities live below the poverty level, but this strongly relates to median family income ($R^2 = .56$). Wealthy cities with few living in poverty can, of course, easily tax residents to provide governmental services for the few residents needing them.

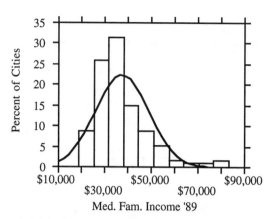

Figure 2.5 Distribution of Median Family Income in Sample

Regionally, the sample cities are well distributed. Table 2.1 shows nearly equal distribution of the cities in the four regions. The *County and City Data Book, 1994* shows the sample cities closely reflect the national distribution of cities. The sample will allow assessing regional differences among the cities. Demographically, the sample cities mirror cities with populations greater than 25,000.

Table 2.1 Sample City Regional Distribution

|  | Regional Frequency Distribution | | |
|  | Count | Percent | National Percent |
|---|---|---|---|
| South | 30 | 25.4 | 26.2 |
| West | 33 | 28.0 | 28.0 |
| Midwest | 30 | 25.4 | 30.7 |
| Northeast | 25 | 21.2 | 15.1 |
| Total | 118 | 100.0 | 100.0 |

**Heterogeneous Cities**

In daily discourse we speak as though we expect some cities to be homogeneous, such as small towns and suburbs, and others to be heterogeneous, such as big cities or industrial towns. Certainly the literature on minority representation emphasizes the heterogeneity between whites and blacks, but some would stress that class may be as important as race. Although much less commonly discussed, we speak of retirement communities that we would expect to be homogeneously elderly and of homogeneous bedroom suburbs.

The data provide three prospective measures of heterogeneity for these cities—percentage minority and two measures of diversity of age and income. Whites in ten cities are a minority. Since a 90 percent minority city is no more diverse than a 10 percent minority city, perhaps subtracting 50 percent in majority minority cities yields a better measure of racial diversity. The distribution of cities on this measure is shown in figure 2.6. More than 52 percent of these cities have fewer than 15 percent minorities. Nearly a quarter of all cities, however, has at least 30 percent minority populations.

The ideal measure of dispersion or diversity would be independent of the mean value in the community. Were the Bureau of the Census to report the standard deviation for age and income for each city, this would be ideal; but they do not. Rather we have percentages falling within various income and age groups. The averages on these groupings for these cities are shown below in

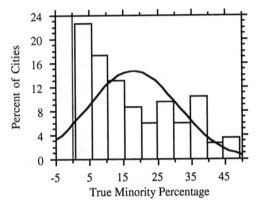

Figure 2.6 Distribution of Sample For True Minorities

table 2.2, followed by the oldest and youngest and wealthiest and poorest cities. Largo, Florida, has the highest median age, forty-seven, with 43 percent of its populace over fifty-five. Bowling Green, Ohio, has a median age of twenty-two with more than 50 percent of its populace between the ages of eighteen and twenty-four.

Table 2.2 Distribution in Grouped Data for Age and Family Income for Different Cities. Shown for Average, Oldest, Youngest, Wealthiest, and Poorest Cities

Distribution of Age

|          | Pct. less than 5 | Pct. 5 TO 17 | Pct. 18 TO 20 | Pct. 21 TO 24 | Pct. 25 TO 34 | Pct. 35 TO 44 | Pct. 45 TO 54 | Pct. 55 TO 64 | Pct. 65 TO 74 | Pct. 75 and Over |
|----------|------|------|------|------|------|------|------|------|------|------|
| Average  | 7.4  | 17.0 | 5.8  | 7.3  | 17.7 | 14.4 | 9.4  | 8.1  | 7.3  | 5.8  |
| Oldest   | 4.4  | 9.7  | 2.8  | 4.6  | 15.3 | 11.4 | 8.7  | 10.7 | 16.3 | 16.0 |
| Youngest | 3.7  | 9.3  | 27.4 | 23.1 | 12.1 | 8.4  | 5.1  | 4.2  | 3.5  | 3.2  |

Distribution of Family Income

|            | <$5000 | $5000- $9999 | $10000- $14999 | $15000- $24999 | $25000- $34999 | $35000- $49999 | $50000- $74999 | >$75000 |
|------------|--------|--------------|----------------|----------------|----------------|----------------|----------------|---------|
| Average    | 6.0    | 9.6          | 9.0            | 17.4           | 15.6           | 17.6           | 15.1           | 9.7     |
| Wealthiest | 4.3    | 6.0          | 4.3            | 9.9            | 8.8            | 13.1           | 15.0           | 38.6    |
| Poorest    | 14.6   | 17.7         | 12.5           | 19.4           | 14.9           | 12.2           | 6.8            | 2.0     |

The central tendency of these distributions is captured by the median age; but to estimate the dispersion with grouped data required a calculation of how many additional years above the median age of a city were needed to include 25 percent of its public. Bowling Green median age of 22 would be half way through the 21 years old through 24 years old category. An estimated 11.6 percent of its population would be one or two years above the median age within the 21-24 category. An additional 13.4 percent must come from older categories. As only 12.1 percent fall within the 25-34 category, an additional 1.3 percent must come from the 35-44 category. This would be an additional 1.5 years. In total, 25 percent of Bowling Green's population must fall between 22 and 36.5.

This is 14.5 for Bowling Green and nearly 23 for Largo, meaning that Bowling Green is more homogeneous with 25 percent of its populace between the ages of 22 and 36.5 as compared with Largo's 25 percent between 47 and 70. A similar measure was computed for family income, although for income the measure is how many dollars above the median family income are needed to include 25 percent of a city's population.

As figure 2.7 shows, the measures of heterogeneity are uncorrelated, meaning that one cannot speak of generally diverse cities as opposed to homogeneous cities. Table 2.3 considers whether central cities, suburbs, and autonomous cities differ in heterogeneity. While these differences typically and expectedly show central cities to be more diverse, only racial diversity in central cities proves statistically significant with a sample of 118.

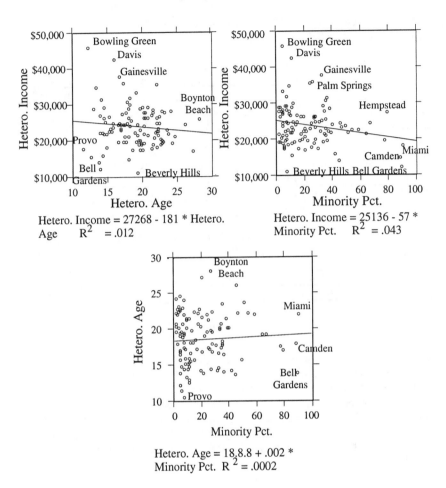

Figure 2.7 Relationships Between Measures of Heterogeneity in Sample Cities

Figure 2.8 presents the relationships between the population of the cities and their heterogeneity on the three measures. Again while the decline in age heterogeneity with population might well be expected, little variance is explained. Similarly, greater racial diversity with increased population is expected, but smaller cities range greatly in minority mix. Little is explained knowing a city's population.

*Chapter 2*

Table 2.3 Heterogeneity in Central Cities, Suburbs, and Autonomous
   Cities in Sample

| | Income Heterogeneity | | | |
| | All Cities | Central Cities | Suburbs | Auto. Cities |
|---|---|---|---|---|
| Mean | $23,868 | $24,228 | $23,107 | $24,248 |
| Minimum | $11,158 | $17,556 | $11,158 | $14,060 |
| Maximum | $45,853 | $31,509 | $29,223 | $45,853 |

| | Age Heterogeneity | | | |
| | All Cities | Central Cities | Suburbs | Auto. Cities |
|---|---|---|---|---|
| Mean | 18.8 years | 19.0 years | 18.1 years | 19.3 years |
| Minimum | 11.4 years | 14.0 years | 12.6 years | 11.4 years |
| Maximum | 28.1 years | 24.0 years | 26.2 years | 28.1 years |

| | Racial Diversity or Heterogeneity | | | |
| | All Cities | Central Cities | Suburbs | Auto. Cities |
|---|---|---|---|---|
| Mean | 18.5% | 28.4% | 15.8% | 17.7% |
| Minimum | 1.4% | 2.3% | 1.4% | 1.9% |
| Maximum | 49.3% | 49.2% | 45.5% | 49.3% |

## Conclusion

Given their random selection, these cities appear quite representative of
American cities with 25,000 people or more. Additionally, they vary greatly in
institutional format and in characteristics of their residents. Both might be expected to influence demands on government as well as the range of actions to
cope with problems and services government might take. This variation far exceeds that among the states, but many of the relationships so commonly discussed, such as homogeneous suburbs and heterogeneous central cities, empiri-
cally prove poorly related or even unrelated.[14]

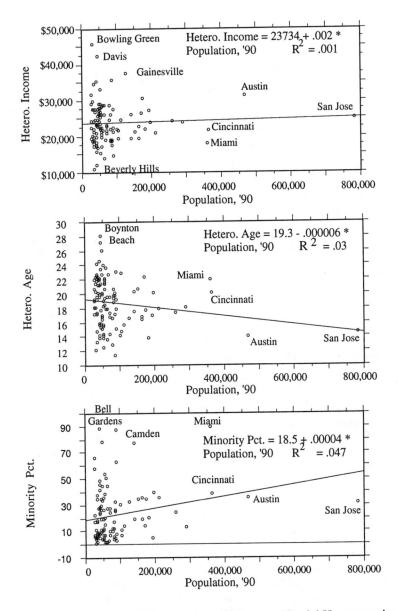

Figure 2.8 Population Effects on Age, Income, and Racial Heterogeneity

# Notes

1. Obviously, I intended to sample 120 cities, not 121.
2. One very cooperative secretary expressed her embarrassment with being unable to find 1988 election results, despite looking "everywhere." Cities have little reason to archive such information. Nevertheless even over this short period record keeping improved greatly in some cities. Early elections were often typed or even hand printed lists while more recent elections were computer printouts. Nevertheless, intercity differences in record keeping were great. In his 1985 study, Luttbeg (1987) called one city after several letters were unanswered. The city secretary admitted that he had received the requests, but offered that he had no method to reproduce the election results. He willingly read the results over the telephone from the blackboard in front of him!

Some cities, especially those in the Northeast, provided photocopies of handwritten ledgers while others provided computer printouts with percentages of votes won and total ballots cast. Sometimes only county clerks or special election authorities could provide election results, but most often the data came from the city secretary's or city clerk's office. Often no office thought it was responsible for such record keeping. Once on being referred back and forth between city and county clerks, a county clerk cited the state's law requiring that the city clerk keep these data. When told that the city clerk had denied having the information, she responded that the city clerk, "Did not know which way she was going through a door!" Eventually, the city clerk hand recorded the data requested. This is all mentioned not to denigrate city secretaries, but to show that the data are only available through the often understaffed offices of busy city secretaries who may make satisfying social science research secondary. The future, thanks to computers, looks brighter.
3. Heywood T. Sanders, "The Government of American Cities: Continuity and Change in Structure," in *The Municipal Year Book 1982* (Washington: International City Management Association, 1982), 181.
4. Sanders reports the mid-Atlantic states for all cities over 2500 have 89 percent partisan elections and New England cities are 46 percent partisan. Sanders, "The Government," 181.
5. Sanders, "The Government," 182.
6. Sanders, "The Government," 183.
7. Sanders, "The Government," 183.
8. Actually, several cities had population over 25,000 in 1990 but declined to below 25,000 by the publication of the *County/City Data Book, 1994* from which these data are taken.
9. *United States Statistical Abstracts, 1993,* 34.
10. *United States Statistical Abstracts, 1993,* 34.
11. Computed from data in *County/City Data Book, 1994.*
12. Computed from data in *County/City Data Book, 1994.*
13. Computed from data in *County/City Data Book, 1994.*
14. Three cities had population declines to below 25,000 after the Census of 1990, meaning that data from the *County/City Data Book, 1994* was unavailable.

Chapter 3

# The Origins of Competition in Municipal Elections

The concept of competition has received much theoretical discussion and research attention, as noted in Chapter 1, and would certainly seem to have ready application to the government "closest to the people." Apart from an extensive research on how members of the U.S. House of Representatives enjoy uncompetitive reelections, both the discussion and the research portray the concept of competition quite simply. A government with open elections but lacking a clear choice of candidates taking clear and alternative policy positions or having only some candidates who are likely to win elections is *not* a true democracy. Earmarks of competitive elections would be at least two candidates seeking each seat, winners facing stiff opposition and winning narrowly, incumbents not always winning, some turnover in those holding public office, and elected officials not spending their entire adult life as public office holders. While this discussion and research might lead to an expectation that the same cities would be labeled "competitive" were we to assess any of a range of measures, such as number of candidates per seat, average winning margin, and incumbents winning, this is not the case. *Winning margin is the best indicator of municipal competition, but it is unrelated to incumbent advantage or turnover.*

## Assessing Competition in Elections

The late V. O. Key's (1949) seminal study of the lack of competition in the American South underlies much of our thinking about the role of competition in American democracy, if not in all democracies.[1] Key attributed the lack of governmental services for indigents in the South to the lack of an opposition political party to compete with the Democrats at the polls. The lack of competition allowed the dominant Democratic Party, or any such unopposed political party, to appeal only to those with money to contribute, the inclination to vote, and the disposition to act when displeased with those who govern. Key argued that competition between political parties was essential to having a viable, responsive, and responsible democracy.

Key's research underlies the continuing concern with competition between political parties at the state level. Since Dawson and Robinson (1963), we have a long and continuing assessment of whether the political parties compete for public offices, such as seats in the state legislature and for governorships.[2] Some see a trend toward improving competition at the state level in these assessments and others do not.[3] While there is increasing awareness that we need to distinguish between the competition for the office of governor and that for the legislature and to consider district level competition as opposed to statewide competition, the research continues to focus on competition between political parties.[4] In the assessment of the role of competition at the local level, however, we have few hints whether some cities see close competition between Republicans and Democrats. Thanks to the reform movement, most cities have nonpartisan elections; thus we have no declarations of political party affiliation by local candidates.

City councils might be studied to see if there are voting blocks and how closely balanced such blocks are, but elections probably afford the best opportunity to assess the level of competition in a city. Instead of noting voting blocks, however, this study focuses on whether elections are competitive. It may be that states or cities with close voting blocks lack competition in their elections. Alternatively competitive elections may not yield closely balanced voting blocks. Tucker and Weber (1992) studying district versus statewide competition make this point. Again at the city level, however, competition may not necessarily be between rivals for differing voting blocks. Individuals' desires to be on the city council may have nothing to do with the policy votes of those they seek to replace. This is a study of competition in elections not between voting blocks.

## Assessing Competition in the U.S. House

The other primary area of research on competition, or the lack of it, comes from the United States House of Representatives. The period between 1952 and probably 1994 saw little evidence of balance between the Democrats and Republicans within the House. The U.S. Senate also showed domination by Democrats.[5] The only competition evident during this period was between the Republican controlled presidency and the Democratically controlled Congress. This competition has attracted much attention under the name of "divided government" rather than "competitive government."[6] Belatedly we have realized that states also have divided government, but there is little research concerning whether divided government states are more competitive and have more responsive government.[7]

The bulk of research on competition in the U.S. House has focused on elections rather than voting blocks. Many concepts derive from this research, such as incumbent advantage, marginal or competitive seats, and the dynamics of how those holding Representative seats can help to assure continuing reelection and careers in the House. Additional concepts have been suggested, such as constituent services to ingratiate the incumbent to constituents, media manipulation, name familiarity, new style, media-based campaigns with astronomical campaign spending, and the increasing role of interests to contribute campaign funds to underwrite such campaigning. We have little closure as to which best explains the lack of competition for public offices or what are called "safe seats" in congressional research. Additionally, many have focused on the role of state legislatures creating districts that assure incumbency advantage.[8] The election outcome in 1994 may, however, refocus interest on voting block competition as well as undercut the explanations for incumbency advantage.

The focus of congressional research on the competitiveness of elections, nevertheless, directs our attention to many measures of competitions in municipal elections.

## Measures of Competition in Elections

If one narrowly wins an election, one has experienced a competitive election. Such a narrow win might motivate the winner to be more responsive to constituent demands. Of course, there are alternative reactions that we might expect. The winner may voluntarily leave office rather than face such a hotly contested election in the future. The winner may seek to discourage future challengers by accumulating substantial and daunting campaign reelection funds. The winner of a competitive election may not be more responsive, but **winning margin** would seem a good measure of how competitive elections are. A seat's marginality or safeness, of course, uses this measure. A winner in a two-candidate race receiving a "safe" 55 percent of the vote has a winning margin of 10 percent. As we saw in chapter 2, the many varieties of municipal elections require a focus on the **winner's margin of victory**.

Another useful measure in assessing electoral competition in municipal elections is the number of candidates vying for each seat up in the election, **candidates per seat**. Most congressional contests see two dominant candidates, one from each of the major political parties; thus the use of the winner's percentage of the vote rather than the winning margin. Many municipal contests see few candidates for each seat, and again the many formats of such contests, such as runoff elections, require some consideration of how to assess the number of candidates for each seat comparably. The most uncompetitive election is one that is uncontested, having a single candidate for each seat. Many candidates per seat afford greater choice and possibly more competition.

We might expect the two measures, candidates per seat and winning margin, to be closely related. At the extreme with only a single candidate and no opposition, the candidate gets 100 percent of the vote with the same winning margin. Each additional candidate takes part of the vote with the winner more narrowly getting victory. It is, of course, possible that the winner will, even in a field of many candidates, win by a wide margin.

Open seats, given their importance at least in congressional research, might well be expected to spur many candidates to run, seeking to replace the retiring incumbent. This proves true in these data (see *Appendix B*). I would therefore hypothesize the relationship shown below.

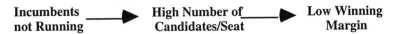

| **Incumbents** | → | **High Number of** | → | **Low Winning** |
| **not Running** | | **Candidates/Seat** | | **Margin** |

Incumbency advantage, the substantially greater than 50 percent chance that the incumbent will win reelection, as noted, holds a dominant conceptual role for congressional election research. Incumbents seeking reelection who win, the percentage of **incumbents winning**, is one of the measures assessed as is the percentage of **incumbents running** and the overall percentage of **incumbents returning** after an election. In all cases this is the percentage of those up for election in the case of cities using staggered elections. Obviously, if only 50 percent of incumbents run and only 50 percent win, only 25 percent return. The measure of incumbents returning is, of course, 100 percent minus the percentage turnover. While the congressional elections of 1992 and 1994 underline the possibility that incumbents may anticipate a coming reelection defeat and voluntarily retire, incumbents running falls short of assessing competition. This is especially the case at the local level where low pay, volunteerism, and the lack of ambition may cause such retirements even without serious challengers.[9]

At some point even the most successful incumbent must either retire, die, or be defeated. Directories of elected officials show when individuals first held public office and when they left. There are two measures in such directories: how long those who have completed their service served, and how long those presently on the council have served. The average tenure of those having served goes back to those in office in 1983 when the first nationwide directory was published.[10] The measure of **tenure of those having completed service** probably best captures whether a city's council regularly runs and wins reelection. This may change over time, however; thus I averaged the time in office of those on the councils at the end of 1992, **tenure of those on present council**. We cannot know how long they will serve, however.

These variables should be related. If incumbents do not run for reelection, they cannot win reelection; and if incumbents do not run or do not win, they cannot return to office. We might be interested in those cities with many incumbents retiring rather than losing because of Prewitt and Eulau's finding of "volunteerism" in San Francisco Bay municipalities in the 1960s.[11] My expectation would be, however, that running and winning are unrelated given that the percentage winning is based on those running. Incumbents not running or not winning will obviously relate to turnover or the percentage of incumbents returning after elections. Finally, a municipality with high turnover, at least over time, should have very short tenure among its incumbents. It is possible, however, that some incumbents escape the turnover and serve long terms. The figure above expresses these relationships.

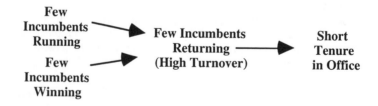

## It is Not Possible to Declare One City's Elections as Clearly More Competitive Than Another's

Key's study of the lack of competition in the American South lead to the expectation that any one measure of competition would serve to identify the more competitive governments or elections. At least at the local level, however, all measures fail to identify the same cities as competitive. Table 3.1 shows four potential measures of competition at two times or rounds of elections.

Average Winning Margins of the winner and Candidates Per Seat hold fairly constant across the two election rounds (also see *Appendix B*). The experience of candidates in the earlier round, typically in the middle 1980s, holds for the most recent round of elections in the late 1980s and early 1990s. The averages for both correlate highly with each round. Average winning margins and candidates vying for each seat seem enduring characteristics of a city's politics. This, however, is not the case for other measures.

The Percentages of Incumbents Running, Winning, and Returning varies greatly from one round of election to the next, as shown in table 3.1. Predicting any one of these attributes of a city's politics from what it experienced in the last or prior round of elections would err greatly. *Any expectation that cities can be easily characterized as having competitive or uncompetitive elections seems dashed by these considerations.*

Table 3.1 Correlations of Cities in Two Rounds of Municipal Elections

|  | Ave. Win. Marg., Recent | Ave. Win. Marg., Prior |
|---|---|---|
| Ave. Win. Marg., Prior | .675 | - |
| Win. Marg., Average | .913 | .913 |
|  | Cands. Per Seat, Recent | Cands. Per Seat, Prior |
| Cands. Per Seat, Prior | .555 | - |
| Cands. Per Seat, Ave. | .881 | .879 |
|  | % Incumbs. Run., Recent | % Incumbs. Run., Prior |
| % Incumbs. Run., Prior | .135 | - |
| % Incumbs. Run., Ave. | .787 | .718 |
|  | % Incumbs. Win., Recent | % Incumbs. Win., Prior |
| % Incumbs. Win., Prior | .112 | - |
| % Incumbs. Win., Ave. | .708 | .753 |
|  | % Incumbs. Ret., Recent | % Incumbs. Ret., Prior |
| % Incumbs. Ret., Prior | .137 | - |
| % Incumbs. Ret., Ave. | .749 | .759 |

As judged by these correlations (and scatterplots in *Appendix B*), incumbents cannot anticipate kind treatment by voters in future elections just because they experienced easy reelection in the past. *Cities experience "episodes" where there is heavy turnover.* While I will want to turn to such episodes in a later chapter, clearly the experience of incumbents varies enormously between rounds of elections.

**Factor Analysis of Competition**

Data on two rounds of elections were gathered to smooth what I thought would be minor changes caused by some incumbents voluntarily retiring or a new ambitious candidate seeking office. Most cities were expected to be consistent between rounds of elections. This was found true for average winning margins and candidates per seat. Cities with few candidates seeking each seat, wide winning margins, and long tenures on their councils were expected to have little turnover as each incumbent sought and won reelection. Obviously, these measures vary from round to round, dashing these expectations. Averages across rounds could be used only with the loss of much information. Eleven measures were used in

Table 3.2 Factor Analysis of Competition Measures

| Factor Analysis Summary | | | Eigenvalues | |
|---|---|---|---|---|
| | | | Magnitude | Var. Prop. |
| Number of Variables | 11 | 1 | 3.19 | .29 |
| Number of Cases | 116 | 2 | 2.46 | .22 |
| Number Missing | 2 | 3 | 1.46 | .13 |
| P-Value | <.0001 | | | |

| | Competition | Old Style Politics | Recent Politics |
|---|---|---|---|
| % Incumbents Run, Recent | .040 | .078 | .769 |
| % Incumbents Run, Prior | .012 | .790 | .056 |
| % Incumbents Win, Recent | .224 | .061 | .631 |
| % Incumbents Win, Prior | .061 | .779 | -.001 |
| Average Winning Margin, Recent | .705 | -.260 | .332 |
| Average Winning Margin, Prior | .725 | .114 | .256 |
| Candidates per Seat, Recent | -.784 | .001 | -.154 |
| Candidates per Seat, Prior | -.705 | -.367 | .204 |
| % Incumbents Returned, Recent | .158 | .053 | .961 |
| % Incumbents Returned, Prior | .068 | .956 | .098 |
| Past Council Members, Years Served | .006 | .593 | .060 |

the factor analysis—incumbents running in recent and prior rounds, incumbents winning in both rounds, incumbents returning in both rounds, candidates per seat in both rounds, average winning margins in both rounds, and average tenure in office for those having completed their office-holding.

Table 3.2 shows the orthogonal rotation of the most prominent three factors, explaining nearly 65 percent of the variance in these measures. This is the most understandable rotation as the two-factor solution finds factors 1 and 2 combining and a four-factor solution breaks apart average winning margin and candidate per seat.[12] I labeled the first factor the Competition Factor because many candidates per seat and narrow winning margins seem to me to best capture the ideas of competition. As noted above, these measures hold across election rounds.

Note that this factor is high when winning margins are greater, thus it is really a "non" competitive factor. To facilitate later analysis, I reversed the sign on this factor; so it is now accurately labeled the **Competition Factor.** The very poor loadings of incumbent success in seeking and winning reelection on this factor would suggest that levels of competition little affect incumbent reelection success. Cities with closely contested municipal elections have nearly the same percentage of incumbents running, winning, and returning as cities with uncontested or poorly contested elections.

Factors 2 and 3 differ mainly in time. Cities with few incumbents running have few winning and thus have high turnover, but there is no consistency in which cities show this turnover across rounds of elections. I characterize factor 2 as "Old Style Politics" rather than just the pattern of the prior round of elections because average tenure on the council loads on the factor. This is a weak loading, however. Overall the three factors do not account for years on the council of those having completed their terms. The recent round of elections seems to be a complete break with the past. While this seems most provocative, I found little support for any hypothesis accounting for the differences.[13]

## Conclusions Concerning Competition

Key's seminal research on the American South certainly leads us to expect the Republican Party could not compete in the South at least in the 1940s, whether one measured voting blocks or the partisan mix in state legislatures, the congressional delegations, winning margins in elections, candidates for each seat, incumbents winning, incumbents running, incumbents returning (lack of turnover), uncontested races, or primary contests. City data shows no such simple pattern.

In a 1985 study of Texas local elections, Luttbeg (1987) first confronted the complexity of competition at the local level.[14] Actually, the data in this nationwide study show less complexity than that in Texas, but multiple dimensions are needed to capture the complexity of data on how competitive a city's council elections are. It may be easier to conceptualize all cities as either elitist or pluralistic, but a continuum would seem more accurate and conceptually rich. It would range from cities where elected officials are held accountable to those where no one challenges incumbents, not out of satisfaction with the job they have been doing but rather because money and support would not be forthcoming. Certainly, the data support this more complex conceptualization.

One factor consistently emerges that would certainly suggest competition. It centers on how many candidates seek each seat on the council and the average winning margin in elections. Cities score consistently on both variables across election rounds (see *Appendix B*). These variable loadings are negatively related, as we would expect. Cities with more candidates per seat have narrower winning margins. This is documented in figure 3.1. Typically each additional candidate decreases the average winning margin by more than 6 percentage points, but clearly few communities have more than two or three candidates for each seat. These are not tight relationships. The first factor nevertheless appears to be the closest to the concept of competition.

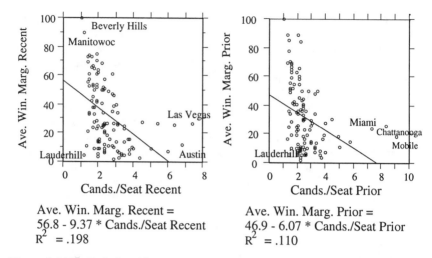

Ave. Win. Marg. Recent =
56.8 - 9.37 * Cands./Seat Recent
$R^2$ = .198

Ave. Win. Marg. Prior =
46.9 - 6.07 * Cands./Seat Prior
$R^2$ = .110

Figure 3.1 The Relationship Between Candidates Per Seat and AverageWinning
Margin

The other factors appear to be best characterized by the turnover experienced in that round of elections. These variables have the largest loadings on these factors. This would suggest that each round of elections would have some cities with substantial turnover, either by way of incumbents voluntarily retiring from office or losing their reelection efforts, others with only modest turnover, and yet others with no turnover. Knowing this for any given round would afford *no* prediction of the next, however. Some other data on these cities bolster this conclusion. Thanks to the directories and information on election timing, for 99 cities we know the percentage of those up for reelection that did not return in every election back to 1983. With my information on the timing of a city's elections and whether staggers are used, I know when there was an election and for how many council members. Missing names after an election, of course, mean turnover. Depending on how cities elect council members, this may give as many as 5 rounds of elections, but it usually adds another round to the two I captured with election data.

While these data cannot be divided into incumbents running and incumbents winning, they do allow an exploration of whether each new election is an independent event in terms of turnover. Is there a history of turnover for each city or is there no predicting turnover? Table 3.3 gives two analyses for the percentage of possible turnover for cities with elections every two years. The analysis shows poor correlations across these five elections, although the signs are all positive. Similarly, the regression analysis shows that turnovers in the four elections preceding the most recent poorly explain turnover in that election. *Each election's turnover seems substantially independent of any prior election's turnover.*

Table 3.3 Analysis of Turnover Over Time in Selected Cities

| Correlation Matrix | Elections | | | |
| --- | --- | --- | --- | --- |
| | Most Recent | - 2 yrs. | - 4 yrs. | - 6 yrs. |
| Most Recent | - | | | |
| - 2 yrs. | .237 | - | | |
| - 4 yrs. | .205 | .037 | - | |
| - 6 yrs. | .121 | .021 | .064 | - |
| - 8 yrs. | .168 | .205 | .099 | .150 |

| | |
| --- | --- |
| Count | 99 |
| Number Missing | 0 |
| R Squared | .114 |
| Adjusted R Squared | .076 |

| Regression Coefficients | | |
| --- | --- | --- |
| Intercept | 28.7 | † |
| | (7.14) | |
| - 2 Years | .206 | ** |
| | (.098) | |
| - 4 Years | .173 | |
| | (.093) | |
| - 6 Years | .091 | |
| | (.099) | |
| - 8 Years | .084 | |
| | (.091) | |
| † Regression coefficient (Standard error) | *** $\alpha \leq .001$ <br> ** $\alpha \leq .01$ <br> * $\alpha \leq .05$ | |

# Is There a Second Aspect of City Politics?

Factors 2 and 3 in table 3.2 appear to be quite specific to the individual rounds of elections rather than enduring characteristics of these cities. Other than Factor 1's capturing of the importance of the number of candidates seeking each council seat and of winning margins, the other data fail to contribute continuing characteristics of the politics of these cities. Incumbents' decisions to seek re-election, their winning of reelection, and the overall rate that incumbents are returned to office vary over time in the same cities. This would suggest that most communities experience occasional crises or "episodes" of unusually turnover on their city councils, and that this turnover poorly relates to competition measures, such as candidates per seat and average winning margins. My concern is how to treat Factors 2 and 3.

While each election may only poorly predict the treatment of incumbents in the next, some cities over time retain more incumbents. I propose another measure on which cities vary greatly, the average turnover on the council for the period 1983 to 1992. Figure 3.2 shows this measure strongly relates to both measures of tenure and in factor analysis (not shown) loads nearly equally on both factors dealing with the return of incumbents. This would suggest that average turnover over many rounds of elections would show high and low turnover cities.

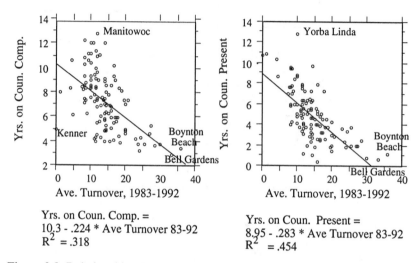

Yrs. on Coun. Comp. =
10.3 - .224 * Ave Turnover 83-92
$R^2$ = .318

Yrs. on Coun. Present =
8.95 - .283 * Ave Turnover 83-92
$R^2$ = .454

Figure 3.2  Relationships Between Average Turnover and Years on the City Council of Those Having Completed Their Terms and Those Presently Serving

Because factor 1 seems to capture the extent of competition in the cities, I will continue the focus on it. A new measure, average turnover for the period 1983-1992, used instead of the two other factors that seem to capture only the experience of incumbents in the most recent and prior rounds of elections, seems to add a second dimension to a city's politics. Figure 3.3 shows these measures are uncorrelated. *Obviously turnover is unaffected by competition, at least in city politics.*

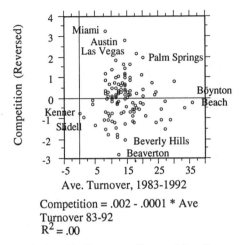

Competition = .002 - .0001 * Ave
Turnover 83-92
$R^2$ = .00

Figure 3.3  Relationship Between Competition Factor
and Average Turnover for the 1983-1992
Period

Figure 3.4 considers the implication of none of the variables having to do with incumbents being related to competition. Certainly the idea that open seats lead to more competition among those seeking that seat has even entered public discussion. At the city level, however, as the figure shows, open seats do *not* encourage competition. *Term limits with the avowed purpose of making seats open every six or eight years to engender competition would seem likely to have little of the intended impact at least in American cities.*

## Accounting for Competition and Turnover in City Elections

While V. O. Key saw the value in competition among political parties for the services provided to the "have nots," institutions were assumed to shape levels of competition. In his later work he saw the use of election primaries as threatening to political parties and thus competition.[15] Even at the state level, however, we might expect that competition would flourish in some states but not in others. Certainly the literature on competition in our cities suggests that both institutions and demography should affect levels of competition.

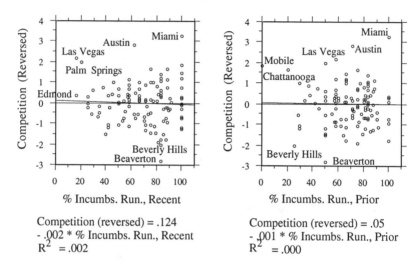

Competition (reversed) = .124
- .002 * % Incumbs. Run., Recent
$R^2$ = .002

Competition (reversed) = .05
- .001 * % Incumbs. Run., Prior
$R^2$ = .000

Figure 3.4   Open Seats in Recent and Prior Rounds and the
Impact on Competition.

## Institutional Factors

As noted in Chapter 1, Svara (1990) sees an institution, the mayor/council form of municipal government, resulting in conflict.[16] The conflict that concerns him is between council members and between the council and the executive. Such conflict discourages good public policy and implementation. While he does not suggest that this conflict might result in competition among those seeking election to the city council, it would seem entirely likely that the different camps in the conflict would seek to increase their strength on the council by electing like-minded individuals and defeating opponents. Certainly, Dahl's (1961) ideas of competition among alternative elites would suggest such a dynamic in the case of conflict among elected or even nonelected decision-makers. This reasoning suggests the mayor/council form cities would have more competition.

Svara's argument would also suggest that a larger council would lack the civility of a smaller council resulting in more conflict. Welch and Bledsoe (1988), however, argue that such a relationship is spurious. Larger cities have both larger city councils, they argue, as well as the greater diversity that leads to greater conflict.[17] We will certainly need to consider the role of the size of a council on the conflict and competition it experiences.

In seeking to account for why some cities have more competitive elections, clearly some see institutional explanations and others see the need for de-mographic controls to assure that institutional variables are indeed the cause of different levels of competition. To deal with various hypotheses and with alter-native hypotheses, I sought to systematically include first institutional variations and then demographic variations in seeking a conclusion that anticipates as yet unexplored theories as well as alternative hypotheses. I also sought uncorrelated independent variables by using factor analysis with orthogonal rotations. No doubt some will view this as atheoretical or counterintuitive, but given our lack of exploration of these issues, I see this course as most illuminating and thorough.

Eleven variables capture the range of institutions used in these cities. While some have had much theoretical discussion, such as the percentage of seats on the council held by representatives elected in districts rather than at-large, each of these differences has been subject to some discussion. Table 3.4 presents the orthogonal factor analysis of institutional variations among American cities, including dummy variables representing four regions. Factor analysis reduces the complexity of analyses by capturing underlying dimensions or the nexus of variables. Fortunately, in this case these dimensions are fairly understandable.

Substantial regional variations in institutions, demography, and policy were not appreciated until late in the analysis. Liebert (1974) noted such regional differences in local government long ago. The "progressive movement," which had its greatest success in shaping western state institutions and least success in the Northeast, along with little specifics dealing with cities in early state constitutions. Historians might have guided a classification of where the Progressives had greatest success for a more refined classification of the states. However, I wanted to retain the same regional controls across all analyses; thus the Northeast is Pennsylvania, West Virginia, and Maryland and all states north and east. The South includes the "border" states of Kentucky and Oklahoma. The Midwest includes states westward to the Rockies including the Dakotas, Nebraska, and Kansas.

No single variable of "reformed" versus "unreformed" can be found to characterize these cities. The first factor, titled **Northeastern Traditional Cities**, includes many of the institutions that might be called "reformed." Notably absent from this factor, however, is the use of nonpartisan elections. Western cities most avoid the more traditional forms of our municipal institutions, using the city manager form, having small city councils elected at-large with long terms of office, and overlapping terms or staggered elections. Northeastern cities, as we might expect, resisted reform efforts and retain traditional institutions. But partisan elections, traditionally viewed as quintessentially unreformed, poorly load on this dimension.

Partisan elections are retained by some cities, but such elections load on the fourth factor along with the use of primary elections. Since only 14 of the 118 cities use partisan elections and only 5 of these are in the Northeast, this is not a regional characteristic. This is also shown by the poor loadings of all regions on this factor. The only fitting label is **Partisan Election Cities**.

The remaining two factors, like the first, have strong regional characteristics. The **Southern, Spring and Runoff Election Cities** factor captures those variables. Runoff elections have been noted to be southern before, but I am unaware of anyone noting the strong southern use of spring rather than fall elections. Municipal term limits are poorly explained by any of these factors, but their use seems more common in the South.

## Table 3.4 Factor Analysis of Municipal Institutions

| Factor Analysis Summary | | | Eigenvalues | |
|---|---|---|---|---|
| Number of Variables | 15 | | Magnitude | Var. Prop. |
| Number of Cases | 114 | 1 | 3.56 | .24 |
| Number Missing | 4 | 2 | 2.26 | .15 |
| P-Value | <.0001 | 3 | 1.56 | .10 |
| | | 4 | 1.47 | .10 |

| | Northeastern Trad. Cities | Southern, Spring and Runoff Election Cities | Midwestern Low Salary Cities | Partisan Election Cities |
|---|---|---|---|---|
| City Manager or Mayor/Council | .651 | -.230 | -.019 | .457 |
| Number on City Council | .775 | -.207 | .105 | -.097 |
| Staggered Elections | -.732 | .109 | .138 | -.109 |
| Term of Office | -.627 | -.184 | -.181 | .253 |
| Percent Districts | .655 | .067 | -.013 | .150 |
| Runoff Elections | -.092 | .640 | -.508 | -.058 |
| Term Limits | -.077 | .387 | -.130 | -.181 |
| Yearly Salary | .094 | .067 | -.631 | .119 |
| Partisan Elections | .081 | -.030 | -.061 | .816 |
| Primary Elections | -.002 | -.163 | .127 | .736 |
| Spring Elections | -.015 | .617 | .358 | -.280 |
| Northeast City | .575 | -.389 | -.287 | -.064 |
| South City | .034 | .880 | -.133 | .040 |
| Midwest City | .151 | -.105 | .730 | .266 |
| West City | -.687 | -.392 | -.305 | -.250 |

Finally, the **Midwestern, Low Salary Cities** dimension shows that the Midwest tends to pay council members poorly and does not use runoff elections to deal with no candidate winning a majority. These four factors explain 59 percent of the variance in municipal institutions.

Table 3.6 presents the regression analysis of the impact of municipal institutions on the reversed **Competition** factor. Before considering these findings, however, I wish to focus on the regional differences in competition in table 3.5. *The West stands out as clearly most competitive and the Midwest as least competitive.*

Table 3.5 Regional Averages for Competition

| Region | Competition Score |
|---|---|
| West | .307 |
| South | .009 |
| Northeast | -.154 |
| Midwest | -.236 |

Two of the four institutional factors in Table 3.6 substantially influence competition. Traditional institution cities in the Northeast, and certain not in the West, lack competition in their elections. To put this more into focus, I will look at the relationships between the high loading variables for both factors. The number of seats on the city council loaded most highly on the **Northeastern Traditional Cities** factor, and the number of candidates per seat and average winning margins loaded on **Competition**. Each additional seat on the council decreases the number of candidates for each seat on average by .091 and increases the average winning margin by .518 percent.

Western cities have few city council members, averaging 6.0, compared with 6.7 for the South, 9.1 for the Midwest, and 10.1 for the Northeast. A plausible dynamic to account for competition being higher in the West would be that the fewer seats do not overcome the limited pool of candidates who might "volunteer" for running.

Table 3.6 Institutional Factors as Explanations for Competition

| Count | 113 |
|---|---|
| Number Missing | 5 |
| R Squared | .158 |
| Adjusted R Squared | .126 |

| Regression Coefficients | | |
|---|---|---|
| Intercept | -.028 | † |
| | (.084) | |
| Northeastern Trad. Cities | -.282 | ** |
| | (.085) | |
| Southern, Spring Election Cities | -.037 | |
| | (.084) | |
| Midwestern, Low Salary Cities | -.249 | ** |
| | (.084) | |
| Partisan Election Cities | -.014 | |
| | (.084) | |

† Regression coefficient $*** \alpha \leq .001$
(Standard error) $** \alpha \leq .01$
$* \alpha \leq .05$

*Chapter 3*

*It would seem that the simple expedient of reducing the size of a city's council would improve competition.* This certainly is not the trend in municipal governance. Moreover, the strong regional patterns might suggest that the West is most likely to have non-traditional institutions and is most competitive. The institutions may not shape competition. If the causality is there, however, efforts to improve representation of different sectors of the city by having more council members may sacrifice competition. Whether larger councils improve representation will be considered in chapter 5.

*Higher salaries would also seem to improve competition.* Just considering the bivariate relationship, a $10,000 increase in council yearly salaries would increase the number of candidates per seat by .47. Again given the strong regional bias to the use of high salaries regional patterns, not salary, may be the cause of this greater competition.

If more competitive elections are the goal, smaller councils with higher salaries might help. The adjusted $R^2$ is only .126, however. Notably term limits, most common in the South, prove to little affect levels of competition. Also while competition between the two major political parties is often seen as the source of competition in elections, the lack of partisan elections in cities little affects competition in elections.

Table 3.7 Institutional Explanations for Average Turnover on City Council

| Count | 114 |
|---|---|
| Number Missing | 4 |
| R Squared | .188 |
| Adjusted R Squared | .158 |

| Regression Coefficients | | |
|---|---|---|
| Intercept | 14.17 | † |
|  | (.517) | |
| Northeastern Trad. Cities | .202 | |
|  | (.519) | |
| Southern, Spring Election Cities | 1.902 | *** |
|  | (.520) | |
| Midwestern, Low Salary Cities | .618 | |
|  | (.517) | |
| Partisan Election Cities | -1.66 | ** |
|  | (.518) | |
| † Regression coefficient (Standard error) | *** $\alpha \leq .001$ ** $\alpha \leq .01$ * $\alpha \leq .05$ | |

Table 3.7 gives the regression for the second aspect of local competition, **Average Turnover** on the City Council. **Southern, Spring Election Cities** have more turnovers on their councils while **Partisan Election Cities** have less. Since the **Southern, Spring Election Cities** and **Partisan Election Cities** prove unrelated to **Competition**, competitive elections must not be at the root of

their turnover.

It is somewhat easier to speculate why partisan election cities have fewer turnovers. The political parties may use ideology or issue positions to recruit candidates rather than relying on economic self-interest or appeals to civic duty to motivate prospective candidates. Such candidates may be more ambitious or may have other rewards than satisfying ones civic duty, such as seeing ones party gain control of the council and pass desired policies.

As with institutional explanations for the level of competition in municipal elections, institutions only account for about 16 percent of the variance in turnover. Institutional factors leave much of the variance unexplained in both competition and turnover.

## Demographic Factors

The residents of American cities vary greatly. The concentration of people in metropolitan areas with the shift from an agricultural economy to a manufacturing and service economy as well as the post-Second World War shift of the middle-class to the suburbs has fundamentally altered us socially. All the included demographic variables derive from the *County/City Data Book, 1994.* using 1990 Census data.[18] We might expect the size or population of the city to be fundamental to municipal politics. Not only does the scale of municipal services entail larger budgets and greater consequences for inefficiency and failures to provide needed services, but also the very interactions between elected officials and their constituents become more structured and impersonal. The American public is quite mobile and as a result many cities, such as St. Louis, have lost population to the suburbs, while others, such as Las Vegas, have grown rapidly. Population and percentage change in population between 1980 and 1992 are among the demographic variables included in this analysis.

Much has been said about the suburbanization of America, usually emphasizing the flight of the middle class from diverse core cities to homogeneous, bucolic enclaves outside the hated masses tightly packed in decaying, industrial, larger cities.[19] The measure developed to capture whether a city is suburban is the population of a city as a percentage of the population of the metropolitan area where it is located.[20] A core city, such as Cincinnati, would hold a substantial percentage of the metropolitan area, as would an autonomous city such as Great Falls. A suburb, such as Beverly Hills, would include but a fraction of the metropolitan population.

Why would suburban politics differ from that of larger cities? The diversity thought true of larger cities underlies much of our expectation of political differences. Diversity drives different needs and expectations of government and leads, presumably, to more significance placed on who wins municipal office and more competition for such offices.[21] I also include many measures of diversity among these cities.

While diversity has become a euphemism for racial and ethnic differences, measures of diversity are not limited to such factors. The percentage of residents that are African-American, Hispanic, and all minorities from the 1990 Census are included. Other measures derive from the wealth and agedness of a city's residents. Wealth, from Key's initial consideration of the importance of competition, is expected to influence residents' demands for services and ability to pay for such services. Presumably, one of the strong factors driving the middle-class to the suburbs was the desire to not pay high taxes to provide services for the urban poor. Median family income should measure the central tendency of this. More educated communities might be expected to press government differently for policies, thus I include the percentage of the city's residents with at least a high school education. As expected, these measures are highly correlated.[22]

Some cities have younger populations. This certainly applied to the suburbs immediately after the Second World War. They were, as a result, the birthplace of the Baby Boomers. The modern Sun City retirement communities represent the opposite end of this scale. The two are likely to differ greatly in the services they expect as well as the taxes they are willing to pay.

I sought a standard deviation measure, but both age and income are reported as categories of unequal size. As initially presented in chapter 2, both diversity or heterogeneity measures start with the median for the city. The measures represent how many years or how much family income would be needed above the median to include 25 percent of the city residents. A homogeneous city would have a small number so heterogeneity is an appropriate name for this measure. None of the measures of diversity correlate.[23] When characterizing a city as homogeneous or diverse, we need to be specific whether we are speaking about African-American percentage of its population, the Hispanic percentage, the age distribution, or the income distribution.

Since Key's documentation of the lack of competition at all levels of southern politics, this has always been an important regional concern. After the realization of the regional differences noted in municipal institutions in table 3.4, I decided to again add the four regions to the factor analysis of demographic variables.

Six orthogonally rotated factors explained 79 percent of the variance in these demographic and region variables. Three factors contributed significantly to explaining competition in city elections. Larger cities have more competition. Independently cities that have a great percentage of their metropolitan area's population, especially common in the Midwest, have less competition, which runs counter to the expectation that suburbs are small cities, politically behaving differently than large cities. The second strongest relationship between the demography factors and competition is for heavily Hispanic and less educated cities to have more competition. The percentage African-American does not load on this factor. No demographic factor proved to explain much of the variance in turnover of city council members.

## Demographic and Institutional Factors

Thus far only the independent effects of institutions and demography on competition, both with region added, have been considered. While we know that large and small cities are more likely to use the mayor/council format and it seems widely believed that heavily minority cities might have at-large elections used against minorities to deny representation, there seems to have been little interest in whether some demographic characteristics cause more use or dependence on some institutions. I would suggest that institutions might merely intervene between demography and competition. Some demographic elements in western cities may cause them to adopt the city manager form and gain the resulting greater competition. Worse, some types of cities may both be likely to adopt certain institutions and to be more competitive. Thus relationships between institutions and competition may even be spurious. Western cities may just be more likely to use the manager form because of state laws and independently to be competitive.

Certainly we do not need to look far to find instances where we might expect demography to shape institutions. In the South, the high percentage of African-Americans and the experience of disenfranchisement during Reconstruction probably motivated the adoption of at-large municipal representation to preclude blacks from winning any council seats. Additionally, the entire discussion of unreformed cities suggests that Northeastern cities resisted the reform movement and retained the mayor/council form of government with large councils and unstaggered terms. Finally, we might expect that the "professionalism" of the city manager form of municipal government might appeal to newly incorporated, middle-class suburbs. It is much more difficult to conceive of how institutions might shape demography, although the "professional" city manager form might attract middle class individuals, making a city manager city even more middle class. They may "shop" for the manager form.

Again resorting to orthogonal rotation, factor analysis gives independent variables, in this case assessing the full nexus of interaction among institutional, demographic, and regional variables without prejudging which is causing which. Table 3.8 shows seven factors account for 68.4 percent of the variance for the 27 variables. Oblique rotation was tried initially but differed little. The independence of factors in the Verimax, orthogonal solution makes further analysis easier and therefore was used.

The table shows the rotated factors are easy to understand. Interestingly, only three factors show both demographic and institutional variable loadings. The first factor, accounting for nearly 19 percent of the variance, includes institutional, demographic, and regional variables. The strongest loading variables on this **Declining Population, Northeastern, Traditional Cities** factor are the institutions that have been labeled "traditional." As implied by this name and as noted by others, these institutions are quite common in the Northeast and quite uncommon in the West. The only demographic variable loading on this factor captures these cities' declining populations. It is possible, of course, that there is not a causal connection between declining population and retention of the older municipal institutions. Northeastern cities may have both without any causality between them. Apart from declining population, this dimension was also clearly evident in my earlier focus on municipal institutions.

### Table 3.8 Factor Analysis of Demographic and Institutional Variables

| Factor Analysis Summary | | Eigenvalues | | |
| --- | --- | --- | --- | --- |
| Number of Variables | 27 | | Magnitude | Var. Prop. |
| Number of Cases | 112 | 1 | 5.02 | .186 |
| Number Missing | 6 | 2 | 4.11 | .152 |
| P-Value | <.0001 | 3 | 2.34 | .087 |
| | | 4 | 2.05 | .076 |
| | | 5 | 1.89 | .070 |
| | | 6 | 1.59 | .059 |
| | | 7 | 1.46 | .054 |

| | Declining Pop., Northeast Trad. Cities | Minority Cities | Partisan Cities | Large, High Salary Cities | MW Non-Sub. Cities | South. Black Cities | Older Pop. Cities |
| --- | --- | --- | --- | --- | --- | --- | --- |
| Manager or M/C | .634 | .094 | .480 | -.003 | .047 | -.121 | .031 |
| Number on C. | .777 | -.061 | -.126 | .074 | .109 | -.249 | .073 |
| Staggered | -.704 | -.104 | -.126 | -.068 | .128 | .059 | -.156 |
| Term of off. | -.626 | .032 | .347 | .182 | .079 | -.180 | .031 |
| Percent Dist. | .651 | -.009 | .098 | .134 | .308 | .050 | -.054 |
| Runoff elect. | -.198 | .040 | -.157 | .410 | -.075 | .558 | .015 |
| Term limits | -.088 | .019 | -.294 | .401 | .159 | .234 | .092 |
| Yearly salary | .076 | .112 | .117 | .871 | -.090 | .014 | -.044 |
| Partisan | .082 | .080 | .736 | -.036 | .015 | .058 | .131 |
| Primary | .014 | .011 | .680 | -.169 | .131 | -.076 | -.081 |
| Spring Elections | -.044 | .037 | -.485 | -.212 | .227 | .457 | -.011 |
| Population, '90 | -.022 | .029 | -.156 | .882 | .126 | -.004 | -.143 |
| Pop. Chg.'80-'92 | -.567 | -.209 | -.190 | .182 | -.137 | .108 | -.297 |
| Pct. Hisp.'90 | -.256 | .657 | -.342 | .032 | -.210 | -.258 | -.261 |
| Pct. Afr.-Am. '90 | .111 | .509 | .271 | .169 | -.083 | .579 | .043 |
| Med. Age '90 | .033 | -.234 | .006 | -.025 | -.093 | .019 | .910 |
| Pct. HS or over | -.244 | -.888 | -.079 | -.017 | -.026 | -.005 | -.151 |
| Med. Fam. Inc. | -.209 | -.607 | -.183 | -.001 | -.429 | -.293 | .069 |
| Pct. Below Pov. | .202 | .815 | .171 | .074 | .180 | .253 | -.076 |
| Minority Pct. | -.111 | .844 | -.050 | .138 | -.195 | .258 | -.143 |
| Hetero. Age | .394 | .166 | .075 | -.100 | .121 | .149 | .758 |
| Hetero. Income | .121 | -.475 | .065 | .084 | -.082 | .247 | -.372 |
| Pct. of SMSA | .074 | .205 | .015 | .200 | .736 | .108 | -.020 |
| Northeast | .607 | .101 | .129 | -.035 | -.604 | -.139 | -.061 |
| South | -.077 | .137 | -.124 | .019 | .030 | .877 | .036 |
| Midwest | .233 | -.195 | .131 | -.176 | .672 | -.232 | .052 |
| West | -.679 | -.042 | -.136 | .188 | -.145 | -.480 | -.097 |

(Institutions: rows Manager or M/C through Spring Elections; Demography: rows Population, '90 through West)

The second factor, **Minority Cities**, is exclusively demographic and closely resembles the earlier demographic analysis. Again, the percentage of African-Americans loads marginally on this factor, although the percentage Hispanic and the total minority percentage both load dominantly. Also as in the earlier analysis, no regional pattern is evident.

The third factor, **Partisan Cities**, is exclusively institutional and is identical to that factor noted earlier. The fourth factor again includes both institutional and demographic variables. The **Large, High Salary Cities** show no regional pattern unlike the earlier, institutional analysis. The inclusion of the demographic, core city versus suburb variable seems to be the reason. Midwest cities are non-suburban, tend to be large, and pay their city council members poorly. Including the core city/suburb variable pulls the Midwest onto another factor, the **Midwest, Non-Suburban Cities** factor.

Factor six mixes institutions and demography again. **Southern, Black Cities** also use runoff elections and spring elections. Notably, the West is strongly negative on this factor and the percentage Hispanic loads negatively. Minorities in the South mean African-Americans but elsewhere, especially in the West, it means Hispanics. The eighth and last factor, **Older Population Cities**, shows neither institutional nor regional loadings and again matches a factor in the earlier demographic analysis.

## Accounting for Competition

I introduce turnout to account for competition. While turnout is not often considered as an institutional variable, the successes in San Diego, Oregon, and elsewhere with mail ballots as well as in other developed democracies with compulsory voting and institutionally initiated registration would suggest that

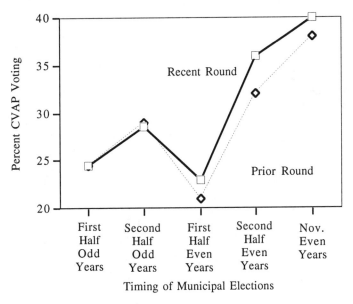

Figure 3.5 Turnout of Citizens of Voting Age by Timing of Municipal Elections

turnout is easily influenced by institutional arrangements. Figure 3.5 shows that not only do fall elections have higher turnout, the highest turnout is in fall elections in even number years, especially when municipal elections coincide with state and national elections. Clearly turnout can be institutionally encouraged with fall elections and by not having staggered terms, but it is also affected by demography.

The conceptualization of the interaction between turnout and competition, however, argues that competition encourages turnout, not the other way around. In the context of city politics, especially in a metropolitan area with suburbanites disinterested in local governance, Prewitt and Eulau's (1969, 1973) San Francisco Bay area study suggests a dynamic in which disinterest and low turnout discourages both ambition for public office and competition for public office.[24] No doubt competition and turnout have a reciprocal relationship, but here I seek to assess the origins of competition and turnover. Average citizen voting age population turnout across the two waves is introduced into the following analysis, as an independent variable.[25]

As in the earlier analyses focusing on institutions and demography separately, in table 3.9 cities with the cluster of institutions, labeled "traditional," lack competition. This is the factor, **Declining Population, Northeastern, Traditional Cities**. The importance of higher council salaries to increased competition continues to show, as the **Large, High Salary Cities** factor. Large cities also prove to have high salaries, perhaps by way of the increased "professionalization" of the city council in such cities as a result of the greater complexity of legislation in larger cities. As the press of business extends the time commitments of those serving on a council, higher salaries permit "full-time" city council members. This is certainly the case at the state level.[26] Both traditional institutions and high salaries retain their regional associations.

The earlier, demographic analysis noted the importance of large population cities to increased competition, independent of how heavily minority, especially Hispanic, the population was. The great impact of high minority cities remains evident in table 3.9, shown as **Minority Cities**, but again such cities are not necessarily large cities. **Older Population Cities** failed to achieve statistical significance in the earlier demographic analysis but proves more important here. Cities with older populations also tend to be those losing population although this is not associated with the Northeast. Since other considerations, such as diversity, load on other independent factors, I can only speculate that few seek elective offices in such cities, dampening competition. *Nationwide, the graying of America seems likely to make city elections less competitive.*

With other factors controlled, cities with higher turnout tend to be those with more competition. Certainly it is possible that turnout may not cause competition but may be the result of competition. However, candidates may seek council seats when they know that incumbents cannot win simply by having an extended group of friends cast votes for them in very low turnout elections. This was certainly suggested in the "volunteerism" analysis.

Table 3.9 The Impact on Competition of Eight Independent
Institutional and Demographic Factors plus Turnout

| Count | 111 |
|---|---|
| Number Missing | 7 |
| R Squared | .314 |
| Adjusted R Squared | .260 |

| Regression Coefficients | | |
|---|---|---|
| Intercept | -.638 | † |
|  | (.225) | |
| Declining Pop., NE, | -.333 | *** |
| Traditional Cities | (.080) | |
| Minority Cities | .282 | ** |
|  | (.085) | |
| Partisan Election Cities | -.053 | |
|  | (.080) | |
| Large, High Salary Cities | .253 | ** |
|  | (.079) | |
| Midwest, Non-Suburban | -.052 | |
| Cities | (.081) | |
| Southern, Black Cities | .045 | |
|  | (.087) | |
| Older Population Cities | -.183 | * |
|  | (.080) | |
| CVAP Voting Average | .024 | ** |
|  | (.008) | |
| † Regression coefficient | *** $\alpha \leq .001$ | |
| (Standard error) | ** $\alpha \leq .01$ | |
|  | * $\alpha \leq .05$ | |

While many factors achieve statistical significance in table 3.9 and these factors account for no more than 26 percent of the variance in competition, few of these relationships provide an opportunity to engineer improved competition. The strongest relationship, that for **Declining Population, Northeast, Traditional Cities,** suggests a dynamic with non-traditional municipal forms encouraging competition at least in cities with increasing population and outside the Northeast. I have noted, however, that western states are most likely to use these non-traditional institutions (table 3.4), to be most competitive (table 3.5), and to have the most rapidly increasing populations (note 24). The entire dynamic may thus be spurious with the West explaining all elements. If so, obviously I could not suggest that cities could be made more competitive by moving them westward.

To explore this possible lack of causality, table 3.9 was redone excluding western cities. The relationships held and now explain nearly 39 percent of the variance in competition. If we consider this from the opposite perspective, excluding the northeastern cities with their rapidly declining populations and strong tendency to use traditional institutions but only being somewhat less competitive, the relationship is weakened, explaining only 21 percent of the variance. It is the Northeast that is different, apparently. Regional differences in the popularity of municipal institutions, in population change, and in competition do not explain this dynamic. Since adding the population change variable to the regression in table 3.9 shows it does not much affect the relationship, I might cautiously suggest that cities wishing to increase competition should adopt non-traditional municipal government institutions. Perhaps contrary to Svara's hypotheses, smaller, at-large elected councils with no distinct executive mayor see their disagreements on the council spreading into elections, enlivening those contests with rival candidates. A professional manager also may be at the root of this greater competition in non-traditional institution cities. Perhaps the "faith" of city managers in development results in quasi-political parties with one pro-growth and pro-manager while the other champions older lifestyles and would replace the city manager.

Table 3.10 Standardized Coefficient Splitting Regression Into Regions

|                                   | West  | Midwest | Northeast | South |
|-----------------------------------|-------|---------|-----------|-------|
| Declining Pop., NE., Traditional  | -.069 | -.503   | -.455     | -.088 |
| Minority                          | .546  | .288    | .409      | .067  |
| Large, High Salary                | .138  | .388    | .358      | .617  |
| Older Population                  | -.184 | -.062   | -.298     | -.287 |
| CVAP Voting Ave.                  | .269  | -.107   | .375      | .463  |

A few factors hold when I split the analysis into the four regions, as shown in table 3.10. While at its weakest in the West, the **Large, High Salary Cities** factor always improves competition, especially in the South. Since large cities have such high salaries, however, the mere act of raising salaries may not encourage competition. Adding yearly salary to the regression in table 3.9, however, shows higher salaries increase competition even when population is controlled. *Cities wishing in improve competition regardless of their populations seem able to do so merely by raising yearly salaries.* Apparently, when there are substantial salaries at stake many will seek public offices.

The remaining relationships are demographic and thus are difficult to use as levers to improve competition. An increased **minority** population encourages competition, except in the Black, South. And cities with **Older Populations**, regardless of region, experience less competition in their elections; but this is quite weak in the Midwest.

# Accounting for Turnover

Table 3.11 extends the analysis to the other measure of a city's politics, **Average Turnover**. The 8 independent variables account for one-fifth of the variance. The demographic factors in earlier analysis little explained turnover; but the combined analysis shows demography does affect turnover. **Southern Black Cities**, as before, have more turnover. The strongest influence on turnover, however, comes from cities using **Partisan Elections**. Surprisingly, they have lower turnover. This may suggest that political parties can retain incumbents once recruited. Southern cities in particular seem to have many incumbents retiring voluntarily.

## Discussion

Several conclusions seem warranted by these analyses. While there are regularities in municipal politics, they tend to be more complex than the literature would suggest. Some findings, while obvious, have never been suggested, and some expectations are unsubstantiated.

*Competition is unrelated to turnover, at least at the local level.* Most fundamentally, elections in American cities do not allow placing cities on a single continuum from those where incumbents face close challenges that they frequently lose to those where few incumbents leave office other than by their personal decision to retire. Competition in municipal elections, as captured by narrow winning margins and many candidates for each elected office, proves unrelated to how many incumbents run, win, or return to office in any given round of elections. Indeed, from one round of elections studied to the next, different cities proved to have high turnover. Incumbent success in each round of elections is largely an independent event. While this might be pleasing for those advocating more democracy at the grassroots, the fact that competition is independent makes it troublesome. *Decisions by incumbents and their challengers rather than levels of public satisfaction or dissatisfaction in competitive elections seem to best account for turnover. Competition is an independent phenomenon, almost a sideshow.* While some cities show enduring competition across the years, the absence of a relationship with turnover leaves in question what the benefits of competition might be. *Competition certainly seems to have no impact on incumbents' concerns about reelection.* I will explore representation and policy impacts of competition in later chapters.

*Traditional institutions discourage competition.* A cluster of four institutions, labeled "traditional," stands out repeatedly. Each institution has an older or "traditional" and a newer form. Traditional cities would have an independently elected mayor who sits as the executive and a separate legislative branch, the city council. Most importantly, such cities have no council appointed city manager that serves as the executive. Such cities represent the opposite pole, the non-traditional form or city manager format. Additionally, traditional cities have larger, district elected councils with all council members up for election each election. They tend to have no overlapping council terms. Lineberry and Fowler (1967) compared "reformed" and "unreformed" city institutions. These labels might have applied except that partisan elections, the quintessential unreformed institution, proved unrelated to this dimension.

Table 3.11  The Impact of Turnover on Municipal Councils of Seven
            Independent Demographic and Institutional Factors Plus
            Turnout

| Count | 112 |
|---|---|
| Number Missing | 6 |
| R Squared | .261 |
| Adjusted R Squared | .204 |

| Regression Coefficients | | |
|---|---|---|
| Intercept | 14.779 | † |
|  | (1.447) |  |
| Declining Pop., NE, | .188 |  |
| Traditional Cities | (.516) |  |
| Minority | .760 |  |
| Cities | (.537) |  |
| Partisan Election | -2.226 | *** |
| Cities | (.518) |  |
| Large, High Salary | -.717 |  |
| Cities | (.507) |  |
| Midwest, Non-Suburban | .444 |  |
| Cities | (.519) |  |
| Southern, Black | 1.541 | ** |
| Cities | (.561) |  |
| Older Population | -.085 |  |
| Cities | (.514) |  |
| CVAP | -.017 |  |
| Voting Average | (.054) |  |
| † Regression coefficient | *** α ≤ .001 |  |
| (Standard error) | ** α ≤ .01 |  |
|  | * α ≤ .05 |  |

Persistently, traditional institutions prove associated with cities with low
levels of competition. I can suggest that small councils raise the identities and
status of council members, thereby encouraging more interest among potential
candidates and more competition. A similar argument can be made for why
competition is less common when districts are used rather than at-large elections. Being a representative of a district would seem to have less status than
representing the entire city; and because of this, few might seek district council
positions, especially when both are present in a city. I suspect also that district
elections might center on single issues, where opposing positions are unlikely
within the district. Perhaps in a city manager city there is more status attached
to the only elected branch of the city government, and again this higher status
attracts more city council candidates and yields greater competition. These ideas
offer little to account for why the remaining characteristic of these non-traditional
institutions, staggered elections, attract more competition. Is there greater status
in being only one half of the council up for election in a given year? Perhaps

prospective opponents see few opportunities in staggered elections and decide they must act now rather than wait two more years in the hopes of challenging a more vulnerable incumbent.

*Region, or probably history, explains the use of traditional but not other institutions.* The factor analyses of institutions as well as the combination of institutions and demography show strong regional patterns. Northeastern cities tend to use traditional institutions, and western cities use non-traditional institutions. These regional patterns would have to be labeled moderately strong and can only be interpreted as reflecting the popularity of different municipal institutions when the state constitutions in different regions were written. The traditional institutions of the Northeast were retained while the popularity of reform institutions caused western state constitutions to specify them for western cities. The only other municipal institution that showed a regional distribution was runoff elections being popular in the South.

*The West is both competitive and uses non-traditional institutions.* As shown in table 3.5, the West is quite competitive in its municipal elections. In conjunction to the above noted pattern of non-traditional municipal institutions to be most common in the West, this suggests that the relationship for such institutions to result in greater competition might be spurious, with the West causing both. However, even outside the West non-traditional institutions prove related to greater competition. The opposite pole of this pattern is the Northeast's use of traditional institutions and relative lack of competition. Perhaps the uniqueness rests with the Northeast, not the West.

*Declining populations are associated with traditional institutions and are less competitive.* In the analysis combining institutions and demography, cities experiencing declining populations prove to have traditional municipal institutions. Viewed from the opposite pole, cities with increasing population have non-traditional institutions. Again I suspected that region caused this association as cities with declining population are mainly in the Northeast as is the use of traditional institutions. In this case excluding the Northeast did weaken the relationship. Nevertheless, population decline is most common in cities using traditional institutions as is less competition for elected offices. Such cities are probably the older core cities of metropolitan areas whose institutions date from an earlier time. If so, it is not the institutions that are causing the decline in competition, but rather the dampening effects of being an elected official in a city losing its population and tax base. Perhaps the declining racial diversity of such cities reduces incentives to win public offices.

*More complex society results in higher salaries and encourages competition.* Consistently the salaries paid to council members have stood apart from other institutions and resulted in more competition. With the addition of demography to the equations, the population of the city closely relates to the salary paid to council members. The dynamic this suggests is familiar in the professionalization of Congress and of state legislatures. As the economy grows more complex and requires full-time council members to resolve the city's problems, few can hold another job. To attract and retain council members higher salaries are necessary. With higher salaries, however, more prospective candidates are interested and will compete for council seats. If this dynamic is correct, of course, few small cities can be expected to raise council salaries, but were they to do so, more competition seemingly would result.

*Apart from traditional institutions and salary, other institutions are unimportant to competition.* Table 3.9 shows only two factors that include institutions contributing much to competition. Term limits, runoff elections, partisan elections, spring elections, and primaries all fail to much affect competition.

*Competition increases in ethnically rich cities outside the South.* Table 3.9 showed several primarily demographic factors that contribute substantially to competition. Cities with substantial minority populations have greater competition. This may again suggest that all forms of heterogeneity contribute to competition, but age heterogeneity and an old population dampen competition. Additionally, income heterogeneity is poorly captured by any of my factors. The redistribution of income by way of government providing services to the poor seems unaffected by the mix of wealth in cities. Cities with many elderly residents lose competition, presumably because few want to deal with the problems of a declining population and tax base city. Apparently race, not income, underlies competition for city council seats when minorities, especially Hispanic minorities, can win and strive to do so. Note that within the South, the **Minority Cities** factor poorly explains competition.

*Cities with partisan municipal elections have sharply reduced turnover.* The other dimension of city politics, turnover, sharply decreases when a city has partisan elections. This may suggest important differences in the recruitment of candidates in partisan and nonpartisan cities.

*Southern cities with many African-Americans have much turnover.* The only other factor shaping turnover is the **Southern, Black Cities** factor that increases turnover. The South has a mean turnover in each election of 16.3 percent compared with 13.7 percent in the West, 12.8 percent in the Midwest, and 13.7 percent in the Northeast.

## Conclusion

All of this seems very complex. Perhaps the strongest finding is that while we can understand the medium level dynamics affecting politics in these cities, we cannot use higher level organizing concepts, such as competition as captured by many variables that we might expected to interrelate. Winning margins and candidates per seat interrelate and most closely reflect our ideas of competitive elections. A second and entirely independent dimension is the average turnover among council members.

While institutions do somewhat affect competition and turnover, the regional pattern of such institutions and the popularity of some institutions only in moderate population cities may suggest they are merely associated with competition and turnover rather than causally related.

*Overall, social engineering with urban institutions, despite the heralded success of the reform movement, seems ineffective.* The primary thrust in institutional change today, moving to district rather than at-large selection of council members, would seem to be swimming upstream as the non-traditional cluster of institutions sees cities adopting at-large rather than district seats. Such cities, however, prove to have neither larger nor smaller minority populations.

70                                    *Chapter 3*

# Notes

1.  V. O. Key, Jr., *Southern Politics* (New York: Alfred A. Knopf, 1949).
2.  Richard E. Dawson and James A. Robinson, "Inter-Party Competition, Economic Variables, and Welfare Policies in the American States," *Journal of Politics* (May 1963): 265-289.
3.. Austin Ranney, "Parties in State Politics," in *Politics in the American States: A Comparative Analysis,* Herbert Jacob and Kenneth N. Vines, eds. (Boston: Little, Brown, 1965), 61-99 versus Harvey J. Tucker, "It's About Time: The Use of Time in Cross-Sectional State Policy Research," *American Journal of Political Science* (February 1982): 176-196.
4.  Harvey J. Tucker and Ronald E. Weber, "Electoral Change in U.S. States: System Versus Constituency Competition," in *State Legislative Careers,* Gary Moncrief and Joel Thompson, eds. (Ann Arbor: University of Michigan Press, 1992).
5.  Stephen D. Shaffer and George A. Chressanthis, "Accountability and U.S. Senate Elections," *Western Politics Quarterly* 44 (September 1991): 625-639; and Alan Abramowitz and Jeffrey A. Segal, *Senate Elections* (Ann Arbor: University of Michigan Press, 1992).
6.  Gary W. Cox and Samuel Kernell, *The Politics of Divided Government* (Boulder, Colo.: Westview, 1991).
7.  Morris P. Fiorina, *Divided Government* (New York: MacMillan, 1992); and Norman R. Luttbeg, *Comparing the States and Communities: Politics, Government, and Policy in the United States,* 3rd ed. (Dubuque, Iowa: Eddie Bowers Publishers, 1998), chapter 9.
8.  Gary C. Jacobson, *Strategy and Choice in Congressional Elections,* 2nd ed. (New Haven: Yale University Press, 1983); and Gary King and Andrew Gelman, "Systemic Consequences of Incumbency Advantages in U.S. House Elections," *American Journal of Political Science* 35 (February 1991): 110-138.
9.  Kenneth Prewitt, *The Recruitment of Political Leaders: A Study of Citizen-Politicians* (Indianapolis: Bobbs-Merrill, 1970).
10.  National League of Cities, *Directory of City Policy Officials* (Washington: National League of Cities, 1983-1992).
11.  Prewitt; and Heinz Eulau and Kenneth Prewitt, *Labyrinths of Democracy* (Indianapolis: Bobbs-Merrill, 1973).
12.  An oblique solution was also considered, but it differed little from that of the orthogonal rotation. Also, the independence of orthogonal factors has benefits in regression analysis.
13.  Exploring the unexpected difference between rounds gives little insight. The timing of rounds of elections varies between cities. For most cities using staggered elections with four-year terms, the most recent round consists of elections in 1991 or 1992 and in 1989 or 1990 for the other stagger. The prior round of elections fell in 1987 or 1988 and in 1985 or 1986. The recent round includes elections in the late 1980s and early 1990s, and the prior round in the middle 1980s. Two rounds of elections for nonstaggered cities with two-year terms, however, could be in 1992 and 1990. Cities with two-year, staggered terms thus with elections every year would also complete two rounds going back in time to only 1989 or 1988. Thus the timing of the rounds differs, making hypothesis development difficult. Perhaps some national happening changed the politics of our cities in the late 1980s.
     To assess this, we partitioned cities into two classes—those with staggered

three- or four-year terms and the others. The factors of the two classes of cities shown in the table below do differ slightly. The 71 staggered, three- and four-year term cities show the pattern shown for all cities, but the other cities differ somewhat. For these other cities, the recent and prior rounds prove even more distinctive. Only average winning margin crosses rounds as a measure of competition. The important findings of this analysis are that all measures do not capture a single dimension of competition in municipal elections, that only Winning Margin and Candidates Per Seat hold across rounds, and that a city's experience with failure to return many incumbents in one election round allows no prediction of how it will behave in the next round of elections. Incumbent election success is unpredictable.

Table  Comparison of Factors in Typical Staggered Three- and Four-Year Terms Cities and Other Cities

Rotated Factor Patterns for Three- and Four-Year Term Staggered Cities

| | | | |
|---|---|---|---|
| % Incumbents Run, Recent | .017 | .152 | .716 |
| % Incumbents Run, Prior | -.229 | -.758 | .084 |
| % Incumbents Win, Recent | .264 | -.159 | .650 |
| % Incumbents Win, Prior | .111 | -.776 | -.075 |
| Average Winning Margin, Recent | .651 | .226 | .337 |
| Average Winning Margin, Prior | .668 | -.065 | .261 |
| Candidates per Seat, Recent | -.832 | -.012 | -.126 |
| Candidates per Seat, Prior | -.835 | .070 | .098 |
| % Incumbents Returned, Recent | .158 | .053 | .958 |
| % Incumbents Returned, Prior | -.028 | -.968 | .039 |
| Past Council Members, Years Served | .082 | -.700 | -.122 |

Rotated Factor Pattern for Other Cities

| | | | |
|---|---|---|---|
| % Incumbents Run, Recent | .270 | .797 | .082 |
| % Incumbents Run, Prior | .843 | .139 | -.044 |
| % Incumbents Win, Recent | -.077 | .652 | -.271 |
| % Incumbents Win, Prior | .694 | .238 | -.017 |
| Average Winning Margin, Recent | -.260 | .249 | -.858 |
| Average Winning Margin, Prior | .233 | .239 | -.753 |
| Candidates per Seat, Recent | -.334 | .036 | .688 |
| Candidates per Seat, Prior | -.775 | .322 | .343 |
| % Incumbents Returned, Recent | .113 | .930 | -.140 |
| % Incumbents Returned, Prior | .897 | .299 | -.079 |
| Past Council Members, Years Served | .319 | .485 | -.234 |

14. Norman R. Luttbeg, "Multiple Indicators of the Electoral Context of Democratic-Responsiveness in Local Government." A paper presented at the annual meetings of the Midwest Political Science Association, Chicago, April 1987.

15. V. O. Key, Jr., *American State Politics: An Introduction* (New York: Knopf, 1956).

16. James H. Svara, *Official Leadership in the City: Patterns of Conflict and Cooperation* (New York: Oxford University Press, 1990), 40.

17. Susan Welch and Timothy Bledsoe, *Urban Reform and Its Consequences: A Study in Representation* (Chicago: University of Chicago Press, 1988), 95-99.

18. U.S. Government Printing Office, *County/City Data Book, 1994*.
19. Arthur J. Vidich and Joseph Bensman, *Small Town in Mass Society* (Garden City, NJ: Anchor Books, 1960).
20. This usually meant the population of the Standard Metropolitan Statistical Area, but some cities with lower populations did not have such a designation. In such cases the population of the county surrounding the city was used.
21. Oliver P. Williams, Harold Herman, Charles S. Liebman, and Thomas R. Dye, *Suburban Differences and Metropolitan Policies: A Philadelphia Story* (Philadelphia: University of Pennsylvania Press, 1965).
22. The correlation is .633. The scatterplot below shows a curvilinear pattern.

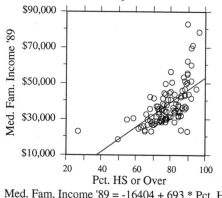

Med. Fam. Income '89 = -16404 + 693 * Pct. HS or over        $R^2$ = .40

23. While the percentage African-American and percentage Hispanic correlate with the overall measure of percentage minority, the two are uncorrelated, as are all other measures of diversity.
24. Kenneth Prewitt, *The Recruitment of Political Leaders: A Study of Citizen-Politicians* (Indianapolis: Bobbs-Merrill, 1970); and Heinz Eulau and Kenneth Prewitt, *Labyrinths of Democracy* (Indianapolis: Bobbs-Merrill, 1973).
25. This was estimated by linear projection between the 1990 Census information on the number of adult citizens and the 1980 Census estimates from the number of citizens among residents.
26. Norman R. Luttbeg, *Comparing the States and Communities*.

Chapter 4

# The Impact of Competition
# in Municipal Elections

Below is the model shown in chapter 1. Chapter 3 evaluated antecedents to competitive elections, but this chapter turns to the relationship between competitive elections and policy. The model suggests an intermediate variable, responsiveness of elected officials, for which I have no data. An explanation of how competition affects policy rests on officials being forced to be responsive because of competitive election. Thus even lacking these data, we should expect competitive and uncompetitive cities to enact different policies. Political theory, however, tends to be vague about what differences we might find. As noted in chapter 1, V. O. Key (1949) saw the scale of government positively related to competition. More competition results in larger scale government. The logic was that a second political party would appeal to the poor and with victory would responsively increase the scale of government to provide promised and wanted services. What happens if the first, middle-class party wins, however? Would it not decrease services and certainly taxes?

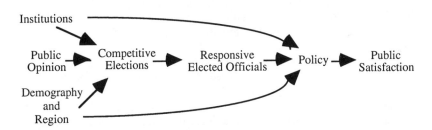

The literature on how congressional elections are won would suggest that competitive elections would result in a reelected incumbent breathing a sigh of relief and a vow to do better next time but hardly any willingness in a poor district to seek to enact more services or in a wealthy district to reduce taxes. The methods of winning elections hardly consider responsiveness. Even if competition engendered more responsiveness, the question remains what the representative would do, especially in a more heterogeneous and difficult to represent district. The analysis that follows merely assesses whether cities with more competitive elections behave differently from those that are uncompetitive. The question of how competition changes policy becomes of interest only if competition influences public policy.

There is still the question of alternative hypotheses as competition is not experimentally introduced into a random sample of cities. If the same characteristics of a city that induce more competitive elections also results in certain policies, we of course have not demonstrated that competitive elections cause policy differences. Regionalism, capturing levels of competition in elections, state law variations, traditions of taxation, encouragement or discouragement of incorporating new cities, and different areas of city expenditures, may suggest causal relationships that do not exist. The analyses that follow must be ever alert to alternative hypotheses.

## Competitive Elections Impact on Public Policy

Available data from the *County/City Data Book, 1994* certainly fail to exhaust actions that cities take. Generally there is no data on the quality of urban services, on efforts to boost city bond ratings, on efforts to induce economic development, on efforts to improve the environment or to make community life better, or to deliver city services equally to all. We can, however, assess dependency on the regressive property tax, on the *scale of government* or expenditures per capita on police, fire, and other services, and finally on the efficiency of local government, such as employees relative to population.

Development is another obvious policy choice. Here we have data that might reflect development, such as reduced unemployment or more jobs. No actual policy decisions that might contribute to development are captured, however.

The *County/City Data Book, 1994* contains much policy information on cities with populations over 25,000. Three of the 118 cities dropped below the 25,000 population figure required for inclusion in this compilation although their populations were above 25,000 in 1990. This chapter will focus on the impact of levels of competition in elections, turnover in office-holders, and turnout of voters on city development, spending for services, and taxes.

Chapter 3 rediscovers Roland Liebert's (1974) long ago observation that even American cities vary regionally in the services they provide. Northeastern cities, frequently with responsibilities even for public education, collect and spend more money than their California counterparts, whose municipal responsibilities are farmed out to multiple special districts, providing everything from education to traffic control and water.

The following analyses include controls for these regional institutional, demographic, and function differences. I conclude that *the three measures of a city's politics, competition, turnover, and turnout, play at best a limited role in shaping a city's decisions on how to spend its resources and how much to tax.* Even municipal institutions little affect these city policies. *Apart from the unique institutions, laws, and responsibilities of cities in the Northeast, institutions and elections little shape policy.*

The federal government partially closed down several times during efforts to pass the 1996 budget. The comedian Jay Leno asked if anyone had noticed, suggesting that it would not be of great importance if the federal government were to close down. Fortunately for us this was just a joke, disparaging government to the applause of his audience. If local governments were to close down, however, we would quickly be in a great mess. Local governments provide most of the governmental services we receive. Despite this, few study the policies and explanations for policy differences among cities. This is not to suggest that there have not been several case studies of either one or a handful of cities (Presthus 1964; Agger, Goldrich, and Swanson 1964; Clark 1968; Tucker and Zeigler 1980; and Stone 1989).

The comparative study of municipal policy is not well developed with only two studies standing out (Rush 1993 and Schneider 1989). Peterson (1981) even rejects such analysis, seeing the states and federal government as all but straight-jacketing cities.[1] City governments are seen as little more than publicly paid officials who help local businesses go about building or developing the city and seeing to traditional services, such as police and fire protection that are developmentally neutral.[2] His argument denies that variations among cities would allow some to excel in development, although he suggests that suburbs must compete against each other for businesses.

American state policy, however, has attracted much research attention. The polar positions on the state research findings hinge on the importance of politics rather than economics in accounting for how states spend their revenues. Unfortunately, this division has yet to be resolved. This chapter turns to competition's impact on municipal policies. Can you fight city hall at the polls, win, and make a difference? The answer seems to be no!

## Competition and City Development or Growth

We often hear that a city is growing and prosperous. Through economic development life in a city is to improve by way of improved municipal services, but also families are personally to benefit from better and higher paying jobs. Since the average city grew 15.5 percent between 1980 and 1992 and only one third of all cities lost population during that period, is all growth just increase in population? Like competitive elections in the previous chapter, economic development is conceptualized as though any measure will yield the same ranking of cities. An economically developing city might certainly be expected to enjoy more jobs, less unemployment, more housing for its residents, more retail sales, and improved median family incomes. Again this unidimensional expectation proves incorrect.

## Measuring Development

Six measures, all derived from available data, might assess city economic development.

### *More Jobs*

Bringing new jobs to the community would seem most fundamental to economic development, especially if they are "good" jobs with high pay. Change in the labor force over the period 1980-1990 would seem to measure this, although population growth would need to be controlled. If population increases beyond the increase in jobs, no one is better off. Another measure of job growth is an increase in the number of manufacturing jobs in the period 1982-1987, but these might not be high paying jobs and might entail attracting polluting industry to town.

### *Lower Unemployment*

Lower unemployment from 1986 until 1991 is also taken as evidence of an improving job climate and economic development. A decrease in unemployment resulting from an increase in the number of jobs in the community would seem quite basic to conceptualizing economic development.

### *Higher Median Household Incomes*

For individuals higher incomes would seem most important in economic development. Certainly if growth and development meant loss of income, voters might oppose growth and might respond to candidates offering to stop growth. Higher median household incomes over the period 1979-1989 would seem an appropriate measure of this.

### *Improved Housing*

Improved housing would indicate development, perhaps even economic development. An increase in the number of housing units between 1980 and 1990 would suggest a demand for additional housing and the attendant jobs to build it would contribute to a city's economy. Were a city to be losing population but retaining its housing, this would not be development. Only 15 percent of cities lost housing units during this period, and the mean was an 18 percent increase. More plentiful housing may, however, not be what we think of when speaking of economic development.

*Increased Retail Sales*

Increased retail sales for the period 1982-1987 provides a potential measure of growth. Increased retail sales in the many states rebating sales taxes to the city where the purchase was made would, of course, yield increase tax rebates to cities, but this would also suggest increasing economic activity.

*A Growing Population*

Most cities are growing, and this may be the fundamental factor underlying growth.

Table 4.1 shows great variation among the cities on these development measures. Apart from an average increase in unemployment, all other measures show growth. The standard deviations and the minimums and maximums show the substantial variation evident in these measures.

Table 4.1 Descriptive Statistics on Measures of City Development

|  | Mean | Stand. Dev. | Stand. Error | Min. | Max. |
|---|---|---|---|---|---|
| Labor Force Chg. 1980-90 | 19.6 | 29.0 | 2.7 | -16.3 | 162.3 |
| Manufacturing Empl. Chg. 1982-87 | 15.9 | 70.1 | 6.5 | -54.1 | 446.2 |
| Unemployment Rate Chg. 1986-91 | 13.1 | 47.9 | 4.5 | -46.3 | 180.6 |
| Median Household Income Chg. 1979-89 | 77.2 | 23.8 | 2.2 | 19.2 | 130.3 |
| Housing Unit Chg. 1980-90 | 17.7 | 25.0 | 2.3 | -7.5 | 133.1 |
| Retail Trade Sales Chg. 1982-87 | 44.3 | 34.6 | 3.2 | -2.2 | 287.8 |
| Population Change 1980-92 | 15.5 | 28.0 | 2.6 | -20.6 | 130.1 |

The question remaining is whether some cities succeed across the full range of these variables. This would mean that we can talk about community development in general; otherwise we have to specify what aspect of development we are considering.

**Dimensions of Growth**

Three factors in table 4.2, explaining 86 percent of the variance, were orthogonally rotated for these six measures of growth. Four variables, suggesting city growth, are captured by the first factor, labeled City Growth. Three variables load equally high on this dimension. One, population change between 1980 and

1992, would seem to be the driving force for this dimension, but providing more jobs is the avowed goal of most city development efforts. Another high loading variable, labor force change between 1980 and 1990, would seem the best expression of this goal, although people in the labor force are not necessarily employed. Finally, housing unit change would seem incidental to the other two variables; but with the small physical scale of local governments, those with jobs in a city need not live in housing within its city limits.

Table 4.2 Factor Analysis of Measures of Growth

| Factor Analysis Summary | | Eigenvalues | | |
|---|---|---|---|---|
| Number of Variables | 7 | | Magnitude | Var. Prop. |
| Number of Cases | 112 | 1 | 3.60 | .51 |
| Number Missing | 6 | 2 | 1.60 | .23 |
| P-Value | <.0001 | 3 | .85 | .12 |

| | City Growth | Family Economic Growth | Manu- facturing Growth |
|---|---|---|---|
| Labor Force Change, 1980-90 | .955 | .132 | .165 |
| Manufacturing Empl. Change, 1982-87 | .203 | .043 | .975 |
| Unemployment Change, 1986-91 | -.020 | .923 | -.019 |
| Median Household Income Change, 1979-89 | .167 | .868 | .075 |
| Housing Unit Change, 1980-90 | .957 | -.031 | .157 |
| Retail Trade Sales Change, 1982-87 | .733 | .195 | .027 |
| Population Change, 1980-92 | .953 | -.029 | .146 |

The second factor deals with two family or individual measures. This dimension of employment and household income is unrelated to that of city growth. By implication at least, proponents of growth argue a tie between residents' well-being and growth. This would appear to be untrue. Finally, only manufacturing employment change loads on the third factor. It captures an unrelated dimension of city growth. Because gaining manufacturing jobs is an uncommon goal for economic development, no further analysis will focus on it.

If a city is increasing in population, it is increasing on many other measures, such as job growth, retail sales, and available housing. Officials in many cities seek praise for "growing" their cities' economies and attracting new employers with jobs. This analysis would suggest that any city increasing in population will experience such growth. Since gaining new jobs is so often the goal of growth, the following analyses will focus on whether competition, turnover, or turnout influence the level of gain in the workforce with other important variables controlled.

Interestingly, the sign on the loading of unemployment on the Family

Economic Growth dimension is positive. As shown in figure 4.1, at least at the aggregate level, cities with high gains in income endure increasing unemployment. Notably, northeastern cities dominate the upper right-hand quadrant, having sharply increasing unemployment during this period as well as sharply higher median family incomes. Without controlling for this region, the relationship would be stronger.

Figure 4.1 Change in Unemployment and Change in Median Household Income

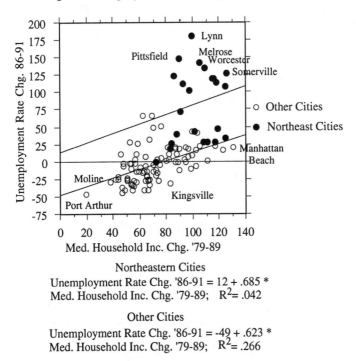

Northeastern Cities
Unemployment Rate Chg. '86-91 = 12 + .685 *
Med. Household Inc. Chg. '79-89;   $R^2$= .042

Other Cities
Unemployment Rate Chg. '86-91 = -49 + .623 *
Med. Household Inc. Chg. '79-89;   $R^2$= .266

The second dimension, Family Economic Growth, especially improving family income, would seem a goal of city development to which voters could identify and pursue in voting, if there were competitive elections and a "pro-growth" "anti-growth" choice in such elections. Competitive elections would seem to facilitate a public preference for such a goal.

**Explaining Growth**

The first dimension of growth focuses on attracting jobs to the city. The equal and strong loadings of both labor force change and population change in table 4.2 strongly suggest that improving jobs is largely a matter of increasing population. Table 4.3 shows that indeed increasing population substantially accounts for increasing the labor force. With little variance left, competition in elections can only marginally affect growth. The negative sign means the limited effect of competition retards a city's growth.[3] City council turnover during the 1983-1992 period and citizen voting age turnout prove equally unimportant. Voter input in competitive elections seemingly can little influence labor force growth as a city's population grows. Perhaps opposing candidates even in competitive elections fail to take opposing sides on city growth and fail to give the public that choice.

Table 4.3 Explaining Growth in the Labor Force

| Count | 114 |
|---|---|
| Number Missing | 4 |
| R Squared | .916 |
| Adjusted R Squared | .914 |

| Regression Coefficients | | |
|---|---|---|
| Intercept | 4.05 | † |
| | (.919) | |
| Population Change, 1980-1992 | .994 | *** |
| | (.029) | |
| Competition (reversed) | -.193 | |
| | (.822) | |
| † Regression coefficient (Standard error) | *** α ≤ .001 ** α ≤ .01 * α ≤ .05 | |

The next analysis concerns improving household incomes, which as discussed above is at least the implicit goal of city growth. Some cities have seen a rapid increase in incomes, several with better than a doubling of income over this ten-year period. Much contributes to this growth. Several plausible hypotheses directed the model in table 4.4. Initially variables on the City Growth factor were thought to contribute nothing to the growth in family or household income because they were on an independent factor. However, a test of the rhetoric of community development thesis that more jobs would be reflected in an improved economic environment for all lead to including labor force change in the model. With population held constant, an increase in the labor force because of more jobs being available should see many families' incomes improve and be reflected in an increase in the median household income.

Similarly, we might expect that increased retail sales should put more money in some families' pockets and raise the median income of the city. As shown in table 4.3, increasing population can drive many changes, such as increasing the size of the labor force as well as increasing retail sales. It is included therefore in the model in table 4.4. Growing unemployment as already noted strongly and negatively relates to improving household incomes in the factor analysis. It is included in the model.

Table 4.4 Explaining Growth in Household Incomes

| Count | 111 |
|---|---|
| Number Missing | 7 |
| R Squared | .791 |
| Adjusted R Squared | .772 |

| Regression Coefficients | | |
|---|---|---|
| Intercept | 33.7 (5.15) | † |
| Unemployment Rate Change, 1986-1991 | .152 (.038) | *** |
| Labor Force Change, 1980-1990 | .819 (.165) | *** |
| Retail Trade Sales, 1982-1987 | -.168 (.047) | *** |
| Population Change, 1980-1992 | -.586 (.166) | *** |
| Median Family Income, 1989 | 1.00 (.113) | *** |
| Minority Percentage of Population, 1990 | .179 (.066) | ** |
| Northeast | 16.2 (4.67) | *** |
| West | 7.71 (3.00) | * |
| Competition (reversed) | 1.82 (1.21) | |

† Regression coefficient (Standard error)  
*** $\alpha \leq .001$  
** $\alpha \leq .01$  
* $\alpha \leq .05$

Median family income and minority percentage of the population were added with the expectation that income would help and substantial minority populations hurt income growth. The Northeast stood out in figure 4.1 and often the West falls at the other extreme. Dummy variables for both were included.

Finally, competition in municipal elections was added. It is, of course, the primary concern. With the exception of competition (also turnover and turnout, although not shown), all variables in the model contribute substantially to explaining the median household incomes of cities.[4]

The strongest explanatory variable in table 4.4 is labor force change. Independent of increased population, more in the labor force strongly increases household income. There is also more income growth in wealthier communities. Generally all variables act as hypothesized, but two have strong negative impacts. Cities with substantial increases in population during this period experienced less growth in their median household incomes. Similarly, greater retail sales retarded income growth. Both are with other independent variables controlled, so retail sales' impact is not a phenomenon of increasing population. Finally, cities with substantial minority populations have faster improvements in median household incomes. While all of these variables largely explain the growth of income, competition adds very little, although the sign is at least positive.

Table 4.5 Explaining Growth in the Labor Force in California and Texas

|                    | California | Texas |
|--------------------|-----------|-------|
| Count              | 21        | 63    |
| Number Missing     | 0         | 5     |
| R Squared          | .878      | .908  |
| Adjusted R Squared | .864      | .905  |

| Regression Coefficients | | | | | |
|---|---|---|---|---|---|
| California | | | Texas | | |
| Intercept | 3.07 | † | Intercept | -2.86 | † |
|  | (3.82) | |  | (2.34) | |
| Population Change, 1980-92 | .950 | *** | Population Change, 1980-92 | 1.07 | *** |
|  | (.087) | |  | (.041) | |
| Competition (reversed) | 1.73 | | Competition (reversed | -.889 | |
|  | (3.00) | |  | (1.90) | |

† Regression coefficient (Standard error)

*** α ≤ .001
** α ≤ .01
* α ≤ .05

## Growth in California and Texas and the Role of Competition

Because of the strong regional influences evident throughout these analyses and because of the weak importance of political factors, such as competition, turnover among council members, and turnout of voters in city elections, further analysis was undertaken within two states. California had 21 cities selected in the random sample, which allowed an assessment of whether political differences among California cities also lack an impact on city growth.

While only 11 Texas cities were randomly sampled, complete data was gathered on an additional 51 Texas cities with population over 25,000. Within state impact of competition, turnover, and turnout was also done within the entire Texas sample. Texas, of course, is not in either of the polar regions, the West and the Northeast, that so often prove different in the analyses. The California and Texas analyses allow assessing the impact of competition when state laws, traditions of local governance, and other regional factors are held constant.

Table 4.5 shows the singular importance of population change and the unimportance of competition also in California and Texas. Nothing new is added here.

Table 4.6 reveals different patterns in California and Texas for what explains Growth in Household Incomes. While unemployment increase hurts the Growth of Household Income in California, Texas follows the national pattern of increased unemployment being found in the cities with the greatest increase in household incomes. An increase in a city's labor force increases income in Texas, as is the case nationally, but such an increase little affects California. California pretty much follows the national pattern of other independent variables affecting household income growth, but Texas shows none of these forces have influence within some states' boundaries. Finally, within California more competitive cities enjoy greater household income growth unlike the national pattern.

## Conclusion

With the exception of a modest relationship within California, political variables fail to much influence the two patterns of city economic growth— growth in the labor force and growth in median household income. New jobs in a community seem largely a question of population change. More or less competitive elections fail to influence such growth.

Growth in household income is largely explained by many variables but political variables, such as competitive elections, turnover of those on the city council, and voter turnout, little affect growth. The exception is that competitive elections in California encourage the growth of household incomes.

Table 4.6 Explaining Growth in Household Incomes In California and Texas

|  | California | Texas |
|---|---|---|
| Count | 21 | 50 |
| Number Missing | 0 | 18 |
| R Squared | .922 | .548 |
| Adjusted R Squared | .870 | .459 |

| Regression Coefficients | | | | | | |
|---|---|---|---|---|---|---|
| California | | | Texas | | | |
| Intercept | 9.69 | † | Intercept | 49.8 | † | |
|  | (11.1) | |  | (14.7) | | |
| Unemployment Rate | -.378 | ** | Unemployment Rate | .346 | ** | |
| Change, 1986-1991 | (.105) | | Change, 1986-1991 | (.124) | | |
| Labor Force Change, 1980- | .085 | | Labor Force Change, | .850 | * | |
| 1990 | (.168) | | 1980-1990 | (.364) | | |
| Retail Trade Sales, 1982- | .006 | | Retail Trade Sales, 1982- | -.040 | | |
| 1987 | (.114) | | 1987 | (.091) | | |
| Population Change, 1980- | .016 | | Population Change, | -.698 | | |
| 1992 | (.152) | | 1980-1992 | (.376) | | |
| Median Family Income, | 1.00 | *** | Median Family Income, | .205 | | |
| 1989 | (.157) | | 1989 | (.342) | | |
| Percent African-American | 1.25 | ** | Percent African-American | .181 | | |
|  | (.315) | |  | (.202) | | |
| Percent Hispanic | .466 | ** | Percent Hispanic | .154 | | |
|  | (.124) | |  | (.114) | | |
| Competition (Reversed) | 5.68 | * | Competition (Reversed) | 1.35 | | |
|  | (2.10) | |  | (1.90) | | |

† Regression coefficient          *** α ≤ .001
  (Standard error)              ** α ≤ .01
                             * α ≤ .05

# Competition and City Expenditures

Some cities have much more extensive and expensive governments, as judged by many measures.[5] Table 4.7 shows this variation across seven variables. Cities average 130 employees per 10,000 population but with substantial variation. This is full-time employees, and several smaller cities report none. Apart from these, the range is from 18 to 423 full-time employees per 10,000 population. General revenue per capita varies from $267 to $2,772, and city taxes per capita varies from $109 to $1,756. General expenditures per capita range from $300 to $3,721. Cities are not entirely dependent on their own resources, however. Intergovernmental transfer revenue per capita varies from

$2.80 to $1,345. Most of this money is earmarked to certain expenditures. Subtracting this money from general expenditures, cities now vary from $235 to $3,412. Intergovernmental transfers do *not* narrow variations in city expenditures.

Table 4.7 Descriptive Statistics on Governmental Effort

|  | Mean | Stand. Dev. | Stand. Error | Min. | Max. |
|---|---|---|---|---|---|
| City Government Employees / 10,000 | 130 | 92 | 9 | 0 | 423 |
| City General Revenue Per Capita | 882 | 520 | 49 | 267 | 2,772 |
| City General Expenditures Per Capita | 779 | 456 | 43 | 300 | 3,721 |
| Intergovernmental Transfers Per Capita | 227 | 269 | 25 | 3 | 1,345 |
| General Expend. Per Capita Intergov. Trans. Per Capita | 676 | 480 | 45 | 235 | 3,412 |
| Property Taxes as Pct. Gen. Rev. | 58 | 30 | 3 | 1 | 100 |
| City Taxes Per Capita | 380 | 262 | 25 | 109 | 1,756 |

Property tax revenues as a percentage of general tax revenues vary from .6 to 100 percent. There is much variance in city taxes, revenues, and expenditures. Sharkansky and Hofferbert (1971) and Dye (1980) long ago noted the importance of a state's wealth to how much it spends.[6] Luttbeg (1998) and others note that city residents' wealth has less impact on city government revenues and expenditures than is the case at the state level.[7]

Median family income relates poorly with city taxes per capita and city general expenditures per capita as shown in figure 4.2, and city taxes show a sharper relationship outside the Northeast. The relationships, however, are weak with outlier cities creating much of the relationship. We should expect only minimal impact of a city's wealth in further analyses.

An additional measure of tax effort derives from these data. Individual per capita income is related to city taxes per capita.[8] The relationship allows predicting taxes based on income. Subtracting predicted taxes from actual taxes per capita yields a measure of tax effort with positive values meaning more taxes than predicted. This measure varies from $516 per capita undertaxed given per capita income to $806 per capita over-taxed.

The *County/City Data Book, 1994* includes city estimates of the percentage of general city expenditures in: education, welfare, health and hospitals, police, fire, highways, and sewage. Because few cities have educational responsibilities, spending in different areas was recalculated per capita, excluding spending for education. Some cities spend a great deal on health and hospitals and receive substantial transfers of state money, perhaps underwriting these expenditures.

*Chapter 4*

There is no way to be certain in these data, however, how such transfers were used in the cities. Therefore, I made no further adjustments.

Figure 4.2 Median Family Income and City Taxes Per Capita and City General Expenditures Per Capita

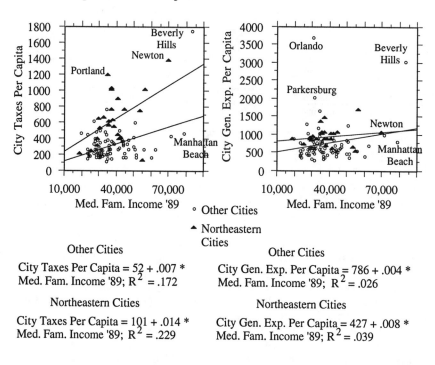

Other Cities

City Taxes Per Capita = 52 + .007 *
Med. Fam. Income '89; $R^2$ = .172

Northeastern Cities

City Taxes Per Capita = 101 + .014 *
Med. Fam. Income '89; $R^2$ = .229

Other Cities

City Gen. Exp. Per Capita = 786 + .004 *
Med. Fam. Income '89; $R^2$ = .026

Northeastern Cities

City Gen. Exp. Per Capita = 427 + .008 *
Med. Fam. Income '89; $R^2$ = .039

Table 4.8 again shows substantial variation among these cities. The highest expenditures go to police, sewage, highways, and fire protection, in that order. As noted, some cities have substantial expenditures for health and hospitals probably with state transfers of funds to cover the city's expenditures to run hospitals for the state. Only 38 of these cities, about one-third, have any per capita expenditures for public welfare. Such expenditures can be found in cities across the country but are most substantial in the Northeast, where the mean is $11.26 per capita.

Table 4.8  Descriptive Statistics on Per Capita City Expenditures
on Different Services

|  | Mean | Stand. Dev. | Stand. Error | Min. | Max. |
|---|---|---|---|---|---|
| Police Exp. Per Capita | 109 | 65 | 6 | 45 | 614 |
| Fire Exp. Per Capita | 68 | 40 | 4 | 0 | 286 |
| Public Welfare Exp. Per Capita | 4 | 11 | 1 | 0 | 67 |
| Health and Hosp. Exp. Per Capita | 29 | 151 | 14 | 0 | 1557 |
| Highway Exp. Per Capita | 68 | 47 | 4 | 15 | 347 |
| Sewage Exp. Per Capita | 92 | 66 | 6 | 0 | 357 |

Table 4.9 Factor Analysis of Areas of City Spending

| Factor Analysis Summary | | Eigenvalues | | |
|---|---|---|---|---|
| Number of Variables | 7 | | Magnitude | Var. Prop. |
| Number of Cases | 113 | 1 | 2.92 | .42 |
| Number Missing | 5 | 2 | 1.18 | .17 |
| P-Value | <.0001 | 3 | 1.01 | .15 |

|  | Trad. Services | Health & Hosp. Services | Welfare Services |
|---|---|---|---|
| General Expenditures Per Capita | .785 | .375 | .209 |
| Public Welfare Exp. Per Capita | -.038 | -.038 | .936 |
| Health and Hosp. Exp. Per Capita | .022 | .973 | -.037 |
| Police Exp. Per Capita | .864 | -.110 | -.198 |
| Fire Exp. Per Capita | .841 | -.029 | .067 |
| Highways Exp. Per Capita | .601 | -.099 | -.342 |
| Sewage Exp. Per Capita | .679 | .079 | .122 |

# Dimensions of Spending

With the exceptions of spending on welfare and on health and hospitals, table 4.9 shows all spending falls on one dimension. If a city spends much per capita on police, it tends to do so also for fire, highways, and sewage. The other dimensions seem specific to a very few cities. Explanation will be sought only for the traditional service dimension.

### Explaining Differences in Expenditures in Cities

Table 4.10 seeks to explain Traditional Service Expenditures in these cities and to see the contribution of competition, turnover of incumbents, and voter turnout. We might expect higher median family income cities to have higher service levels given prior research on the importance of wealth. The Minority Percentage of a city might also be expected to relate to Traditional Service levels. This is largely an argument that rests on the low incomes of minorities, thus with median family income already in the model, the direction this variable's contribution is uncertain. Similarly, suburbs that are wealthy might have high service levels while poor suburbs may not.

Finally, previous work with these data shows the importance of the median age of a city's population as well as the impact of higher pay for city council members. Table 4.10 includes all of these variables plus the level of competition in city elections. Average turnover on the city council and voter turnout were also added to the initial model. Since they so little affect Traditional Service Levels, they are excluded in table 4.10.

Table 4.10 Explaining Traditional Service Levels

| Count | 111 |
|---|---|
| Number Missing | 7 |
| R Squared | .233 |
| Adjusted R Squared | .189 |

| Regression Coefficients | | |
|---|---|---|
| Intercept | -3.83 | † |
|  | (.800) | |
| Median Family Income, 1989 | .024 | * |
|  | (.009) | |
| Median Age, 1990 | .072 | *** |
|  | (.021) | |
| Minority Percentage of Population, 1990 | .014 | * |
|  | (.005) | |
| Municipality's Percentage of SMSA | .003 | |
|  | (.004) | |
| Yearly Salary of City Council Members | .031 | ** |
|  | (.011) | |
| Competition (reversed) | -.162 | |
|  | (.098) | |
| † Regression coefficient (Standard error) | *** $\alpha \le .001$ | |
|  | ** $\alpha \le .01$ | |
|  | * $\alpha \le .05$ | |

Nearly 20 percent of the variance in Traditional Services is explained. Wealthy cities have higher service levels, as hypothesized, but more minorities independently increase service levels. Cities with older publics have sharply higher service levels. Again this is understandable of a more dependent population. Again, higher paid city councils lead to higher service levels, perhaps out of the belief among politicians that this will gain them reelection. Suburbs are no more likely to have higher services expenditures than are core cities.

While the relationship with increased competition falls just short of statistical significance, more competitive cities, with all of these other factors held constant, have lower per capita expenditures across these traditional municipal services. While this is understandable in the context of elected officials being held accountable for expenditures being too high, V. O. Key's hypothesis concerning the importance of competition would seem refuted, at least at the local level. As government can redistribute wealth by providing services to those needing them from revenues largely provided by the more wealthy, a city with competition might be expected, he would argue, to respond to the need for services of the poor. In cities, however, competition reduces governmental service levels.

## Traditional Spending in California and Texas and the Role of Competition

While several nonpolitical and noninstitutional variables partially explain Traditional Service Levels in the random sample, the focus on California and Texas cities finds Median Age of a city's population proves statistically significant only in California and irrelevant in Texas. This may be the low median age in Texas cities, 29.9, versus 32.1 in California and 32.4 in the random sample and low variance also in Texas with a standard deviation of 2.7 versus 4.9 in California and 4.3 in the random sample. The increase in traditional services with increased family income in Texas largely parallels that in California, although this is too weak to reach statistical significance in either state.

Higher salaries, the only institutional variable of importance in the random sample, prove unimportant in either Texas or California. Competitive elections in California decreases Traditional Service levels but increases them ever so slightly in Texas. Turnout and turnover have no significant impact in either state.

Service levels for these typical or traditional city services respond to demography but only to one institution in the random sample, higher city council salaries. Even this proves unimportant in California and Texas cities. Competitive elections discourage expenditures for these services, except in Texas, but always the importance of competition is slight. Demographic characteristics of cities, mainly how old their public is, rather than institutional, political, or wealth characteristics shape the extent of traditional services in a city.

*Chapter 4*

## Competition and the Scale of Local Government

Five variables would seem to capture the scale of local government. A city with higher general expenditures per capita also has more government employees per

Figure 4.3 The Interrelationship Between City Expenditures and City Revenues
With the Northeast Separated

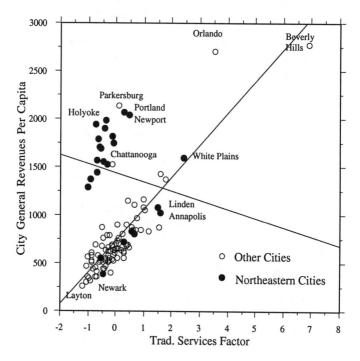

Northeastern Cities
City General Revenues Per Capita = 1433 - 93.4 *
Trad. Services Factor; $R^2$ = .027

Other Cities
City General Revenues Per Capita = 728 + 331 *
Trad. Services Factor; $R^2$ = .68

10,000 population, higher general revenues per capita, more taxes per capita, and makes more of a tax effort. One dimension explains 73 percent of the variance in these variables, and general revenues per capita loads on this factor at .918.

Therefore, only general expenditures per capita will be used in the analysis of the scale of government in these cities, and competitive elections impact on the scale of government.

Figure 4.3 shows several things. First, more services require more revenues. The relationship without the Northeast separated is (City General Revenues Per Capita = $882 + $258 * Trad. Services Factor; $R^2$ = .246). This is in the expected direction but quite weak. Second, most of the northeastern cities and only two other cities stand apart from most cities, having very high revenues for the level of traditional services they provide. Perhaps in providing non-traditional services, such as education, welfare, and health and hospitals, such

Table 4.11 Explaining General Revenues per capita

| Count | 112 |
|---|---|
| Number Missing | 6 |
| R Squared | .849 |
| Adjusted R Squared | .836 |

| Regression Coefficients | | |
|---|---|---|
| Intercept | -32.8 | † |
| | (196) | |
| Median Family Income, | -.003 | * |
| 1989 | (.002) | |
| Median Age, 1990 | 3.10 | |
| | (5.05) | |
| Minority Percentage of | -1.62 | |
| Population, 1990 | (1.26) | |
| Municipality's | .666 | |
| Percentage of SMSA | (.990) | |
| City General Expend. per | .837 | *** |
| capita | (.047) | |
| Northeastern Cities | 513 | *** |
| | (54.6) | |
| Competition (reversed) | 2.85 | |
| | (22.8) | |
| Average Turnover 1983- | 5.27 | |
| 92 | (3.56) | |
| CVAP Voting Average | 4.10 | * |
| | (2.03) | |

† Regression coefficient     *** $\alpha \leq .001$
  (Standard error)         ** $\alpha \leq .01$
                         * $\alpha \leq .05$

cities cannot compete with other cities in traditional services. Third, the relationship between Traditional Services and General Revenues Per Capita is quite strong with northeastern cities excluded. Clearly, any focus on City General Revenues per capita needs to consider the distinctiveness of the Northeast.

Table 4.11 shows the model to account for a city's general revenues per capita. As in the analyses in table 4.10, the wealth, age, and racial diversity of a city's population are anticipated to affect its general revenues. Additionally, suburbs are again expected to differ from core cities and autonomous cities. The Northeast, as noted in figure 4.3, stands apart. Since spending differs greatly among cities, a city's general expenditures might drive the need for additional revenues. Finally, competition in elections, turnover of council members, and voter turnout, the primary focus, are added to see if they affect policy.

A city's expenditures make necessary its revenues, but also northeastern cities have far greater revenues than cities in other regions ($513 per capita) even apart from their higher per capita expenditures. Revenues poorly and negatively relate to the wealth of a city's residents. Similarly, revenues poorly and negatively relate to the size of a city's minority population.

Voting turnout does increase a city's revenues, or possibly residents in a city with high revenues vote to secure the best use of these funds. If so, however, competitive elections play no role. Indeed, once again competitive elections afford voters no different policies than is evident with the lack of competition.

## General Revenues in California and Texas and the Role of Competition

As in the general case, in California and Texas, a city's general expenditures drive its revenues. In these two states, however, nothing else much affects revenues. The wealth of cities in these two states proves to have virtually no effect. Certainly competition, turnover, and voter turnout have no significant effect.

## Conclusion

Since northeastern cities standout in table 4.11 along with expenditure levels, it is not surprising that a focus on cities outside that area would find expenditure levels alone influence revenues. We learned earlier that apart from northeastern cities' unique mix of services, only an older population and to a lesser degree higher salaries for city council members provide additional impetuses for traditional services. Higher salaries for city council members played no role in traditional services in Texas or California. Service levels and amount of revenue and taxes are regional phenomena not affected by institutions, politics, competition, or even economics.

## Dependence on Property Taxes

Key's concern with government's responsiveness to the poor is further assessed in table 4.12, considering explanations for the dependence on regressive property taxes. The model includes: median family income with the expectation that

Table 4.12 Explaining Dependence on Property Taxes

| Count | 112 |
|---|---|
| Number Missing | 6 |
| R Squared | .463 |
| Adjusted R Squared | .432 |

| Regression Coefficients | | |
|---|---|---|
| Intercept | 37.1 | † |
| | (11.9) | |
| Median Family Income, | -.166 | |
| 1989 | (2.58) | |
| Minority Percentage of | .067 | |
| Population, 1990 | (.135) | |
| Municipality's | .227 | * |
| Percentage of SMSA | (.107) | |
| Northeastern Cities | 45.4 | *** |
| | (5.78) | |
| Competition (reversed) | -4.82 | |
| | (2.45) | |
| CVAP Voting Average | .433 | * |
| | (..208) | |

† Regression coefficient    *** $\alpha \leq .001$
(Standard error)       ** $\alpha \leq .01$
                         * $\alpha \leq .05$

wealthy cities would favor this regressive tax, minority populations with the opposite expectation, a municipality's percentage of its metropolitan area expecting again that suburban self-interest would motivate use of a regressive tax, and a dummy of northeastern cities, because such dependence is known to be common in that region. Additionally, competition, turnover, and turnout were considered. Turnover was removed as it had little effect.

The model explains a good deal of the variance in dependence on property taxes, but the Northeast is the best contributor. When the analysis is split between northeastern and other cities, little variance is explained and no remaining variable is statistically significant. Depending on the property taxes is merely a characteristic of northeastern cities.

Table 4.13 Explaining Dependence on Property Tax In California and Texas

|  | California | Texas |
|---|---|---|
| Count | 21 | 58 |
| Number Missing | 0 | 10 |
| R Squared | .452 | .338 |
| Adjusted R Squared | .158 | .245 |

| Regression Coefficients | | | | | | |
|---|---|---|---|---|---|---|
| California | | | Texas | | | |
| Intercept | 36.7 | † | Intercept | 34.9 | † |
|  | (21.7) | |  | (9.34) | |
| Municipality's Percentage of SMSA | -.240 | | Municipality's Percentage of SMSA | -.069 | |
|  | (.177) | |  | (.045) | |
| Median Family Income, 1989 | .075 | | Median Family Income, 1989 | 1.00 | ** |
|  | (.321) | |  | (.176) | |
| Percent African-American | -.068 | | Percent African-American | .216 | |
|  | (.614) | |  | (.139) | |
| Percent Hispanic | -.218 | | Percent Hispanic | .093 | |
|  | (.190) | |  | (.079) | |
| Competition (Reversed) | 1.29 | | Competition (Reversed) | 3.64 | * |
|  | (4.86) | |  | (1.46) | |
| Average Turnover, 1983-1992 | -.162 | | Average Turnover, 1983-1992 | .154 | |
|  | (.664) | |  | (.095) | |
| CVAP Voting Average | .215 | | CVAP Voting Average | -.176 | |
|  | (.218) | |  | (.261) | |

† Regression coefficient     *** α ≤ .001
  (Standard error)            ** α ≤ .01
                              * α ≤ .05

## Dependence on the Property Tax in California and Texas and the Role of Competition

   Table 4.13 presents the analyses for California and Texas. In California while no variable achieves statistical significance, suburbs are inclined to depend on the property tax as hypothesized. Also, the higher the Hispanic percentage in the city public, the less a city is dependent on the property tax. Competition, turnover, and turnout prove to have little influence on such dependency.

   In Texas several variables achieve statistical significance, but those that are important in Texas seldom are those important in California. Texas cities with higher family incomes are more dependent on the property tax as hypothesized but not confirmed with the entire sample. As in California, Texas suburbs are more likely to depend on the property tax. The percentage Hispanic plays little role in Texas. Finally, competition increases dependence on the property tax in Texas and this relationship is statistically significant.

## Considering the Impact of the Problem of Crime

The relationships thus far considered fail to weigh the importance of the problems faced by the community. Data for this are limited to police and welfare expenditures per capita, which are part of Traditional Services. Table 4.14 presents analysis for police expenditures per capita using two models, one without considering the volume of serious crime in the city and one including it. The independent variables are those used in table 4.10 plus the percentage of a city's population living below poverty as poverty might drive investment in police to prevent crime.

As in table 4.10, older population cities, those with more wealthy residents, and those with high minority populations, especially Hispanic populations, have higher expenditures, here for police only. The yearly salary for city council members, while still positively related to expenditures, fails to influence police expenditures as much as it did all traditional services. Northeastern cities again prove distinctive having sharply lower police expenditures regardless of wealth or minority populations. Finally, cities with high minority populations have higher police expenditures per capita.

Competition (and other political characteristics of these cities in analysis not shown) fails to affect expenditures much. More competition does seem to reduce expenditures, however.

The severity of the crime, however, greatly affects a city's expenditures for police, but this effect is largely independent of the other independent variables. Implausibly, northeastern cities lower their already low expenditures for police even more when they are experiencing more crime. High Hispanic population cities prove less distinctive when the seriousness of their crime rate is introduced into the model. Similar analyses on public welfare expenditures show the severity of poverty in a city greatly influences its welfare expenditures, but the age of the population as well as wealth plays little role. Competition remains irrelevant.

### Police Expenditures per capita in California and Texas and the Role of Competition

A focus on what explains police expenditures and the importance of crime to those expenditures in California and Texas again adds little. Police expenditures in Texas are poorly explained even with the addition of the amount of serious crime.[9] The explanation for California police expenditures closely parallels that

Table 4.14 Explaining Police Expenditures per capita and Considering the Crime Problem

|                    | Without Crime | With Crime |
|--------------------|---------------|------------|
| Count              | 111           | 111        |
| Number Missing     | 7             | 7          |
| R Squared          | .409          | .474       |
| Adjusted R Squared | .357          | .422       |

| Regression Coefficients | | | | | |
|------|------|------|------|------|------|
| **Without Crime** | | | **With Crime** | | |
| Intercept | -220 | † | Intercept | -234 | † |
|  | (54.2) |  |  | (51.5) |  |
| Median Family Income, 1989 | 4.00 | *** | Median Family Income, 1989 | 4.00 | *** |
|  | (1.00) |  |  | (1.00) |  |
| Median Age, 1990 | 3.85 | ** | Median Age, 1990 | 3.58 | ** |
|  | (1.22) |  |  | (1.16) |  |
| Percent African-American | .829 |  | Percent African-American | .336 |  |
|  | (.451) |  |  | (.410) |  |
| Percent Hispanic | 1.41 | ** | Percent Hispanic | 1.28 | * |
|  | (.520) |  |  | (.495) |  |
| Municipality's Percentage of SMSA | -.091 |  | Municipality's Percentage of SMSA | -.117 |  |
|  | (.262) |  |  | (.248) |  |
| Yearly Salary of City Council Members | 1.00 |  | Yearly Salary of City Council Members | 1.00 |  |
|  | (1.00) |  |  | (1.00) |  |
| Percent Living Below Poverty | 3.60 |  | Percent Living Below Poverty | 2.90 |  |
|  | (1.58) |  |  | (1.51) |  |
| Northeastern Cities | -38.0 | ** | Northeastern Cities | -34.0 | * |
|  | (13.4) |  |  | (13.1) |  |
| Competition (Reversed) | -7.73 |  | Competition (Reversed) | -9.98 |  |
|  | (6.07) |  |  | (5.79) |  |
|  |  |  | Serious Crimes per 100,000 people | .005 | *** |
|  |  |  |  | (.002) |  |

† Regression coefficient *** α ≤ .001
(Standard error)     ** α ≤ .01
          * α ≤ .05

for all cities, although median family income is not as important, and median age and percent living in poverty are more important. Competitive elections in California reduce police expenditures. Serious crime in a city does encourage expenditures in California but not to the degree noted elsewhere.

Region strongly influences local policies. This is especially true relative to dependency on the property tax and expenditures apart from those labeled

Traditional Services. *Consistently three measures of the nature of city politics, competition, turnover, and turnout, fail to account for differences in municipal policy.* An institutional difference, high salaries for city council members, proves to influence overall service levels, what I call Traditional Services. No other policy showed any impact of salary differences. *There is a strong regional pattern to the use of various municipal institutions, but these institutional differences have no impact on city policies.*

# Notes

1. Paul E. Peterson, *City Limits* (Chicago: University of Chicago Press, 1981), 13.

2. Peterson, *City Limits*, 32.

3. The impact of competitive elections alone on an increasing labor force is: Labor Force Chg. 80-90 = 20 + 5.6 * Competition (reversed); $R^2$ = .037. This is statistically significant at the .05 level.

4. For competition alone the relationship is Med. Household Inc. Chg. 79-89 = 77 + 2.7 * Competition (reversed); $R^2$ = .013. For competition, turnover, and turnout the equation is Med. Household Inc. Chg. 79-89 = 66.8 + 2.02 * Competition (reversed) - .064 * Ave Turnover 83-92 + .430 * CVAP Voting Ave.; $R^2$ = .059

5. For a very thorough consideration of how a limited number of cities spend their revenues see Terry N. Clark and Lorna C. Ferguson, *City Money* (New York: Columbia University Press, 1983).

6. Thomas R. Dye, "Taxing, Spending and Economic Growth in the American States," *Journal of Politics* 42 (Winter 1980): 1085–1107; and Richard I. Hofferbert, "The Relation Between Public Policy and Some Structural and Environmental Variables in the American States," *American Political Science Review* (March 1966): 73-82.

7. Norman R. Luttbeg, *Comparing the States and Communities: Politics, Government, and Policy in the United States* (New York: HarperCollins, 1992), chapter 6.

8. Since City Taxes are per capita, per capita money income is used in the relationship rather than median family income. The relationship is City Taxes per capita = 9.4 + .02 * per capita money income. $R^2$ = .31.

9. The adjusted R squared is only .085 for the 8 independent variables excluding serious crimes per 100,000 people and increases to only .246 with serious crime added.

# Chapter 5

# Improving Representation of Those Normally Underrepresented

At least since the success of the reform movement in undoing the political machines of American cities, those in positions to influence public policy have seen political institutions as providing the leverage needed to affect desired changes in our politics (Welch and Bledsoe 1988, 4-9). Among the many institutional changes advocated by reformers was the movement to at-large rather than the older, single member, district-based, municipal elections that were viewed as narrow and parochial (Christensen 1995, 125). Since reformers only advocated at-large selection at the local level rather than at all levels of government, they obviously most intended to weaken urban machines rather than to extend these ideas throughout our institutions. Seemingly, if at-large elections were desirable, they would also apply to state and national offices.

Certainly the courts and the Department of Justice, at least during the Bush presidency, believed that the institutional format for choosing representatives could shape the representation of minorities. It probably never occurred to them that this would advantage Republicans. The same idea led to federal courts ordering many cities to move from at-large selection of city council and school board members to district elections. An extensive literature in political science suggests that African-American representation improves with an institutional change from multimember at-large (city wide) elections to single member, district elections (Gelb 1970; Jones 1976; Karnig 1976; Taebel 1978; Robinson and Dye 1978; Cottrell and Fleischman 1979; Karnig and Welch 1981; Davidson and Korbel 1981; Engstrom and McDonald 1981, 1982, and 1986; Bullock and MacManus 1987 and for the opposition point-of-view see: Cole 1976; MacManus 1978 and 1979). More recent work, however, suggests a decline of this effect in the 1980s (Welch 1990); nevertheless, she concludes that "Blacks are still most equitably represented by district elections"(1072).

Professor Welch has the trend right, but now her conclusion about "equitable" representation of African-Americans no longer holds. Apart from the African-American percentage of a city, no other factor, including district selection of municipal council members, contributes to more "equitable" representation. The same holds for Hispanics. Federal court ordered adoption of district selection rather than at-large selection of city council members, given the gains in

99

representation of both minorities as well as women, no longer can be expected to improve the situation.

Such changes with those typically underrepresented achieving more "equitable" membership on councils were expected to lead to different policies that better reflected the preferences of constituencies previously unheard on the council. The analysis of policy differences between city councils better reflecting the minority percentages of their city shows no impact. The more accurate representation of African-American, Hispanic-Americans, and women fails to shape policies in municipalities. Efforts to improve such representation, while no doubt of great importance to those involved, bears little fruit in public policies.

## The Role of Competition in Minority Representation

The literature discussed in Chapter 1 touches little on the question of representation other than improving that of minorities and women. With the exception of Svara's (1990) statement that the manager form does not harm such representation,[1] no literature suggests a role for other political variables, such as competition. The literature on accurate minority representation on city councils rests on a single premise, that representatives, not sharing the racial or gender demographics of constituents, fail to represent them in policy. This chapter will consider the role of competition in representing minorities and women.

Previously, competition for public offices played little role in the question of representing minorities, probably because it was thought that competition could be sacrificed to achieve more accurate demographic representation. Our pluralistic thinking leads to the expectation that moving from more demographically heterogeneous, at-large districts to smaller more demographically homogeneous districts would result in the loss of competition and the loss of the compromises necessary to win election in larger, more heterogeneous districts. Competition thus becomes a dependent variable, reduced by the change from at-large districts to single member districts.

There are, however, several reasons to expect an independent role for competition improving the demographic representation of minorities. First, competition in a minority defined district may subvert the intent of drawing the district if the minority's majority vote in such a district is divided among several minority candidates, resulting possibly in a white candidate winning. It is also conceivable that the winning minority candidate may appeal to whites and win election with little minority support, and once elected such a candidate may poorly reflect the minority's concerns.[2] Apparently, for minority districts to function as intended, competition should be most limited. Furthermore in the at-large case, the lack of competition may result in the victory of a minority candidate. Just consider a city lacking competition where only five candidates, one a minority, seek five at-large seats. The lack of competition results in perhaps a token minority representative, but minority representation, nevertheless. Competition may subvert the impact of moving to district elections.

Second, the community studies, perhaps too swiftly dismissed by political science, also suggest the importance of competition. In a closed community, such as Floyd Hunter (1953) found, moving from at-large to district elections could hardly be expected to affect minority representation. Indeed, in such a city even accurate demographic representation of minorities would little suggest that anyone in the general public, whether majority or minority, influences public policy. Finally, even in Dahl's (1961) world, competition among elites, not minority representation, was seen as influencing responsiveness to the public. Luttbeg (1988) found that Texas cities with large African-American populations lacked the levels of competition found elsewhere, suggesting an effort to remove politics from city elections thereby reducing the potential influence of minorities. In short while the focus of this research is African-American representation on city councils, competition should be considered an independent variable along with institutional formats, such as at-large versus district elections.

## The Broad Question of Representation

Thus far, the discussion has focused on whether minorities and women have their representative share of city council seats. This is but one consideration of representation, however. We know from case studies and from research at other levels of government that representatives seldom are representative from other demographic perspectives. Education, occupational status, and income levels of representatives at all levels differ substantially from their constituents, which means we need to suspect bias in the policies they enact. This has been called the demographic representativeness or the Sharing Model of Representation (Erikson, Luttbeg, and Tedin 1980). Luttbeg's (1998) research with superior data on state legislators would suggest great difficulties with the expectation that failure to represent minorities also reflects other biases and that only failure to represent minorities biases public policies. Neither prove true in his data.[3]

### Minority and Women Council Members

Data availability, however, greatly limits my consideration of the question of representation. The *National Rosters of Black Elected Officials* allows the identification of African-Americans serving on city councils over time and first names of council members, with follow-up to National League of Cities' yearly *Directory of City Policy Officials* to track names. City secretaries were asked when necessary to account for uncertainties in records from other sources. Similarly the *Directories* allowed tracking the percentage of women back to 1983. No similar techniques allow the identification of other minorities such as Hispanics or Native-Americans. These data will allow me to assess changes in representation of African-Americans and women over the period 1983 to 1992.

While late 1992 telephone calls gave then current information on the number of African-Americans, Hispanics, and women on each council, the patience of those at the other end of the telephone as well as their unfamiliarity with those serving in the past precluded noting all minorities serving on councils in the past. These late 1992 percentages of each city council that are African-

American, Hispanic, or women will be the dependent variables in the following analyses. The overtime data will also be used.

**More Representative Cities**

Table 5.1 shows the typical city has few representatives from any of these groups. Svara's (1991) 1989, stratified sample survey of city council members shows 26.4 percent female, 10.0 percent African-American, and .9 percent Hispanic council memberships.[4] Other than the percentage Hispanic, my figures are similar.[5] Typically, minorities and women remain a minority on the average city council. There are, however, minority and women controlled city councils. The range for each variable is substantial. Only nine of the 118 cities (8%) have no women council members, but 68 (58%) have no African-Americans and 99 (84%) have no Hispanics. Only three cities lack representatives from all of these groups.

Table 5.1 Three Measures of City Council Representation

|  | Percentage of Women on City Council 1992 | Percentage of African-Americans on City Council 1992 | Percentage of Hispanics on City Council 1992 |
|---|---|---|---|
| Mean | 25.8 | 9.8 | 3.4 |
| Standard Dev. | 16.3 | 14.4 | 9.1 |
| Minimum | 0.0 | 0.0 | 0.0 |
| Maximum | 85.7 | 80.0 | 60.0 |

In discussions at the most abstract level, some cities are dismissed as dominated by "businessmen" (Shefter 1989); but more specific studies of the impact of underrepresenting African-Americans seldom consider the broader questions of whether all groups are represented on the city council (Heilig and Mundt 1984). Figure 5.1 shows that cities better representing African-Americans fail to do so for Hispanics and women. There is no indication that some cities better represent all groups. There is no relationship between the number of women, Hispanics, or African-Americans on city councils. Each will need to be analyzed separately.

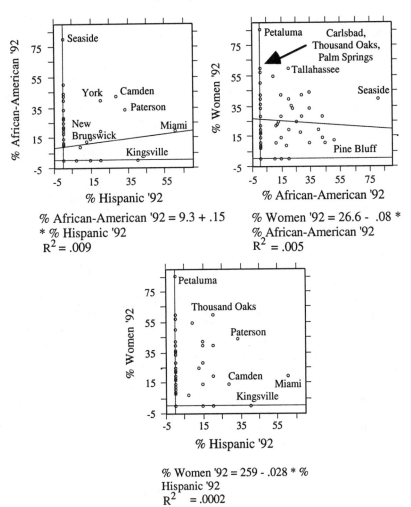

Figure 5.1 The Relationship Between African-Americans, Hispanics, and Women on City Councils

## District and At-large Elections

The size of each city's council and the number of district selected seats allows calculating the percentage of seats elected by districts. In contrast to prior work dividing councils into all at-large, all district, and mixed, this continuous percentage will be used here. A "mixed" council with only one council member selected at large, usually the one designated the mayor, differs little from an exclusively district-based council. Similarly, such a "mixed" council differs greatly from a "mixed" council with a minority of the council members coming from districts. Since the courts will usually settle for less than total "district" rather than "at-large" selection of council members, using a "mixed" category wastes information.

A voluntary survey by the International City/County Management Association (1993) with 818 cities over 25,000 population found 49 percent with at-large selection, 12 percent with district selection, and 39 percent mixed. The comparable percentages in this sample are: at-large, 46 percent; district, 13 percent; and mixed, 42 percent. The sample again appears representative.

The percentage of city's council seats from districts loads on factors stressing more traditional institutions, as noted in chapter 3 and *Appendix B*. The prominent institutional variables loading on this factor in order are: (1) the number of seats on the council; (2) the percentage district; (3) whether staggered elections are used; and (4) whether the form of government is city manager or mayor/council. Cities scoring high on this factor have the traditional municipal format of many council members selected from districts in unstaggered elections and use the mayor/council format. Since the use of partisan elections fails to load on this factor, it is labeled "traditional," rather than "unreformed."

Chapter 3 sought an understanding of both institutional and regional contributions to competition in municipal elections. Table 3.4 presented factor analysis of all institutional characteristics for the sample cities as well as four regional dummy variables. In this analysis the dimension of traditional institutions captured by the Northeastern, Traditional Cities factor would seem an appropriate control but without the regional characteristics. The same analysis of institutions without regional dummies yields a **Traditional Institutions** factor, as shown in *Appendix B*. This traditional institution factor scores might be used rather than the percentage selected from districts as an independent variable. As noted in the introduction to this chapter, however, both scholars and the courts have focused on the use of districts rather than at-large seats. Therefore, this measure will be used. However, other aspects of traditional institutions may be important to the following analyses, thus the traditional factor scores will be included in some models.

## Accuracy in Representation

Figures 5.2, 5.3, and 5.4 show the percentage of city council members who are women, African-American, and Hispanic relative to the population percentages of those groups. The lower left to upper right dark diagonal shows what would be perfect representation. Figure 5.2 on the representation of women will receive no further consideration as the actual relationship, while not statistically significant, is nearly the opposite of what we might expect, as the percentage of women in the city increases slightly, given its small range, the percentage of women on the council declines.

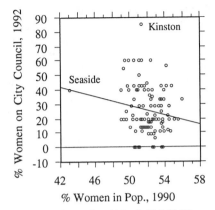

$$\% \text{ Women on Council} = 111 - 1.64 * \% \text{ Women in Pop.}$$
$$R^2 = .029$$

Figure 5.2 Women in the Public and Women on City Councils

Figures 5.3 and 5.4 show both African-American and Hispanic presence on city councils increases as their respective percentages of the population in the city increase. The relationship is weaker for Hispanics and only nineteen of these cities (16%) have any Hispanic representation. Given limited data the further exploration of the impact of misrepresentation must be limited to under-representing blacks. To do so we might focus on the ratio of African-American council members relative to those in the public. Such a ratio, however, would

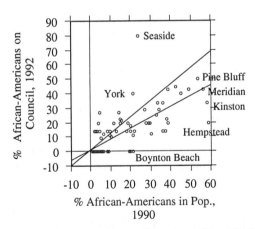

$$\% \text{ African-American on Council} = 1.07 + .744 * \% \text{ African-American in Pop.}$$
$$R^2 = .583$$

Figure 5.3  African-Americans in the Public and African-Americans on City Councils

be zero were there no African-American council members regardless of how many African-Americans lived in the city. We think that there is greater misrepresentation when the percentage in the population is substantial. To capture this distinction I merely subtract the percentage of African-Americans in the population from those on the council. Because I do not consider overrepresentation of African-Americans to reflect better representation, especially when one African-American is on the council to represent very few blacks within the public, I set positive values to zero or perfect representation. More negative values reflect poorer representation. Again I will be assessing the impact of accurate African-American representation not of accurate representation across all types of biases among city council members.

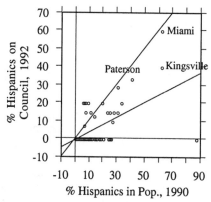

%  Hispanics on Council = -.662 + .415 * % Hispanics in Pop.
$R^2$ = .365

Figure 5.4 Hispanics in the Public and Hispanics on City Councils

## Assessing the Origins of Representation

I sought to explain the African-American percentage of each city council with five independent variables—(1) the African-American percentage of the public; (2) the percentage district rather than at-large elections; and (3) the three measures of competition, turnover, and turnout from chapter 3. Most prior analyses sought to explain the ratio of the percentage of African-Americans on the council to that in the public. Ratios can exceed 1.0 and such values indicate declining representation or over representation of minorities. Keeping the African-American percentage in the community as an independent variable, explaining the percentage on the council, avoids this problem. The second independent variable is the percentage of a city's council selected from single member districts. With so many cities using a mix of districts and at-large elections and with a range among the mixed cities from 43 percent district to over 90 percent district, using the percentage districts retains this variance. Subsequent analyses use similar models for Hispanics and women.

Table 5.2 Explaining Minority and Women Council Members:
The Impact of Using Districts

|  | African-Americans on City Council | Hispanics on City Council |
|---|---|---|
| Count | 115 | 115 |
| Number Missing | 3 | 3 |
| R Squared | .587 | .365 |
| Adjusted R Squared | .579 | .354 |

**Regression Coefficients**

| African-Americans on City Council | | | Hispanics on City Council | | |
|---|---|---|---|---|---|
| Intercept | .253 (1.39) | † | Intercept | -.445 (1.22) | † |
| Percent African-American | .740 (.059) | *** | Percent Hispanic | .412 (.054) | *** |
| Percent Districts | .022 (.022) | | Percent Districts | -.005 (.018) | |

|  | Women on City Council |
|---|---|
| Count | 118 |
| Number Missing | 0 |
| R Squared | .080 |
| Adjusted R Squared | .064 |

**Regression Coefficients**

| Women on City Council | | |
|---|---|---|
| Intercept | .93.8 (45.2) | † |
| Percent Women | -1.24 (.872) | |
| Percent Districts | -.093 (.037) | * |

† Regression coefficient (Standard error)

*** α ≤ .001
** α ≤ .01
* α ≤ .05

This first model shown in table 5.2 includes only the percentage African-Americans in the public and the percentage use of districts. It explains nearly 58 percent of the variance; but the correlation of .76 between the African-American percentage of the council and that in the public means that this one independent variable explains all the variance. The percentage use of districts explains nothing. Welch (1990) with her late 1980s data reports a decline in the impact of using districts from that noted earlier. Engstrom and McDonald (1981) using earlier data, for example, found that the African-American percentage of the public explained 47 percent of the variance in the percentage African-American on the council, leaving much to be explained by other variables. The percentage of African-Americans in these cities in 1992 explains 58 percent of the variance leaving little to explain for other variables, including the use of districts.

Hispanic representation follows a similar but weaker pattern. What variance is explained centers on the Hispanic percentage of the population, and the percentage of districts adds nothing. Only the representation of women is much influenced by districts rather than at-large selection. The percentage of women in the population does not vary much, from 43 percent to 56 percent, and little explains the presence of women on city councils. While the use of district selection hurts their presence on the city council, the model accounts for only 6 percent of the variance.

Table 5.3 adds levels of competition, turnover, and turnout to the models. Overall, none add much. Explained variance is little affected by the addition of levels of competition, average turnover for the period 1983-1992, or voter turnout, although competition in all three cases improves representation. The percentage use of districts remains statistically significant for fewer women on the council, but the model still little explains the variance.

The final models add the traditional institutional factor and several other possible independent variables. The percentage of both African-Americans and Hispanics are added to all models on the theory that representing one minority or women may be at the expense of others.

The more complex model in table 5.4 adds some to our understanding of the representation of African-Americans. The adjusted explained variance increases only from .58 to .62 with the addition of percent Hispanic and the heterogeneity of income variable, but we now see that the percentage of Hispanics in the public hurts the representation of African-Americans on city councils independent of the African-American percentage of the population. This may suggest that Hispanics do not support African-Americans at the polls, that Hispanics in strong numbers may be preoccupied with seeking their own representation, or that Anglos may, if given a choice of minority candidates, prefer the Hispanics. This, however, is a very weak influence.

The addition of percent Hispanic and income heterogeneity does strengthen the tie between more competition and more representative councils. The influence of turnover and turnout, however, are quite weak and not statistically significant. Cities with publics with disparate income distributions have fewer African-American representatives. This variable was added because, to use Key's words, the "haves" would oppose improving the representation of "have nots" of any race and that this would be most evident when there is more of a gulf between the "haves" and "have nots." This appears to be the case and is accentuated when the "have nots" are black.

Table 5.3 Explaining Minority and Women Council Members: The Impact of Using Districts and Other Variables

|  | African-Americans on City Council | Hispanics on City Council |
|---|---|---|
| Count | 114 | 114 |
| Number Missing | 4 | 4 |
| R Squared | .597 | .358 |
| Adjusted R Squared | .579 | .328 |

### Regression Coefficients

| African-Americans on City Council |  |  | Hispanics on City Council |  |  |
|---|---|---|---|---|---|
| Intercept | 5.32 (3.77) | † | Intercept | -3.64 (2.86) | † |
| Percent African-American | .707 (.062) | *** | Percent Hispanic | .350 (.060) | *** |
| Percent Districts | .037 (.023) |  | Percent Districts | -.005 (.018) |  |
| Competition (Reversed) | 1.71 (.972) |  | Competition (Reversed) | .896 (.801) |  |
| Average Turnover, 1983-1992 | -.218 (.154) |  | Average Turnover, 1983-1992 | .162 (.119) |  |
| CVAP Voting Average | -.085 (.082) |  | CVAP Voting Average | .053 (.063) |  |

|  | Women on City Council |
|---|---|
| Count | 116 |
| Number Missing | 2 |
| R Squared | .126 |
| Adjusted R Squared | .086 |

### Regression Coefficients

| Women on City Council |  |  |
|---|---|---|
| Intercept | 89.7 (47.4) | † |
| Percent Women | -1.23 (.914) |  |
| Percent Districts | -.093 (.039) | * |
| Competition (Reversed) | .549 (1.66) |  |
| Average Turnover, 1983-1992 | -.169 (.251) |  |
| CVAP Voting Average | .246 (.135) |  |

† Regression coefficient (Standard error)

*** $\alpha \leq .001$
** $\alpha \leq .01$
* $\alpha \leq .05$

109

Table 5.4 Institutional, Demographic, and Competition Explanations for African-American Representation in 1992

| Count | 111 |
|---|---|
| Number Missing | 7 |
| R Squared | .647 |
| Adjusted R Squared | .620 |

| Regression Coefficients | | |
|---|---|---|
| Intercept | 14.7 | † |
| | (5.50) | |
| Percent Hispanic | -.034 | |
| | (.081) | |
| Percent African-American | .747 | *** |
| | (.063) | |
| Percent Districts | .029 | |
| | (.035) | |
| Traditional Institutions factor | .145 | |
| | (1.43) | |
| Heterogeneity of Income | -.392 | * |
| | (.161) | |
| Competition (Reversed) | 2.34 | * |
| | (1.04) | |
| Average Turnover, 1983-1992 | -.209 | |
| | (.151) | |
| CVAP Voting Average | -.076 | |
| | (.086) | |
| † Regression coefficient (Standard error) | *** α ≤ .001 ** α ≤ .01 * α ≤ .05 | |

The complete model for representation of Hispanics proves slightly more complex in table 5.5 than earlier when only the percentage Hispanic in the public proved of much influence. Now both average turnover and average voter turnout encourage better representation of Hispanics. Neither much influenced better representation of African-Americans. By contrast, competition encouraged Hispanic representation. Finally, western cities are less likely to have better represented Hispanics, although this is not a phenomenon of western cities using non-traditional institutions or having more competition, as both are part of the model. Contrary to the pattern earlier noted for African-American representation on city councils, where the percentage Hispanic adversely affected African-American representation, the percentage of a city's population that is African-American positively influences Hispanic representation. Like the earlier analysis, the relationship is quite weak.

Table 5.5  Institutional, Demographic, and Competition Explanation for Hispanic Representation in 1992

| Count | 111 |
|---|---|
| Number Missing | 7 |
| R Squared | .347 |
| Adjusted R Squared | .289 |

| Regression Coefficients | | |
|---|---|---|
| Intercept | -2.62 | † |
|  | (3.70) | |
| Percent Hispanic | .284 | *** |
|  | (.055) | |
| Percent African-American | .024 | |
|  | (.045) | |
| Percent Districts | -.007 | |
|  | (.024) | |
| Traditional Institutions factor | -1.91 | |
|  | (1.13) | |
| Heterogeneity of Income | -.140 | |
|  | (.109) | |
| Competition (Reversed) | .101 | |
|  | (.695) | |
| Average Turnover, 1983-1992 | .261 | * |
|  | (.101) | |
| CVAP Voting Average | .126 | * |
|  | (.060) | |
| Western City | -4.69 | * |
|  | (1.80) | |

† Regression coefficient     *** $\alpha \leq .001$
(Standard error)              ** $\alpha \leq .01$
                             * $\alpha \leq .05$

The full model assessment of the representation of women in table 5.6 greatly changes our explanations. The importance of the use of district selection of council members ceases to have much influence, presumably because other Traditional factor institutions better capture the variance in representation of women. Newer municipal institutions, such as the city manager form or smaller councils, encourage women serving on the city council. Contrary to the effects of heterogeneous incomes on African-American and Hispanic representation, here the effect is positive. Voting turnout also encourages women on the city council. There is much variance unaccounted for in the representation of women, but region seems unimportant. No regional control expanded the explained variance or altered the importance of other variables.

Table 5.6 Institutional, Demographic, and Competitive Explanations of the Representation of Women in 1992

| Count | 111 |
|---|---|
| Number Missing | 7 |
| R Squared | .240 |
| Adjusted R Squared | .180 |

| Regression Coefficients | | |
|---|---|---|
| Intercept | 5.56 | † |
|  | (9.21) |  |
| Percent Hispanic | -.029 |  |
|  | (.135) |  |
| Percent African-American | .013 |  |
|  | (.105) |  |
| Percent Districts | .015 |  |
|  | (.058) |  |
| Traditional Institutions factor | -6.49 | ** |
|  | (2.39) |  |
| Heterogeneity of Income | 1.00 | * |
|  | (.270) |  |
| Competition (Reversed) | 1.35 |  |
|  | (1.75) |  |
| Average Turnover, 1983-1992 | -.203 |  |
|  | (.253) |  |
| CVAP Voting Average | .295 | * |
|  | (.145) |  |
| † Regression coefficient (Standard error) | *** $\alpha \le .001$ | |
|  | ** $\alpha \le .01$ | |
|  | * $\alpha \le .05$ | |

Competition in municipal elections improves representation of minorities and women, especially African-Americans. Voter turnout improves representation both of Hispanics and women. Turnover on the city council also encourages Hispanic representation, but it negatively influences African-American and women representation. All of these measures fall short of the influence of the racial mix of the city in the case of minorities and to a somewhat lesser degree non-traditional municipal institution in the case of women. Especially for African-Americans, the models explain the variance in representation evident in American cities.

## The Impact on Municipal Policies of African-American Representation

Table 5.7 replicates table 4.3 but adds accuracy of African-American representation to the model. This adds little. Increased population remains the best predictor of an increased labor force. When African-Americans have more accurate representation on city councils, however, growth in the labor force is retarded. Like competition, representation of African-Americans little shapes cities' successes in attracting a larger labor force.

Table 5.7 Explaining Growth in the Labor Force

| Count | 114 |
|---|---|
| Number Missing | 4 |
| R Squared | .917 |
| Adjusted R Squared | .914 |

| Regression Coefficients | | |
|---|---|---|
| Intercept | 3.51 | † |
| | (1.10) | |
| Population Change, 1980-1992 | .997 | *** |
| | (.029) | |
| Competition (reversed) | -.184 | |
| | (.823) | |
| African-American Representation | -.131 | |
| | (.146) | |
| † Regression coefficient (Standard error) | *** α ≤ .001 ** α ≤ .01 * α ≤ .05 | |

Table 5.8 assesses the importance of African-American representation relative to other contributing factors in explaining growth household incomes. Compared to table 4.4 the only real impact of more representation of African-Americans is a decline in the importance of the percentage minorities, not any real impact of better representation. As in table 5.7, the negative sign means that better representation dampens the increase in incomes.

Table 5.8 Explaining Growth in Household Incomes

| Count | 111 |
|---|---|
| Number Missing | 7 |
| R Squared | .798 |
| Adjusted R Squared | .778 |

| Regression Coefficients | | |
|---|---|---|
| Intercept | 33.6 | † |
| | (5.08) | |
| Unemployment Rate | .146 | *** |
| Change, 1986-1991 | (.038) | |
| Labor Force Change, | .822 | *** |
| 1980-1990 | (.163) | |
| Retail Trade Sales, 1982- | -.173 | *** |
| 1987 | (.047) | |
| Population Change, | -.582 | *** |
| 1980-1992 | (.164) | |
| Median Family Income, | 1.00 | *** |
| 1989 | (.112) | |
| Minority Percentage of | .125 | |
| Population, 1990 | (.071) | |
| Northeast | 17.2 | *** |
| | (4.64) | |
| West | 9.04 | ** |
| | (3.04) | |
| Competition (reversed) | 2.18 | |
| | (1.21) | |
| African-American | -.416 | |
| Representation | (.215) | |

† Regression coefficient (Standard error)

*** $\alpha \leq .001$
** $\alpha \leq .01$
* $\alpha \leq .05$

## Traditional Service Policy

As table 5.9 indicates, better representation of African-Americans adversely shapes Traditional service levels in cities but only weakly. As in table 4.10, the most significant influences are wealthy cities spending more and older cities needing more spending. Overall, the model little explains variation in such traditional municipal services.

Table 5.9 Explaining Traditional Service Levels

| Count | 111 |
|---|---|
| Number Missing | 7 |
| R Squared | .235 |
| Adjusted R Squared | .183 |

| Regression Coefficients | | |
|---|---|---|
| Intercept | -3.83 (.803) | † |
| Median Family Income, 1989 | .024 (.009) | ** |
| Median Age, 1990 | .071 (.021) | *** |
| Minority Percentage of Population, 1990 | .013 (.006) | * |
| Municipality's Percentage of SMSA | .003 (.004) | |
| Yearly Salary of City Council Members | .031 (.012) | ** |
| Competition (reversed) | -.151 (.101 | |
| African-American Representation | -.009 (.017) | |

† Regression coefficient  *** α ≤ .001
(Standard error)  ** α ≤ .01
 * α ≤ .05

## General Revenues

Again in table 5.10 nothing is added by better African-American representation. The effect of better representation is to hold revenues down. Voter turnout is still positively associated with higher revenues.

*Chapter 5*

Table 5.10 Explaining General Revenues per capita

| Count | 112 |
|---|---|
| Number Missing | 6 |
| R Squared | .849 |
| Adjusted R Squared | .834 |

| Regression Coefficients | | |
|---|---|---|
| Intercept | -32.1 | † |
| | (197) | |
| Median Family Income, 1989 | -3.00 | |
| | (2.00) | |
| Median Age, 1990 | 3.08 | |
| | (5.09) | |
| Minority Percentage of Population, 1990 | -1.65 | |
| | (1.37) | |
| Municipality's Percentage of SMSA | .673 | |
| | 1.00) | |
| City General Expend. per capita | .837 | *** |
| | (.047) | |
| Northeastern Cities | 513 | *** |
| | (54.9) | |
| Competition (reversed) | 3.11 | |
| | (23.3) | |
| Average Turnover 1983-1992 | 5.24 | |
| | (3.61) | |
| CVAP Voting Average | 4.10 | * |
| | (2.04) | |
| African-American Representation | -.227 | |
| | (3.97) | |
| † Regression coefficient (Standard error) | *** $\alpha \leq .001$ ** $\alpha \leq .01$ * $\alpha \leq .05$ | |

## Dependence on Property Taxes

Table 5.11, adding the measure of African-American representation, again shows no impact and the results are nearly identical to those in table 4.12. Cities better reflecting the African-American percentage of their population among their city council members are less dependent on the property tax, even with the Northeast region as part of the model. Voter turnout again with the Northeast region controlled encourages dependence on the property tax.

Table 5.11 Explaining Dependence on Property Taxes

| Count | 112 |
|---|---|
| Number Missing | 6 |
| R Squared | .463 |
| Adjusted R Squared | .427 |

| Regression Coefficients | | |
|---|---|---|
| Intercept | 36.7 (12.0) | † |
| Median Family Income, 1989 | -.163 (2.32) | |
| Minority Percentage of Population, 1990 | .049 (.146) | |
| Municipality's Percentage of SMSA | .232 (.108) | * |
| Northeastern Cities | 45.4 (5.81) | *** |
| Competition (reversed) | -4.65 (2.51) | |
| CVAP Voting Average | .433 (.209) | * |
| African-American Representation | -.146 (.424) | |

† Regression coefficient (Standard error)

*** α ≤ .001
** α ≤ .01
* α ≤ .05

## The Impact of Crime on Police Expenditures

Chapter 4 assessed the impact of the social problem of crime on police expenditures. Cities with more serious crimes had higher police expenditures per capita. Table 5.12 extends this analysis to include how accurately the city represents African-Americans. As the table shows more accurate representation of African-Americans contributes nothing to our explanation police expenditures, although the sign is negative, meaning that better representation reduces police expenditures regardless of other influencing factors.

*Chapter 5*

Table 5.12  The Impact of African-American Representation on per capita Police Expenditures

| Count | 111 |
|---|---|
| Number Missing | 7 |
| R Squared | .478 |
| Adjusted R Squared | .420 |

| Regression Coefficients | | |
|---|---|---|
| Intercept | -237 | † |
| | (51.8) | |
| Median Family Income, 1989 | .400 | *** |
| | (.100) | |
| Median Age, 1990 | 3.57 | ** |
| | (1.16) | |
| Percent African-American, 1990 | .163 | |
| | (.504) | |
| Percent Hispanic, 1990 | 1.27 | * |
| | (.496) | |
| Municipality's Percentage of SMSA | -.090 | |
| | (.252) | |
| Yearly Salary of City Council Members | 1.00 | |
| | (1.00) | |
| Percent Living Below Poverty | 3.00 | |
| | (1.52) | |
| Northeastern Cities | -33.7 | * |
| | (13.1) | |
| Competition (reversed) | -9.41 | |
| | (5.85) | |
| Serious Crimes per 100,000 people | .005 | *** |
| | (.002) | |
| African-American Representation | -.812 | |
| | 1.01) | |

† Regression coefficient (Standard error)

*** $\alpha \leq .001$
** $\alpha \leq .01$
* $\alpha \leq .05$

## Conclusions on African-American Representation

In no instance does the better representation of African-Americans contribute at a statistically significant level to the different public policies. The conclusions from the analysis are unchanged by the addition of this variable. The models would also suggest that African-American representation cannot be improved using district elections. Any improved responsiveness to the needs of African-Americans on American city councils seems overwhelmed by other factors to the degree that our measures of policy tap such needs. Increased use of district elections no longer contributes to better representation. Only an increasing percentage of African-Americans in a city results in more African-American council members, although at less than a proportional rate. But cities with the number of African-Americans on their councils reflecting their percentage in the population prove indistinguishable from those poorly representing African-Americans.

## Conclusion

Figure 5.4 shows the percentage of African-Americans on the sample cities' councils increasing by about one percent every 3 years, which is, as shown, less rapid than the increase in percentage of women on city councils. Taken in conjunction with the facts that twenty-eight of these cities overrepresent African-Americans and that 58 percent of the variance in the African-American representation on city councils is explained by their percentage of the city's population,

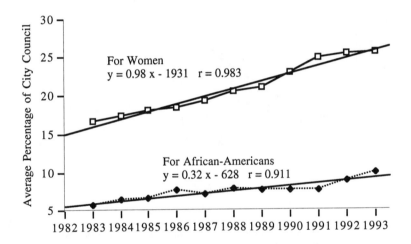

Figure 5.4  Trends for Women and African-Americans in Percentage of City Councils, 1983-1993

this suggests that somehow the last twenty to thirty years have resolved the representation of African-Americans in American city governance. The movement to district elections would seem at least partially responsible. Certainly the period when cities have changed to use more district selection coincides with an improvement in African-American representation. It would thus appear that the success of this institutional change has all but washed out its influence. But like that other great success in using institutions to alter urban politics, the reform movement, can we really ascribe change to the institution? Perhaps resistance to accurate African-American representation, like the strength of urban machines, was declining before those advocating the reform won success.

The combined national random and Texas samples yield 22 instances where a city changed to using more district-based council seats during the period there are data, typically from all at-large to a mix of district and at-large seats. Figure 5.5 overlaps the percentage of African-American council members at the time of the change and for years before and after. A city making the change in 1988 would be shown as -1 in 1987 and +1 in 1989. The number of cities averaged for each year decreases at both ends of such analysis, as this is outside the period for which data are gathered. Figure 5.5 shows data where there were 10 or more observations.

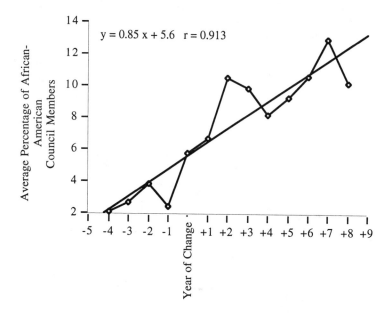

Figure 5.5 The Impact of a Change Toward District Elections in Twenty-two Cities Where Change Was Captured in Data Collection (Averages Based on Fewer Than 10 Cities Were Excluded

The regression line for these cities has a much greater slope than the average shown in figure 5.5, as African-American council members increases by .85 per year rather than .32. What is most striking, however, is that the data show the increase predates the change to more district-based selection of council members. The data around the change show a sharp one-year decline the year before the change and a rebound in the year of the change, but no great change the year after the change. Speculatively, this might suggest that the institutional change was incidental or perhaps even a symbolic act with the tenor of the times propelling receptive cities to facilitate more accurate African-American representation. The sharp decline in African-American council members the year before the change and the sharp increase two years after the change may speak to the dynamics of this process or may be just instabilities introduced by the few cities in this analysis. Nevertheless, in these cities African-American representation had improved before the move to more district elections, and the move failed to accelerate this change.

I have already noted that the slope of American-American representation on the council in these cities is steeper than for all cities, suggesting that there is greater willingness to increase the number of African-American representatives in these cities. This receptivity may rest on a higher percentage of African-Americans in these cities, 19.1 percent, than in the random sample cities, 12.0 percent as well as a greater deficit in African-American representation. These cities average 5.96 percentage points too few African-American representatives

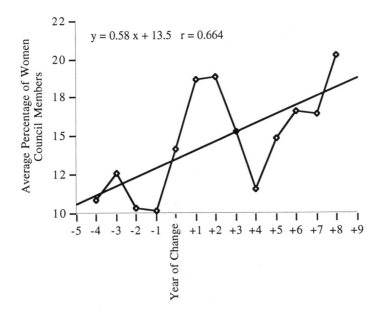

Figure 5.6 The Impact of a Change Toward District Elections in Twenty-two Cities Where Change Was Captured in Data Collection (Averages Based on Fewer Than 10 Cities Were Excluded)

given the percentage of African-Americans among their public versus -3.76 percentage points for the random sample.[6] Earlier data for these cities may well show no increase in African-American representation until just five to ten years before the change to district elections. The change in willingness may, of course, rest on the threat that federal courts may order the change. Apparently the institutional change to districts is itself not responsible for improving African-American representation.

Figure 5.6 gives the data for women council members in these cities. While the slope of African-Americans on the city council was steeper for these cities than for the entire sample, for women it is shallower, .58 rather than .98. It would seem that African-American representation, at least in these cities is the primary goal. More specifically, women on these city councils have gained additional representation at a slower rate than has the entire city sample while African-Americans have gained representation at a faster rate than the sample.[7] Figure 5.6 shows, however, that in the sample the growth of women council members is unrelated to that for African-Americans.

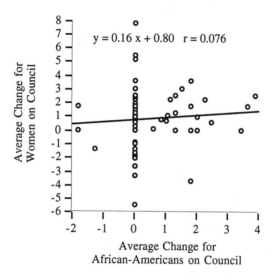

Figure 5.7 The Relationship Between Changes in Women and
African-Americans on City Councils

These data may suggest that the dynamics of a city's welcoming, or at least accepting African-American representatives and the eventual movement to at least greater use of district elections, may dominate public attention with the unintended result being that the growth of woman representation is retarded. Certainly, figure 5.7 shows a much more erratic pattern than that shown in figure 5.5 and in figure 5.4. As with interpreting year to year changes around the time of the change to more district elections in figure 5.5, the instability of the data given the small sample size may be the best explanation.

## Other Changes With the Move Toward Districts

Data on African-Americans and women on these city councils could be gathered back to 1983. While I sought two complete waves of municipal elections (typically four staggered elections), frequently I have election data back only to 1986 or 1985. As a result I have data on elections before and after moving to more district selection for only three cities. These data suggest, however, that moving to more districts reduces competition. Table 5.10 shows the averages before, at the time of the change, and after for these cities. The change to more district selection seems adverse to competition.

Table 5.10  Election Changes as a Result of Change to Greater Use of District Selection of Council Members in Three Cities

|  | Before Change | At Change | After Change |
|---|---|---|---|
| More Incumbents Run | 50.9 | 75.0 | 75.9 |
| More Incumbents Win | 45.8 | 66.7 | 100.0 |
| Winning Margin Temporarily Drops | 50.3 | 24.8 | 58.2 |
| Candidates per Seat Temporarily Rises | 1.8 | 3.0 | 1.6 |
| Turnout Increases | 15.2 | 19.5 | 25.2 |

Institutions little affect the representation of African-Americans on city councils in the 1990s. Even in those cities that moved to electing a larger percentage of their council members from single member districts, the improvement in representation of African-Americans predated the change and was not accelerated by the change. Since we also could find no policy evidence that the accurate representation of African-Americans shapes policy differences, and since improving representation precedes the move to more district selection, this change may be symbolic after the victory was won.

**The General Question of Representation**

It is unfortunate that I lack data on other dimensions of city council representation of characteristics of constituents, especially characteristics where the council's characteristics are minority characteristics, such as education and income. I do have the ratio of women on the council to that in the population that is such a characteristic. Men dominate city councils but typically are in a minority in the population. I repeated all the analysis shown for representation of African-Americans for women. In no instance did the ratio of women on the council play a statistically significant role in accounting for policies, but also in every case all institutional and demographic variables that proved important for the analysis focusing on African-American representation held for women and no other factors were added. The results in terms of statistically significant relationships proved identical. Recalling that figure 5.1 showed no relationship between the number of women and the number of African-Americans on a council, this analysis may mean one of two things. If the representation of women and African-Americans taps the underlying dimension of how representative each city's council is of constituents, representation is unimportant in the performance of democratic governance in my cities. Since the percentage of women and of African-Americans on city councils is uncorrelated (figure 5.1), it seems improbable that we could speak of some cities being generally more representative of African-Americans, Hispanics, or women.[8] Alternatively, if neither captured measure of representation correlates with the underlying dimension of representativeness, additional data needs to be gathered to assess the question fully. I suspect such research would prove useful.

At this time and given available data on representativeness, institutions neither encourage nor discourage representation. Furthermore, misrepresentation has no policy significance.

# Notes

1. James H. Svara, *Official Leadership in the City: Patterns of Conflict and Cooperation.* (New York: Oxford University Press, 1990), 79.

2. Jerry Polinard, Robert Wrinkle, and Tomas Longoria, Jr., "The Impact of District Elections on the Mexican-American Community: The Electoral Perspective," *Social Science Quarterly* (September 1991): 608-614.

3. Norman R. Luttbeg, *Comparing the States and Communities: Politics, Government, and Policy in the United States* 3rd ed. (Dubuque: Eddie Bauer, 1998), chapter 9.

4. James H. Svara, *A Survey of America's City Councils: Continuity and Change* (Washington: National League of Cities, 1991), 12, 14.

5. Since he got only a 44 percent return and his sample is not a random sample, we would suggest that the error might be in the National League of Cities Survey.

6. No other demographic characteristics differ much from these cities to the random sample.

7. Actually, among the twenty-two cities used here are several from the Texas sample.

8. The analysis suggests that there is a single dimension with accuracy of representing African-Americans loading negatively.

# Chapter 6

# Episodes of Total Turnover in 29 City Elections

Much was made of the congressional elections of 1994. The Republicans took control of both the House of Representatives and the Senate. With the defeat of many Democratic incumbents and the change of control, many commented that the American public had changed its mind. This is probably an exaggeration on the part of Republicans interested in furthering their aims as well as on the part of the media eager to gain audience. As evidence of a public choice at the polls, it pales in comparison with the episodes evaluated in this chapter. I will be focusing on 29 cities that had an election in which no incumbent was returned to office, either because they were defeated at the polls or chose to retire voluntarily.

## Identifying Episodes of Total Turnover

These data, discussed earlier, derived from election returns, directories, and institutional information from city secretaries, show how many city council members were up for each election. I also know their names. When election results showed incumbents not winning or when their names disappeared from directories, these are turnovers. Incumbents may not have run for reelection, or they may have lost a reelection effort. Some might say that a defeat is sending more of a message than an incumbent not being available for defeat because he or she chose to retire from office. Voluntarily retiring incumbents may, however, have already received the message, knowing that they would lose. I chose to look at the entire turnover picture, hoping to disentangle in further analysis whether there was a message in the voting outcome.

### Learning the Message

Probably a message was intended in how Americans voted in the congressional elections of 1994. Unfortunately, we cannot know what that message was nor whether it was the same for even all of those voting against incumbent Democrats. This is true despite the great claim-taking by the Republicans, the despondency of the President and First Lady, the substantial editorializing, and the many public opinion polls. Consistent changing from voting for the Democrat to the Republican candidate by as few as 5 percent of all voters could have resulted in the changes in Congress seen in 1994. Perhaps only five to ten percent of all voters were sending a message. Discerning the voters' message at the local level is even more difficult. Fleeting data and recollections of local elections, the media's inattention to such elections, the absence of any opinion polls, and many communities' desires to present a positive face on happenings to continue to attract new investment, a sentiment often shared by local newspaper editors, makes reconstructing these events most difficult.

*Informants*

In the cities with at least one total turnover election, I sent the questionnaire in *Appendix C* to all candidates in the election, to the mayor, to the city manager, if there is one, to the editor of the newspaper serving the city, and to the city secretaries. Often in recent elections I merely sent the questionnaire of candidates involved who still served on the city council to their council address. I also consulted city telephone directories to get many addresses; and all else failing, sent sealed, addressed, and stamped envelopes with the questionnaires to city secretaries to forward to candidates. Later I sought respondents by telephone, especially when I had ambiguous responses or needed to ask pointed questions. All information was obtained anonymously.

*The Questionnaire*

My question was simply what happened? Having briefly refreshed the respondent's memory by noting the election in question, the questionnaire's first question is, "What factors do you think explain what happened in the election?" Anticipating some unwillingness to be candid but dependent on voluntary completion of the questionnaires, I structured it to gradually narrow responses until the next to last question asks those involved to, "Please check the scenario that best applies" with fixed alternatives. Each of these alternatives was taken from prior research examples. Finally, respondents were asked, "What impact did this election have in your city?" If a message was intended by voters, I assumed that respondents would say it did affect the city.

I foresaw a range of explanations. Because the typical council includes only eight members and better than 70 percent use two staggers on their council, even total turnover involves typically no more than four incumbents. The lowest level of message from voters may be no message but merely that all incumbents left the city, died, or retired after many long years of low pay, public service. Obviously this could not be true were some defeated at the polls or in primaries. Many explanations entail decisions by incumbents or challengers that failed to define a message from the public because no policy alternatives were involved. Frequently the impact on the city question in these instances was answered "no impact." Such explanations might be expected were incumbents to view themselves as "volunteers," who serve out of a sense of civic duty. In some instances incumbents imposed "term limits" on themselves. When their allotted time expired, they would no longer seek reelection.

## The Nature of Episode Cities

There are alternative explanations for the turnover episodes noted in these cities. Episodes might be more common at the municipal level than at the state or national level because councils are much smaller legislative bodies, meaning that it is easier for 4 incumbents to change as a result of an election than half of a state lower house or the U.S. House of Representatives. I first considered whether it was easier to have turnover episodes in some cities. All 29 episode cities use staggered elections as compared with 71 percent of the entire sample. Additionally, episode councils average 6.1 members as compared with the sample's 7.8. Only one episode happens in a city with 10 or more council members. The chances of total turnover are more likely in the episode cities merely by only half of a smaller council being up for election. This is not to say that there are not equally small councils with staggered elections that do not experience total turnover. Nearly 63 percent of such cities had no such episode in the two rounds of election evaluated here.

Table 6.1 shows that when I consider the size of the council and the use of staggered elections, the use of staggered elections best explains episodes of total turnover, but together they explain 13.6 percent of the variance in such episodes.[1] Clearly the ease of a total turnover partially but not exhaustively accounts of these episodes.

Table 6.1  The Size of City Councils and the Use of Staggerred Elections as Explanations for Episodes of Total Turnover

| Count | 118 |
|---|---|
| Number Missing | 0 |
| R Squared | .151 |
| Adjusted R Squared | .136 |

| Regression Coefficients | | |
|---|---|---|
| Intercept | .198 | † |
|  | (.141) | |
| Number on City Council | -.019 | |
|  | (.012) | |
| Staggered Elections | .279 | ** |
|  | (.091) | |

| † Regression coefficient | *** $\alpha \le .001$ |
|---|---|
| (Standard error) | ** $\alpha \le .01$ |
|  | * $\alpha \le .05$ |

**Institutional Differences**

While most of the episode cities have a single rather than multiple election with total turnover, they prove to be cities with less incumbent reelection success. Table 6.2 shows this. In episode cities, fewer incumbents run, win, and return to office and more candidates vie for seats and win by narrower margins. Turnout is somewhat lower. These episodes are not out of character for these cities.

Table 6.2 Comparing Elections in Episode and Entire Sample Cities

| | Incumb. Running | Incumb. Winning | Incumb. Returning | Recent Winning Margin | Cand./ Seat | CVAP Voting | Turnover 1983-92 |
|---|---|---|---|---|---|---|---|
| Episode | 55.9 | 58.0 | 32.9 | 27.8 | 2.84 | 24.5 | 15.2 |
| Sample | 69.0 | 73.9 | 51.5 | 33.1 | 2.52 | 25.7 | 14.2 |

| | | | | Prior | | | |
|---|---|---|---|---|---|---|---|
| Episode | 65.5 | 65.2 | 46.1 | 24.2 | 2.58 | 24.0 | |
| Sample | 69.4 | 78.9 | 56.8 | 31.7 | 2.50 | 25.0 | |

Institutionally, these cities are less inclined to use districts, averaging only 19.3 percent districts rather than 39.3 percent, and they have somewhat lower salaries, which might suggest more volunteerism. Episode cities are more likely to use the city manager format, 78.6 percent versus 61.0 percent in the sample. All of this would suggest that the episode cities would have more competition, higher turnover, and are less traditional in governmental format.

They are, however, only slightly more competitive, averaging .158 on the **Competition Factor**, only a portion of a standard deviation from the sample mean. I have already noted that they average somewhat higher turnover and lower, not higher, turnout.

Since episodes is a dichotomous dependent variable, table 6.3 and those that follow will use logit regression analysis. Except that all episodes happened in staggered cities making coefficients uninformative, table 6.3 indicates only 79 percent of the episode cities have city managers. The other variables add little. The model only successfully predicts one episode city. Only the West proves important in the second part of the table. As noted earlier, staggered elections along with other non-traditional institutions are much more common in the West. The West also has 19 of the 29 episode cities. Once the West is introduced into the model, institutional variables explain little. Alone the West allows 78.8 percent correct predictions. Adding the other variables raises this to 80 percent.

Table 6.3   Variables From the Traditional Factor Explaining Episodes of Total Turnover

| Without Regions | | With Regions | |
|---|---|---|---|
| Count | 115 | Count | 115 |
| Number Missing | 3 | Number Missing | 3 |
| R Squared | .239 | R Squared | .302 |

| | Predicted 0 | Predicted 1 | Percent Correct | | Predicted 0 | Predicted 1 | Percent Correct |
|---|---|---|---|---|---|---|---|
| Observed 0 | 83 | 3 | 96.5 | Observed 0 | 75 | 11 | 87.2 |
| Observed 1 | 28 | 1 | 3.5 | Observed 1 | 12 | 17 | 58.6 |
| | | Total Correct | 73.0 | | | Total Correct | 80.0 |

**Logistic Model Coefficients**

| Without Regions | | | With Regions | | |
|---|---|---|---|---|---|
| constant | -16.7 | † | constant | -17.8 | † |
| | (2419) | | | (2459) | |
| Number of City Council | -.256 | | Number of City Council | -.164 | |
| | (.181) | | | (.184) | |
| Staggered Elections | 17.9 | | Staggered Elections | 17.6 | |
| | (2419) | | | (2458) | |
| Manager or Mayor/Council | -.095 | * | Manager or Mayor/Council | -.651 | |
| | (.619) | | | (.739) | |
| Percent District | -.005 | | Percent District | -.006 | |
| | (.009) | | | (.010) | |
| | | | West | 1.480 | ** |
| | | | | (.570) | |
| | | | Northeast | -.301 | |
| | | | | (.998) | |

† Logistic coefficient   $*** \alpha \leq .001$
 (Standard error)   $** \alpha \leq .01$
   $* \alpha \leq .05$

## Demographic Differences

While these cities have more women council members (36% versus 26%), African-Americans and Hispanics are less prominent on their councils (African-Americans 4.3% versus 9.8% and Hispanics 2.9% versus 3.4%). The less prominence of minorities on these councils in part reflects their fewer numbers in these cities as noted below.

Cities experiencing at least an episode of total turnover are demographically distinct on few variables. While they are somewhat smaller in population with a mean of 74,242 versus 83,832 in the sample, they are rapidly growing cities with a mean change over the period 1980 to 1992 of 29.8 percent increase versus 15.5 for the sample. Only four episode cities experience population decline.[2]

*Chapter 6*

## Table 6.4 Explanations for Episodes of Total Turnover

| Without Regions | | Selected With Regions | |
|---|---|---|---|
| Count | 114 | Count | 114 |
| Number Missing | 4 | Number Missing | 4 |
| R Squared | .320 | R Squared | .413 |

| | Predicted 0 | Predicted 1 | Percent Correct | | Predicted 0 | Predicted 1 | Percent Correct |
|---|---|---|---|---|---|---|---|
| Observed 0 | 80 | 6 | 93.0 | Observed 0 | 81 | 5 | 94.2 |
| Observed 1 | 13 | 15 | 53.6 | Observed 1 | 10 | 18 | 64.3 |
| | | Total Correct | 83.3 | | | Total Correct | 86.8 |

### Logistic Model Coefficients

| Without Regions | | | Selected With Regions | | |
|---|---|---|---|---|---|
| constant | -21.0 (7.39) | † | constant | -18.2 (5.68) | † |
| Population, 1990 | -1.71 (4.54) | | Percent Hispanic, 1990 | -.081 (.054) | |
| Population Change, 1980-1992 | .013 (.010 | | Median Age, 1990 | .173 (.074) | * |
| Percent Hispanic, 1990 | .019 (.043) | | Percent High School Ed. or higher, 1990 | .136 (.051) | ** |
| Percent African-American, 1990 | -.050 (.036) | | Competition (Reversed) | .707 (.371) | |
| Median Age, 1990 | .178 (.080) | * | Average Turnover on Council, 1983-1992 | .090 (.051) | |
| Percent High School Ed. or higher, 1990 | .194 (.075) | ** | CVAP Voting, Average | -.063 (.028) | * |
| Median Family Income, 1989 | -.044 (.041) | | West | 3.13 (.863) | *** |
| Municipal Percent of SMSA | -.006 (.014) | | | | |
| Competition (Reversed) | .553 (.374) | | | | |
| Average Turnover on Council, 1983-1992 | .069 (.048) | | | | |
| CVAP Voting, Average | -.029 (.026) | | | | |

† Logistic coefficient
(Standard error)

*** α ≤ .001
** α ≤ .01
* α ≤ .05

Given this population increase, the earlier noted pattern of adopting non-traditional institution, in particular staggered election, and the low prominence of minorities in episode cities, table 6.4 considers to models of demographic, regional, and political origins of episodes of total turnover in these cities. The second model differs from the first only in adding a control for cities in the West and excludes variables that only weakly influence whether a city has episodes.

Two demographic attributes, median age and percentage with at least a high school education, encourage episodes. They remain influential in the reduced model when the West control is introduced. In the second model, voting turnout discourages episodes, perhaps suggesting that an electorate that has a say sees little need to "throw the rascals out," but higher competition only weakly influences fewer episodes. As in table 6.3, the West is strongly more likely to experience such episodes, here even with its unique demography controlled. Demographic attributes of cities influence whether there will be an episode of total turnover, especially if we consider the West as a demographic variable. The selected model can correctly predict 87 percent of the cases, but only eighteen of the episode cities are correctly predicted.

## Policy Differences

While the episode cities have higher overall services, as judged by their mean of .239 on the **Traditional Services** factor, police expenditures per capita are much higher at $136 versus $109 and public welfare lower at $.40 versus $3.71. Taxes per capita are slightly lower at $364 versus $380, and tax effort much lower at $88 less per capita than predicted based on median family incomes as compared with a mean of $.05 over predicted for the sample. These cities have fewer city government employees with 104 per 10,000 population while the sample cities have 130. Only 45 percent of their tax revenues comes from the property tax as compared with 58 percent of the entire sample. Unemployment during the 1986-1991 period increases only by 3 percent in these cities versus 13 percent in the sample. These cities seem unlikely prospects for a public protest centered at the polls to throw the rascals out. These episode cities are not "tax and spend" cities. In fact they seem fairly efficient with higher traditional services and lower per capita taxes, low tax effort, and fewer city employees per 10,000. They do not even greatly depend on the regressive property tax.

Table 6.5 shows two models focusing on possible policy sources of public dissatisfaction that might result in episode of total turnover. The second model only adds a control for the West. Two policies in the first model modestly contribute to such episodes. Cities with higher levels of traditional services and those less dependent on property taxes have fewer episodes. Again the West sweeps up variance in not depending on property taxes, but higher traditional services do contribute to episodes. Interestingly, higher taxes little affect the probability of episodes of total turnover, and the sign is negative. Economic success in increasing the labor force somewhat encourages episodes as does improved median family income. Neither model successfully predicts episodes more than 41 percent of the episodes, suggesting that policies are not the underlying source of episodes of total turnover.

*Chapter 6*

## Table 6.5 Episode Cities and Policy Differences

| Without Regions | | With Regions | |
|---|---|---|---|
| Count | 112 | Count | 112 |
| Number Missing | 6 | Number Missing | 6 |
| R Squared | .203 | R Squared | .274 |

| | Predicted 0 | Predicted 1 | Percent Correct | | Predicted 0 | Predicted 1 | Percent Correct |
|---|---|---|---|---|---|---|---|
| Observed 0 | 79 | 4 | 95.2 | Observed 0 | 74 | 9 | 89.2 |
| Observed 1 | 17 | 12 | 41.4 | Observed 1 | 17 | 12 | 41.4 |
| | | Total Correct | 81.3 | | | Total Correct | 76.8 |

### Logistic Model Coefficients

| Without Regions | | | With Regions | | |
|---|---|---|---|---|---|
| constant | -.093 (1.17) | † | constant | -.422 (1.36) | † |
| Yearly Salary on City Council | -.055 (.036) | | Yearly Salary on City Council | -.053 (.037) | |
| Labor Force Change, 1980-1990 | .013 (.008) | | Labor Force Change, 1980-1990 | .008 (.009) | |
| Median Household Income Change, 1979-1989 | .027 (.014) | | Median Household Income Change, 1979-1989 | .018 (.015) | |
| Traditional Service Factor | 1.21 (.509) | * | Traditional Service Factor | 1.28 (.567) | * |
| City General Expenditures Per Capita | -.002 (.001) | | City General Expenditures Per Capita | -.002 (.001) | |
| Property Taxes as Pct. Gen. Rev. | -.022 (.010) | * | Property Taxes as Pct. Gen. Rev. | -.011 (.011) | |
| City Taxes, Per Capita | -.002 (.002) | | City Taxes, Per Capita | -.002 (.002) | |
| | | | West | 1.75 (.589) | ** |

† Logistic coefficient
(Standard error)

*** α ≤ .001
** α ≤ .01
* α ≤ .05

## Conclusion

While the analyses have shown some variables distinguish between cities that experience episodes of total turnover and those that do not, they have best explained those that do not. The best that we have done is to explain about two-thirds of cities experiencing episodes. Also while understanding the important uniqueness of the West is important, it is dissatisfying in that it gives little policy-making leverage. We cannot recommend that cities be moved to the

West. Table 6.6 represents the effort to better explain episode cities and to pull out the essence of why western cities are different. It is candidly only partially theory driven.

The analysis in table 6.6 starts with the realization that some cities have a better opportunity for episodes because of the small councils and use of staggered elections for those council members. It is more likely that you will have an episode of total turnover when you only have two incumbents up for election rather than having ten incumbents up for election. As previously noted, all episode cities use staggered elections and only one has a council of 10 or more members.

While most of the analyses have usefully distinguished between Hispanic and African-American minorities, to do so fails to include other minorities and suggests that the dynamics of how minorities affect local politics is not affected by their combined percentages rather than their individual percentages.

Earlier we noted the strong influence on voter turnout of having municipal elections on the same date as state and national elections. Voter turnout has been a minor influence in explaining episodes, but it might also affect candidate behavior. When its influence on episodes is compared with actual turnout, a congruent with state and national election date proves most important.

Finally, an exploration of the elements of the measure of competition reveals the strong importance of how often incumbents win. Earlier this was not important in characterizing a city's competition in elections, but it must be important to increase the probability of episodes. Again this is probably candidate behavior rather than voter behavior. Incumbents always winning discourages challengers and precludes episodes of total turnover.

The five variables in the first model of table 6.6 successfully predict nearly 83 percent of the episodes. Staggered elections, of course, increase the probability of an episode, but the others discourage episodes. Clearly if more total turnovers are desired, staggered elections, smaller councils, and elections at time away from state and national elections should be implemented. A larger minority population would also seem to discourage turnover. Speculation based on this seems dangerous, but further hypothesis testing would seem warranted. Finally, while it is easy to conceive of explanations for the relationship between increased percentage of incumbents winning and few episodes, why a city would have such high success is less clear. Certainly, Floyd Hunter would have a ready explanation, namely that an elite controls their politics and elections.

The second model merely adds the West. Before its importance was evident even with other variables already in the model, but here it contributes little and hurts the prediction of episode cities. The western cities use staggered elections more (100% versus 60%), have smaller city councils (average of 6 versus 8.6 members), have fewer minorities (19.9% versus 23.2%), have fewer incumbents

Table 6.6 Five Variables That Best Account for Episodes of Total Turnover

| Without Regions | | Selected With Regions | |
|---|---|---|---|
| Count | 115 | Count | 115 |
| Number Missing | 3 | Number Missing | 3 |
| R Squared | .550 | R Squared | .569 |

| | Predicted 0 | Predicted 1 | Percent Correct | | Predicted 0 | Predicted 1 | Percent Correct |
|---|---|---|---|---|---|---|---|
| Observed 0 | 82 | 4 | 95.4 | Observed 0 | 82 | 4 | 95.4 |
| Observed 1 | 5 | 24 | 82.8 | Observed 1 | 8 | 21 | 72.4 |
| | | | 92.2 | | | | 89.6 |

**Logistic Model Coefficients**

| Without Regions | | | Selected With Regions | | |
|---|---|---|---|---|---|
| constant | -7.88 (3508) | † | constant | -9.19 (3593) | † |
| Staggered Elections | 20.3 (3508) | | Staggered Elections | 19.8 (3593) | |
| Number of City Council | -.442 (.197) | * | Number of City Council | -.363 (.199) | |
| Percent Minorities | -.043 (.020) | * | Percent Minorities | -.036 (.021) | |
| Average Percentage of Incumbents winning | -.120 (.032) | *** | Average Percentage of Incumbents winning | -.110 (.033) | *** |
| Municipal Elections on Same Day as State and National Elections | -2.43 (1.36) | | Municipal Elections on Same Day as State and National Elections | -3.02 (1.41) | * |
| | | | West | 1.22 (.763) | |

† Logistic coefficient (Standard error)

*** $\alpha \le .001$
** $\alpha \le .01$
* $\alpha \le .05$

winning reelection (68.8% versus 79%), and more often use state and national election dates as their municipal election date (20.6% versus 1.2%). Apart from this little is unique about western cities.

Episodes of total turnover are not common and surprisingly are little related to the policies or tax levels enacted by city councils. Apart from incumbent reelection success and possibly the changes in it by substantial minority populations, politics seems to have little impact on episodes of total turnover. What would look to be the ultimate measure of a dissatisfied public, throwing all the rascals out, seems to hinge on characteristics of cities and their elections where this impact was unanticipated. It is entirely possible that western city council members do show the "volunteerism" noted by Eulau and Prewitt (1969) in their San Francisco Bay area study, and this results in episodes of total turnover. Western cities do have fewer incumbents seeking reelection

(64.1% versus 71.5%) which might be expected among volunteers, but fewer running incumbents also win reelection, as noted above. Similarly, I might suggest that a racially homogeneous city may find few willing to bother with being council members for reasons other than a sense of civic duty, again making voluntary retirement and episodes more likely.

## Episodes of Competition in Individual Cities

I now turn to accounting for why twenty-nine cities experienced an episode of competition during the period of these collected data. As noted much earlier, twelve cities in the sample have term limits. Several of them were initially identified as episode cities, but none were instances of all incumbents leaving office because of the limit on how many terms they could serve. Typically, however, some being forced out because of term limits disrupted voting coalitions or resulted in others deciding it was a good time to leave. Often also when the mayor was forced out by term limits, several incumbents would seek that office with one or none able to win it. The analysis below excludes the two episode cities with term limits, because I cannot be certain whether these limits influence candidates to behave differently.

Episodes of competition in these cities fall into two types. The first type, labelled **Volunteerism**, evidences career choices and other actions by council members and those seeking such offices. The motives for seeking or not seeking reelection rest on actions by incumbents and challengers. Obviously incumbents not seeking reelection because they have moved from the community or have died give the electorate no opportunity to express its satisfaction or dissatisfaction with their actions while in office. Of course, it would be rare for all incumbents up for election to die or move from the community. Most commonly incumbents left office voluntarily. Of course we all know of instances where those retiring from an office to go back to their first love of teaching or to devote more time to their family are a pretense. A questionnaire sought the informant's judgment whether he or she thought there was more to voluntary retirement than being tired of serving at low pay and enduring nimbycrats (Not In My Back Yard). When in doubt, I took the question on whether the episode had a significant impact on the community as pivotal. A no impact response would suggest volunteerism. I would also classify as volunteerism an instance where a young, ambitious for higher office, challenger defeats an incumbent based on the primary argument that it is "time for a change."

An Illinois city gives as example of a **Volunteerism** episode. One incumbent died before the election, another moved to another state, and the third retired because of old age. No informant thought the turnover had any impact on the city. Another example is an Ohio city where two incumbents, having served eleven and twelve years on the council, voluntarily retired while a third ran for municipal judge. A California city gives another example. The two incumbents agreed that two terms on the council were enough although the city had no term limits.

The second type of episode is my primary interest. These episodes I will call **Choice Taken**. In these instances the electorate had a choice of retaining incumbents who had taken stands in their votes on the council or supporting their challengers. This would be what we classically view as the public holding elected representatives accountable.

An example of **Choice Taken** is a California community with three incumbents up of elections. Two chose to not run and the third was defeated with informants saying that two unpopular decisions had led to the turnover. Those decisions were to redesign the central shopping plaza in the city and to buy a controversial piece of art. Ideologically the resulting change in the council shifted it to the right on social issues. Another California city provides a second example. The electorate defeated a large community development referendum that was advocated by the three incumbent council members who chose not to run for reelection. The council moves toward opposition to the "growth" policies reflected in the rejected community development program. In a third city unpopular acts, closing two branch libraries to save money, the relocation of a high school athletic field, and demotion of the police chief, led to several challengers successfully using the campaign appeal that it was time for a change, as one incumbent had served seventeen years. All incumbents were defeated.

Some **Choice Taken** elections are troublesome, such as a Montana city where two incumbents took opposite positions on a controversial issue and both lost. Perhaps the electorate reasoned that they wanted a clean sweep and fresh thinking? Also some cities showed an issue basis for the defeat of only some incumbents. In one California city, one incumbent fulfilled his commitment to serve only one term, while another's ill wife and daughter distracted him during the campaign. The winning, well-financed challenger played on "anti-incumbent" sentiment and a water rate increase. In turn he was indicted and had to resign. The defeated incumbent was appointed to serve out the term. I did code these as "choices taken" episodes.

Two cities showed elections where incumbents with prickly and blunt personalities were defeated. These were not coded as **Choice Taken** episodes.

### Conclusion

Only eleven cities have even one election that suggests the public's influence in holding policy-makers accountable. This is out of more than 400 elections. We hardly see in the elections closest to the people an electorate that uses its votes to shape policies. Only one variable proved statistically significant in predicting **Choice Taken** episodes—they are more common in the West.

# Conclusion

Since the coefficients in the follow-up analysis of only the **Choice Taken** cities are quite low, it is unlikely that a much larger sample would pull them to something more meaningful. While I have some confidence in characterizing the episodes in these cities, I do note that few **Choice Taken** episodes involved long term policies, such as the development of wealth or commitment to well-funded police forces. Possibly, even when episodes of total turnover are more likely, few involve a real choice of policy direction of the city. Perhaps changes in policy direction rather than episodes of turnover should be studied. Such a study, given the fleeting nature of city data, would be quite difficult; and we have no basis of even guessing how common such changes might be. I can only conclude here that if elections are the basis of such changes, implying that the public is the impetuous for the change, such changes must be very infrequent.

We might anticipate when to expect such changes in policy. A community experiencing a massive influx of minorities where few lived before might expect its political culture to change with its ethnic culture. Finally, older cities, especially core cities, seeing the exodus of the middle-class to the suburbs, might lack the resources to continue public policies that were adopted in the past. The process of change in the councils of such cities might better be characterized as evolutionary rather than sharp changes evident with all council members being replaced. All of this discussion, however, would suggest that we will not find elections where the public makes a choice among alternative candidates taking opposing policies.

# Notes

1. Since all episodes of total turnover are in staggered election cities, in logit regression, which is appropriate given a dichotomous dependent variable, the use of staggered elections little contributes to correct predictions.

2. These cities are somewhat better educated with 83.5 percent with a high school education or above versus 77.7 percent for the sample cities. This, as expected, is reflected in higher incomes, $42,402 versus $37,427, and fewer living in poverty, 6.7 percent versus 10.0. Minorities are only 16.8 percent of the population of episode cities versus 22.2 percent of all sample cities. These cities tend to be more suburban with their population typically being 16.1 percent of the metropolitan area versus 21.7 percent of the sample cities.

# Chapter 7

# The Dynamics of American Municipal Elections in the 1990s

Many of the conclusions of this study will probably be controversial. As these methods fall short of experimental control, some variables that both account for dependent and independent variables of interest may not have been controlled. Therefore some relationships may yet be spurious. While I feel confident that those variables to which prior literature alerts us have been controlled, perhaps the literature has ignored some explanatory variables. Certainly, I know of no suggestion in the literature that closely contested municipal elections are most prevalent in the West.

Except in a few circumstances, this study lacks change data. While time series data would strengthen demonstrations of causal relationships between variables, such data seem important in later stages of studying relationships rather than at the preliminary level of gaining an understanding. Interrupted time-series analysis seems best suited when a single and abrupt change takes place, such as a move away from all at-large elections to the use of single member districts. Even then, of course, we need to be alert to complications of why some cities enact such a policy while others do not. Time-series data also involve the question of what lag to use. Certainly, a thorough comparative analysis is only a first step in understanding.

This random sample is sufficiently large to dampen the impact of a single community's uniqueness. New York City is not like all cities or even all large cities. It is difficult to get the accurate institutional information I have. Often when the terminology is not shared, such as the distinction between by place and by district, or is just a classification, such as that between all district, all at-large, and mixed, I have been able to measure more accurately. Probably the most important data added here, however, is the complete election data on candidates seeking election for each seat in each election for the 118 city sample. These data permit a thorough examination of the levels of competition in municipal elections; and in turn, these measures allow analyses of what impact competition has on policy in cities. These complete data allow a comparative analysis of the dynamics of American city politics, at least for cities with more than 25,000 residents in the 1990s. Additionally, their number allows controls for related variables.

# A Summary of Findings

In this discussion I will take some liberties with ignoring some relationships to push toward broader generalizations, having already noted all relationships in the earlier analyses. I seek to summarize and to synthesize. It is difficult to order these conclusions, but generally those most central to our focus on competition come first followed by other important and related concerns.

1.  **Competition in city elections varies greatly among cities but has little or no impact on city politics or policies.**

Average winning margins best characterize "competitive" city elections, but the number of candidates seeking each seat is strongly related. Incumbent reelection success is unrelated to such closeness in winning. Some cities have representatives typically serving a long time, regardless of how narrowly they first won election and thereafter reelection. The range of averages for turnover on these city councils varies greatly. There was no turnover in either the 1986 or 1990 elections in Kenner, Louisiana. Only one council member left the council during this study, and he resigned in midterm. Those on the council have served for 10.7 years as of 1992. At the other extreme, Boynton Beach, Florida, had an average turnover of 36 percent per election, with council members serving on average only 3.4 years. To borrow from Bledsoe's perspective (1993), this means that some cities do not encourage the development of leadership potential on their councils as members leave too quickly to have mastered leadership skills.

The range of averages for narrowness of winning margins is from 1.7 percent in Cincinnati, Ohio, in both the 1989 and 1991 elections to 100 percent in Beaverton, Oregon, where no candidate had an opponent between 1986 and 1992. We might well expect that candidates in Cincinnati were nervous and those in Beaverton not. Whether this caused the Cincinnati council to be responsive, we can only speculate, but this comparative analysis would suggest not.

Table 3.9 shows competition proves lowest in the declining population, northeastern cities with the more traditional mayor/council form of government. It is also higher in cities with younger populations, especially when turnout is high, in larger cities with high salaried councils, and in cities with substantial minority populations. All of these relationships are statistically significant with other important variables also in the model. Southern cities have higher turnover, while cities with partisan elections have lower turnover. Both relationships are with other institutional and demographic factors controlled, although no demographic characteristic relates to turnover. Both are also statistically significant. The lower turnout in partisan cities would seem a blow to those who see political parties as providing the organization voters need to participate effectively in elections.

Characteristics of cities affect their competitiveness, turnover, and turnout. Strikingly, competition, turnover, and turnout largely fail to influence any assessed city policy. If we were to characterize Key's competition hypotheses as saying that greater competition would induce larger scale government, these data offer little support. More competitive cities *fail* to stand out for having higher taxes, greater tax effort, more traditional services, higher police expenditures, more city employees, and less dependency on the regressive property tax. Similarly, turnover fails to discourage larger government. Other variables substantially influence the growth of a city's labor force, its increased family income, its provision of traditional municipal services, its taxes and dependence on property taxes, but competition, turnover, and voter turnout are unimportant to any of these.

**2. City institutions, policies, and even politics have strong regional characteristics.**

A city's demography influences its policies. In turn the people living in cities differ greatly from one region to another. Midwestern cities have smaller scale governments, and cities with older populations have larger scale governments. Regional preferences for certain institutions or regional patterns of politics may confound an understanding of what causes municipal policy differences.

Table 7.1 Correlations Between Measures of Municipal Institutions and Regions

|  | Traditional Inst. Factor | Manager or M/C | Number on Council | Staggered Elections | Length of Term | Percent District |
|---|---|---|---|---|---|---|
| Manager or M/C | .728 | | | | | |
| Number on Council | .801 | .450 | | | | |
| Staggered Elections | -.752 | -.540 | -.451 | | | |
| Length of Term | -.499 | -.107 | -.454 | .350 | | |
| Percent District | .766 | .496 | .549 | -.362 | -.199 | |
| West | -.528 | -.437 | -.346 | .407 | .437 | -.352 |
| Northeast | .416 | .358 | .365 | -.354 | -.298 | .172 |

Several regional differences between western and northeastern cities also complicate the explorations of the dynamics of municipal policies. Western cities prove substantially more competitive, and midwestern and northeastern cities less competitive (see table 3.5). Northeastern cities tend to use the traditional municipal government forms, such as large councils, the mayor/council form, district elections, and non-staggered terms, and western cities disdain such forms of government (see table 7.1). The relationship between form of municipal government and competition thus may derive from regional characteristics rather than institutions causing competition. The path analysis in table 7.2 shows that while the West is more competitive and achieves additional competition by its adoption of non-traditional municipal institutions, these institutions themselves directly affect competition. This conforms with the impact of the control for the West on the explanations of competition in chapter 3. Traditional municipal institutions suppress competition even apart from the regional patterns of institution adoptions. Nevertheless, region influences both which institutions are used and levels of competition. If we ignore controls for region, we exaggerate the impact of institutions.

Table 7.2 Influences of the West and Traditional Institutions on Competition

|  | Direct Effects | Indirect Effects | Total Effects |
|---|---|---|---|
| The West | .10 | .13 | .23 |
| Traditional Inst. Factor | .24 |  | .24 |

Table 7.3 presents the regional relationships for different policies. Correlations greater than .40 are shown in bold. The Northeast stands out on many measures, and different signs from one region to another are quite common. Again, region proves important in explaining variations among American cities. When studying states, most differences vanish if the South is excluded; but when studying the cities, most differences vanish by excluding the West or the Northeast.

Table 7.3 Correlations Between Measures of Policy and Regions

|  | West | Northeast | South | Midwest |
|---|---|---|---|---|
| Competition | .203 | -.124 | .012 | -.119 |
| Traditional Services Factor | .047 | -.015 | .011 | -.044 |
| Labor Force Change | **.368** | -.189 | .134 | **-.305** |
| Median Family Income Change | .190 | **.552** | -.245 | **-.441** |
| City Gov. Emp. Per 10,000 Pop. | **-.392** | **.555** | .009 | -.216 |
| City General Rev. Per Capita | -.184 | **.542** | -.125 | -.231 |
| City Taxes Per Capita | -.041 | **.507** | -.189 | -.224 |
| City General Rev. from Prop. Taxes | **-.408** | **.624** | -.106 | .004 |
| Tax Effort | -.222 | **.601** | -.107 | -.214 |

Correlations greater than .300 are shown in bold.

3. **The use of district rather than at-large elections has *no* impact on representation of minorities.**

The success of African-Americans in gaining representation on a city council does not necessarily mean Hispanics and women will also be represented well in that city. *We cannot speak broadly of some councils allowing better representation of those traditionally excluded.* Although there is little variation in the percentage of women in the population of cities, more African-Americans and more Hispanics greatly improves their respective representation on city councils. Other demographic characteristics of cities or institutional variations do not influence the accuracy in which these groups are represented on the council. Recently even the use of districts little affects minority representation on councils. When demographic, institutional, and regional characteristics of the cities are considered in tables 5.4-5.6, minorities gain only from their higher percentage of the population and women only from using non-traditional municipal institutions. Competition, turnover on the council, and voter turnout little contribute to explaining variations in representation.

The model predicted below suggests the use of districts in the selection of city councils might provide an indirect linkage to accurate representation of African-Americans on their city councils. This path analysis is shown in table 7.4.

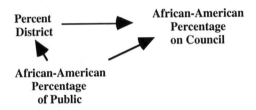

Table 7.4 Influences on African-American Percentage on Council

|  | Direct Effects | Indirect Effects | Total Effects |
|---|---|---|---|
| A-A Percentage of Public | .76 | .00 | .76 |
| Percentage District | .06 |  | .06 |

The table shows no indirect path to more accurate African-American representation by way of cities with more substantial African-American populations adopting district selection of city council members. By the 1990s the percentage African-American in the public became the strongest influence. Districts contribute slightly but only directly.

The use of districts rather than at-large selection of council members is not equally common in all types of American cities. Using district elections relates strongly to cities using the "traditional" format (table 3.4). Other elements of this format are the mayor/council form of city government, large city councils serving short terms, and having all members up for election each election. Rapidly growing cities seldom have such traditional institutions (table 3.8). Greater minority populations are not characteristics of such cities, however. In the 1990s at least, the use of districts or at-large selection of council members is incidental to the influence of how numerous African-Americans or Hispanics are in a city's public. Earlier no doubt, some cities used at-large selection to deny African-Americans their just percentages on city councils. The federal court efforts of the 1970s and 1980s focusing on the South apparently undid those efforts.

**4.  The accurate representation of those previously underrepresented on city councils has *no* impact on the policies of cities.**

Available policy information on cities provides only limited perspective on council policy actions. I lack information on African-American and Hispanic employment by cities. At least African-American employment seems responsive to accurate representation on city councils (Kerr and Mladenka 1994). Lacking information on service delivery throughout the city precludes saying whether accurate representation fails to affect biases against the working class or minority areas. I also lack information on the use of incentives to attract businesses to the city, or a city's active support for chamber of commerce efforts to attract new businesses, but we have measures of the success cities have in "growing" their economies. Desirable specific information on ordinances and practices in cities would include hearing what all segments of the public had to say, receptivity in zoning decisions to the idea that land owners have a right to make a profit on their investments, park planning from the perspective of all using such parks, tight overseeing of the actions of police, and interactions with other governments in the area.

Nevertheless, city taxing, spending, and economic growth do show much about its policies. Expenditure data in cities falls in two dimensions, the scale or size of government and the extent of traditional services. Additionally, data on each city's success in growing its economy, labor force, and housing relative to its increase in population allows assessing at least the success of such policies. Controlling other contributing factors, the accuracy of African-American representation on the city council affects no assessed policy (see tables 5.7-5.12). Accurate representation of African-Americans negatively influences growth in the labor force and in median household incomes, levels of traditional municipal services, general revenues, dependence on the property tax, and policy expenditures per capita, although these tend to be most modest contributions to the explained variance.

**5.  American cities vary greatly in size, minority percentage and heterogeneity, growth, and size relative to the surrounding metropolitan spread, but suburbs and core cities do not represent the poles of diversity, growth, and population size.**

American cities *cannot* be arranged from more populous, older, core cities with substantial minority populations to newer, smaller but growing, suburbs with few minorities. Cities in the sample can be easily ordered along a dimension of the percentage of their population of the surrounding metropolitan area. Core cities should be high on this variable, and suburbs low. Table 7.5 presenting the correlations between various characteristics of American cities in the 1990s, shows a complex pattern. It is not the case that population, diversity, and being a core city all connote urbanism (Christensen 1995, 33). Population is unrelated to anything demographically, and cities that include a substantial percentage of their metropolitan area's population, my definition of core cities, only dominant characteristic is low family income. The minority percentage of such cities as well as the percentage African-Americans or Hispanic, however, are independent of this dimension. Core cities need not be diverse nor suburbs lily white. A city's population and population growth are also independent of whether it is a suburb or a core city. Suburbs do not necessarily include only young families, and core cities not necessarily include the elderly.

Table 7.5 Correlates of Urbanism

| | Pop. | Pop. Chg. | % Hisp. | % A-A. | % Min. | Med. House Income | % HS Ed. | Med. Age | Het. Age | Het. Income |
|---|---|---|---|---|---|---|---|---|---|---|
| Pop. Chg. | .197 | | | | | | | | | |
| % Hisp. | .223 | .140 | | | | | | | | |
| % A-A. | .097 | -.165 | .010 | | | | | | | |
| % Min. | .218 | -.019 | **.676** | **.730** | | | | | | |
| Med. H. Income | -.061 | .207 | -.137 | **-.396** | **-.386** | | | | | |
| % HS Ed. | -.096 | **.331** | **-.535** | **-.452** | **-.684** | **.633** | | | | |
| Med. Age | -.117 | -.193 | -.279 | -.098 | -.258 | .205 | .027 | | | |
| Het. Age | -.174 | **-.465** | -.196 | .194 | .012 | **-.320** | **-.374** | **.641** | | |
| Het. Income | .028 | .058 | -.218 | -.083 | -.207 | .128 | **.389** | -.152 | -.111 | |
| % Metro. | .227 | -.140 | -.043 | .080 | .047 | **-.437** | -.140 | -.092 | .182 | -.039 |

Correlations greater than .300 are shown in bold.

The percentage of African-Americans and Hispanics are unrelated in American cities (r = .01). Those with many Hispanics have low percentages having completed at least high school and a broad mix of family incomes in the city. Heavily African-American cities, however, prove most common in the South. Neither a high percentage of Hispanics (r = -.043) nor of African-Americans (r = .080) relates to whether a city is a core city or a suburb. Notably, median family income, while lower in both heavily African-American (r = -.396) and minority (r = -.386) cities, proves only weakly associated with more Hispanic populations (r = -.137). Finally, population, population change, and a city's percentage of the metropolitan area are very weakly related. Large cities weakly tend to be core cities (r = .227) and are growing (r = .197).

**6.  Two institutions have a small effect on competition in American cities, the number on the city council, and the salaries paid to city council members.**

Institutions for municipal governance and elections are the result both of fashion and demographics. Thus, apart from the movement back to using single member districts rather than multimember, at-large districts, cities are moving away from the institutions labeled "traditional" and toward more recently fashionable institutions. Traditional institutions, of course, include the mayor/council form, large councils, and non-staggered elections as well as district selection of council members.

Demographic attributes and institutions prove to have some impact on competition, representation, and policy. Combining demography and institutions in the factor analysis in table 3.8, reveals only three of the seven underlying factors have a nexus between demography and institutions. Cities with increasing populations embrace non-traditional institutions, such as the city manager form, staggered elections, small councils, and at-large elections. Also cities with large populations have high yearly salaries. Finally, southern cities that tend to have substantial African-American populations use runoff elections. The first two of these include institutional features that seem more important. I turn to the question of whether even the limited role of institutions is the result of demography shaping institutions and thus indirectly influencing competition, representation, and policy. Using path analysis, I sought to evaluate the following model.

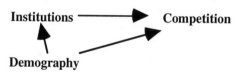

The first of the analyses (shown in the first path analysis in table 7.6) assesses the direct influence of increasing population on Competition and its indirect influence through the Traditional factor. Traditional institutions prove nearly as influential as the direct and indirect effects of increased population. The remainder of the table shows the paths for other variables.

Only the number of council members much influences competition directly more so than indirectly as a result of increased population. More council members discourage competition, and cities with increasing population are likely to have few council members. This relationship holds without controls as the overall correlation between number of council members and competition is -.36. Hypothetically, it may be difficult to find enough candidates; thus large councils see few candidates vying for each seat and less competition in elections. Alternatively, it may have to do with public capability. Large councils may be a blur of individual council members forcing a reliance of name familiarity when voting. Table 7.7 shows the number on the council decreases competition with demographic factors controlled. While populous cities have more competition and reduce the influence of the size of a city council, size nevertheless remains important.

Table 7.6 Influences on Competition

|  | Direct Effects | Indirect Effects | Total Effects |
| --- | --- | --- | --- |
| Increased Population | .13 | .10 | .23 |
| Traditional factor | .22 | | .22 |

|  | Direct Effects | Indirect Effects | Total Effects |
| --- | --- | --- | --- |
| Increased Population | .19 | .04 | .23 |
| Mayor/Council Form | .12 | | .12 |

|  | Direct Effects | Indirect Effects | Total Effects |
| --- | --- | --- | --- |
| Increased Population | .10 | .11 | .21 |
| Number on Council | .32 | | .32 |

|  | Direct Effects | Indirect Effects | Total Effects |
| --- | --- | --- | --- |
| Increased Population | .25 | .04 | .29 |
| Staggered | .09 | | .09 |

|  | Direct Effects | Indirect Effects | Total Effects |
| --- | --- | --- | --- |
| Increased Population | .32 | .12 | .44 |
| Percent District | .09 | | .09 |

All other institutions little influence competition. In the case of higher percentages of district rather than at-large selection, however, increasing population influences competition both directly as well as indirectly through the non-use of districts in such cities. As noted, districts are less competitive. Overall, table 7.6 shows some instances where institutions influence competition and many others where they do not. Similarly, increasing population proves stronger as a direct influence on competition than institutions, but the indirect path through institutions mainly proves weak.

Table 7.7 Number of Council Members and Demographic Factors Influence on Competitition

|  | Number on City Council | Plus Demo. Controls |
|---|---|---|
| Count | 116 | 114 |
| Number Missing | 2 | 4 |
| R Squared | .129 | .322 |
| Adjusted R Squared | .122 | .278 |

| Regression Coefficients | | | | | |
|---|---|---|---|---|---|
| **California** | | | **Texas** | | |
| Intercept | .811 (.215) | † | Intercept | 1.24 (1.46) | † |
| Number on City Council | -.103 (.025) | *** | Number on City Council | -.087 (.026) | ** |
|  | | | Population, 1990 | .003 (.0008) | *** |
|  | | | Population Change, 1980-1992 | .003 (.003) | |
|  | | | Median Age, 1990 | -.001 (.021) | |
|  | | | Median Family Income, 1989 | .004 (.009) | |
|  | | | Percent HS Ed. or More | -.015 (.014) | |
|  | | | Minority Percentage | .008 (.007) | |

† Regression coefficient (Standard error)

*** $\alpha \leq .001$
** $\alpha \leq .01$
* $\alpha \leq .05$

Large cities with high city council salaries also had higher competition. Table 7.8 assesses whether higher salaries have any direct influence on competition. Higher salaries, which may be viewed as an institutional variable, directly affect competition, presumably by attracting candidates eager to earn that salary. The direct and indirect effects of larger cities exceed the influence of salary, and the indirect effect with population shaping competition through its effects on salaries proves substantial. Nevertheless, smaller cities might improve competition somewhat by raising council salaries.

Table 7.8 Influences on Competition

|  | Direct Effects | Indirect Effects | Total Effects |
|---|---|---|---|
| Large Population | .22 | .13 | .35 |
| High Council Salaries | .19 |  | .19 |

**7. Institutions do play a limited independent role in shaping city policies and expenditures.**

The logic above for conclusion #6 is that demography shapes institutions, with institutions having only modest independent impact on competition. This would again hold for community policies. I again assessed this model.

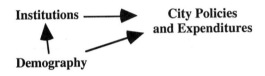

**Institutions ⟶ City Policies and Expenditures**

**Demography**

While table 7.9, assessing this model, shows many weak relationships, the consistent pattern reveals institutions exceeding the direct and indirect effects of demography. The first three path analyses examine municipal expenditures for police. All show vanishingly little direct effects of a city's population or population change. There are some indirect effects through institutions, but the largest effects are the direct effects of the institutions independent of a city's population or population change. Higher salaries, smaller city councils, and having a higher percentage of council members elected at-large all contribute to higher police expenditures, independent of population or population change. Speculatively, to win elections politicians make campaign promises to strengthen the police and on winning do so. Even though larger cities pay higher council salaries and cities with decreasing populations retain larger councils and district elections, the institutions chiefly affect police expenditures, not the demography.

The fourth path analysis down also assesses this pattern as the Traditional Services factor mainly captures police expenditures per capita. Here the direct and indirect effects of higher city council salaries both shape expenditures.

The last three path analyses shown in table 7.9 center on the relationships of increasing populations and the negative end of the Traditional factor for institutions, the use of non-traditional city managers, smaller councils, at-large elections, and staggered terms. Here there are direct and negative effects of increasing population and some indirect effects through non-traditional institutions. The institutions themselves, however, have an even larger direct and negative influence on the number of city employees for each 10,000 population, per capita level of municipal taxes, and percentage of revenues coming from the property tax. The non-traditional institutions of cities with increasing populations themselves independently result in smaller scale government.

Table 7.9 Influences on Policy

| Police Exp. PC | Direct Effects | Indirect Effects | Total Effects |
|---|---|---|---|
| Population | .01 | .09 | .10 |
| Salary | .12 | | .12 |

| Police Exp. PC | Direct Effects | Indirect Effects | Total Effects |
|---|---|---|---|
| Increased Population | .01 | .08 | .09 |
| Number on Council | .23 | | .23 |

| Police Exp. PC | Direct Effects | Indirect Effects | Total Effects |
|---|---|---|---|
| Increased Population | .00 | .09 | .09 |
| Percent District | .24 | | .24 |

| Traditional Services | Direct Effects | Indirect Effects | Total Effects |
|---|---|---|---|
| Population | .05 | .18 | .23 |
| Salary | .25 | | .25 |

| Employees/10K Pop. | Direct Effects | Indirect Effects | Total Effects |
|---|---|---|---|
| Increased Population | .19 | .18 | .37 |
| Traditional Factor | .39 | | .39 |

| City Taxes PC | Direct Effects | Indirect Effects | Total Effects |
|---|---|---|---|
| Increased Population | .09 | .10 | .19 |
| Traditional Factor | .21 | | .21 |

| Rev. as Pct. Prop. Tax | Direct Effects | Indirect Effects | Total Effects |
|---|---|---|---|
| Increased Population | .14 | 19 | .33 |
| Traditional Factor | .41 | | .41 |

**8. While institutions and demography influence municipal voting turnout, turnout little shapes city politics or policies.**

*Appendix B* finds three institutional variables, spring elections, staggered terms, and the use of districts, all dampen turnout (table 8). Additionally, three demographic variables, lower turnout in the South, higher turnout in cities with higher incomes, and higher turnout when the community shows diversity in incomes, also greatly influence voter turnout. Higher incomes and heterogeneity of incomes encourage turnout. More educated cities vote less with income controlled. Although this is not statistically significant, it runs counter to expectations based on individual data.

Table 7.10 Demographic and Institutional Sources for Greater Voting Turnout

| Count | 115 |
|---|---|
| Number Missing | 3 |
| R Squared | .428 |
| Adjusted R Squared | .391 |

| Regression Coefficients | | |
|---|---|---|
| Intercept | 28.2 | † |
| | (6.74) | |
| Spring Elections | -6.05 | ** |
| | (1.83) | |
| Staggered Elections | -8.32 | *** |
| | (2.09) | |
| Percent District | -.019 | |
| | (.023) | |
| South | -6.02 | ** |
| | (2.18) | |
| Median Family Income, | .309 | ** |
| 1989 | .104) | |
| Heterogeneity of Income | .357 | * |
| | (.167) | |
| Percent HS Ed. or Over | -.151 | |
| | (.116) | |
| † Regression coefficient | *** $\alpha \leq .001$ | |
| (Standard error) | ** $\alpha \leq .01$ | |
| | * $\alpha \leq .05$ | |

Table 7.10 considers these variables and their impact on turnout. With both demographic and institutional variables included, the percent of seats selection using districts proves unimportant. Also as in the analyses in *Appendix B*, better educated cities prove less likely to turn out in elections. As before the South votes less and spring and staggered elections result in lower voting turnout.

The analysis of the influence of competition on various policies in chapter 4 also included the impact of voting turnout. Greater voting turnout is positively associated with cities with higher general revenues as shown in table 4.11, and these cities also tend to depend more on property taxes, even when we control for region (table 4.12). Apart from these counter examples, turnout little affects policy. *The policies of low turnout cities are not significantly different from those of high turnout cities.* If an active electorate insists on what it prefers in policy, that policy is no different from the policies in apathetic electorate cities.

9.  **There is nothing about elections in American cities or in the dynamics of their politics that would suggest this is a government "close to the people."**

The rhetoric of politics often includes the argument that government should not be centered in Washington, D.C., but closer to the people at the local level. In this argument few make a distinction between whether local means at the state level or really at the local level. While this idea no doubt derives from when cities were increasingly providing local service for an increasingly dependent urban public, it provides little insight into why this might be true. Presumably such a government is more responsive, although it may have inadequate resources to deal with problems. Such responsiveness implies that voters more closely monitor actions by local representatives and swiftly act to remove the unresponsive in elections.

The previous conclusion shows that public participation in municipal elections fails to prove important to the politics of a city. Also competitive municipal elections little affect a city's policies. While political scientists stress the importance of turnout, competition, and the lack of turnover in "safe" districts for the U.S. House of Representatives and in state legislatures, there certainly are differences between local democracy and the larger democracies of state and national governments that might make them more responsive even without voter turnout and competition in elections. Chief among these might be the greater ease that local representatives have in learning constituent sentiments. By not being set apart from constituents and being among them daily, local representatives may better sense community opinion. Only if they feel it is their obligation to enact those opinions into policy, even without electoral threats, could this greater awareness result in responsive public policy.

Of course, this presumes that local elective office holders are aware that competition in elections is unrelated to their remaining in public office for another term. They may believe they are likely to be challenged successfully unless they are responsive. Alternatively the "volunteers" of Eulau and Prewitt (1973) may see no need to be responsive. These are all empirical questions beyond the scope of this research. Can officeholders accurately predict public opinion or district opinion? Do they feel electorally challenged? Are local representatives aware of instances in which unresponsive municipal leaders lost reelection efforts? Student research that I have conducted strongly suggests that certain fabled instances "demonstrate" to many elected officials that you can lose unless you are responsive. Elected officials at all levels recalled one instance in which many school board members were defeated because of how they had voted on a policy.

Presumably by not being a class apart from the public, local leaders may be more demographically representative of the public and even by enacting their personal preferences may respond to public opinion. While it may seem doubtful that those coming forth to seek local elective offices, when the pay is poor at best, do so out of altruistic motives, the media pay less attention to the private lives of local representatives allowing them a more normal life. Thus more normal individuals might tolerate such offices. I can only conclude that more information is needed about local elected officials. Are they "volunteers" as Prewitt (1970) and Eulau and Prewitt (1973) found in the San Francisco area at the time? Are they demographically representative? Is there evidence that public service personally benefits them economically or otherwise?

## Conclusion

The sample cities show substantially different policies. Competition in their elections also varies greatly. One of two conclusions must hold: either competition fails to influence policies, or I have not validly measured competition or exhaustively measured policy.

### If Competition Fails to Influence Policy

Perhaps at the local level, as at all other levels of government, we expect change to be easier than it is. In the dynamics by which public policy is made, we have seen that demographic characteristics do influence the policies that cities enact. How can this happen without democratic accountability? Policy makers cannot or do not ignore what their public is like in voting policies, but why? Democratic government is certainly supposed to be more than differing when the city is in the Northeast or has a larger minority population. I have *not* demonstrated that the public in competitive elections fails to influence policies differently than when elections afford them no choice. What I think has been demonstrated is that such influence pales in comparison to other influences. Perhaps those elected in competitive contests struggle endlessly to improve policy as they promised but fail to have the needed resources or to overcome other sources of resistance. It is hackneyed, but maybe the public has influence at the margins. Perhaps with similar problems and similar resources, cities would prove responsive when elections were competitive.

The analyses of episodes of complete turnover hardly encourage expectations that when policy makers wrong the city through their unresponsiveness, we could expect competition will increase. We might assess the importance of occasional competition in some cities to policies enacted. Ethically, social scientists cannot experiment in a community by engendering competition, even if we knew how to do so. But we could study cities over time capturing policies before and after competition. I cannot be sanguine, however, about encouraging such laborious research. Alternatively, we might monitor a large number of cities and their policies. When there is a sharp break with previous policies, we might focus on whether competitive elections preceded that change.

*Should We Focus on the Personal Characteristics of City Council Members?*

Regardless of how they end up in public office, through competitive elections or not, working class council members may support different policies than middle class members. Previous research would suggest that the middle class is greatly overrepresented in all legislative bodies, perhaps because they are more comfortable seeking voter support, because they have the time when "amateur" status means you cannot make a living as a public representative, or because they take the positions that are likely to get support from those who contribute to campaigns and vote. Regardless, a city with less class bias among its city council members may enact different policies.

Perhaps true competition is when both working class and middle class council members must interact to make policy. Or perhaps middle class cities get representative council members merely because the middle class is likely to run for office. Possibly the population growth of most cities dooms the prospects of old time council members being like their recent arrival constituents.

*Could a Quality Electorate Achieve Influence on City Policies?*

Regretfully, I have no data other than turnout to explore the dynamics of public involvement in city governance. These data reveal substantial variations in voting turnout and some weak evidence that greater competition and greater public participation are associated. But neither competition nor turnout seems to affect policies. The question is whether a subset of instances of greater public involvement does affect policies in some cities. Certainly we would expect variations in the quality of public participation as we saw true for turnout. Electorates in some cities may be more informed of prior decisions, may have rational formed preferences for public policies, and may see the instrumentality of voting for one candidate rather than another based on those preferences. Is what happens in city governance entirely determined by elite decisions, such as whether to run or to seek reelection, or can a "quality" electorate achieve its preferences through how it votes?

I am not sure that assessing a "quality electorate" would be easy, and it certainly would be expensive to do for a large number of cities. With such data, however, we could assess whether the electorate can affect public policy. Voting in competitive elections would not seem to be the vehicle for expressing this "quality," as neither proves important to policy. Perhaps, no present electorate has achieved the level of "quality" needed to prove important.

I should also note that many cities, especially those in the West, have voter initiative. Perhaps behind the greater participation and competition in California, and the West in general, is greater public familiarity with expressing one's views on city policy questions.

## If We Need to Validly Assess Competition

Perhaps competition, even close competition, between candidates offering nothing more than "I am better than he is!" falls short of what we mean when we use this concept. It would be quite difficult to assess the quality of the campaign appeals made in elections by rival candidates. Luttbeg did gather newspaper advertisements during the last several weeks in the 1985 Texas municipal and school board elections, as part of the overall study of the role of print media in local elections (Luttbeg 1988). While these ads were never systematically assessed, impressionistically they seldom, if ever, rose above claims to be "more qualified," "a true family man," or "having done a good job." In few, if any, instances did the voter know what policy positions she was prospectively getting with a vote for one candidate rather than for the other.

Perhaps the subset of "truly" competitive elections needs to be studied, those where the candidates take opposing positions on issues likely to be quickly enacted into policy. This research might need to go beyond paid advertisements to observe this. If the "new style" of presidential and congressional campaigns, where no stands are taken on hard issues but only on style issues, such as being against crime and for better education, has reached municipal elections, such research might need to solicit candidate stands on such issues or use survey research to assess public agreement on where the candidates fall on such issues.

Finally at the local level, I should note, most have the option of "voting with their feet." Given the range of municipal policy and given the concentration of Americans in metropolitan areas, many could "shop" for public policies of their choice by moving to a desirable city, if such a choice is available (Schneider 1989). Moving for policy reasons, while inconvenient, may be easier than seeking to achieve those policies more indirectly by the careful election of selected candidates. Certainly the importance of factors that have substantial regional components to accounting for policy variations in chapter 5 would suggest that this "shopping" might entail moving from one region to another. Typically, region explains about one third of the variance in the policies. Your right to move, perhaps from one region to another, may be more important than your right to vote.

# Trends

What does the future hold? Some trends are evident. The use of districts in heavily minority cities has given minorities proportional if not accurate representation. There has been a movement to district elections, no doubt, pushed by federal court actions. If the courts realize that the further use will probably contribute nothing to improving minority representation, this institutional trend might cease. Paralleling this improvement of minority representation on city councils has been the growth of women serving on councils. This may or may not be the result of increasing use of districts. The analysis in chapter 5 would suggest it is unrelated and thus might continue, even were fewer cities to adopt district selection of council members.

Increasing salaries with the attendant reduced turnover in office seems like a continuing trend. Cities will continue to growth in population, making its business more complex, taking more time, and necessitating higher salaries to justify the time commitment council members are called to give.

Term limits seem to be increasingly common. These data show this is curiously most common in cities with histories of high turnover on their councils. Term limits, as shown, discourage candidates from seeking office. The trend toward term limits may make the volunteerism noted in the San Francisco Bay area more prevalent, as candidates must be recruited out of a sense of civic duty rather than as a representative or a person with strong views on policies.

Figure 1 in *Appendix B* shows over time, incumbents have been winning less often, a decline of 1.6 percentage points each year; but the winner's margin has been increasing by over one percentage point each year. No other measure of the nature of municipal elections shows a consistent trend. It is hard to reconcile the meaning of both trends. Having incumbents who increasingly lose might suggest voter dissatisfaction, but if so, why are winning margins increasing?

Volunteerism may be increasing as low pay, more demands on the time of council members, and more citizen complaints discourage prospective candidates from seeking election and retaining their offices after initial election. Incumbents may lose or quit, but a limited candidate pool may discourage competitive elections. If only one candidate per seat can be recruited, competitive elections are unlikely.

Minorities seem likely to be an ever increasing percentage of most cities. Since a high percentage of minorities improves competition, future municipal elections may be more competitive. There are forces that would seem likely to decrease competition in our cities as well as increasing minority percentages that might increase competition; obviously much would depend on the mix in a particular city.

Growth in population seems likely to continue. Average cities grew by 15.5 percent over the 1980-1992 period. This seems unlikely to slow. Growth may be the goal of many city managers, business owners, and council members; but apart from a very few cities, it is inevitable given the population growth of the country.

Several other trends can be seen, not in these data, but in national patterns. States and federal governments seem increasingly likely to both provide money for local use but also to set standards to which cities must comply. This might well further discourage anyone from seeking city council seats.

The money spent in local campaigns as for state and national offices probably increases every year. This would mean that others would "own" a piece of each council member and further discourage candidates who are unwilling to grovel for bucks.

While these data show no trend in declining turnout over the 1985-1992 period, nationwide turnout for state and national offices shows only occasionally deviations from a steady decline since 1960. Perhaps local participation would also show such a decline from this longer perspective, or perhaps the 25 percent voting rate shown in these data is as low as turnout will get. Turnout did not have any substantial impact on city politics and policies, so this trend may have no import.

Finally, the trend for American cities to have multiple newspapers results in no competition among papers. There is no thorough research on the question of whether large newspapers devote much time to cities that are a fragment of their audience or how such coverage affects competition in cities. An electorate that does not know of local policies may not be able to cast votes for or against those responsible.

Nothing in any of these trends seems likely to improve competition or voter turnout. The increased mobility of Americans along with the proliferation of suburbs in most metropolitan areas, however, may make it easier to vote with your feet while shopping for city policies. If cities are in competition with each other for residents and businesses, will they act to reduce policy differences among them and offer lower prices (taxes) and poorer services? This is the behavior of grocery and other stores. Or will they specialize into being a good place to raise children, a cheap place for the elderly to live, a safe and luxurious place where you can be confident of your investment, or the only place where the poor can afford to live? All of this negates any need for democratic governance at the local level. Probably no one moves to a city because its elections are competitive, its voters more participant, or its policies more reflective of city opinion, but they may do so for its taxes and services.

# Appendix A

# Cities in the Sample

| | | | | | |
|---|---|---|---|---|---|
| AK | Little Rock | IL | De Kalb | NV | Las Vegas |
| AK | Pine Bluff | IL | Downers Grove | NY | Binghamton |
| AL | Mobile | IL | Moline | NY | Hempstead |
| AZ | Mesa | IL | Oak Lawn | NY | White Plains |
| CA | Bell Gardens | IL | Quincy | OH | Bowling Green |
| CA | Beverly Hills | IL | Rockford | OH | Cincinnati |
| CA | Buena Park | IL | Wheaton | OH | Cleveland Heights |
| CA | Carlsbad | IN | Marion | OH | Elyria |
| CA | Clovis | IN | South Bend | OH | Lakewood |
| CA | Concord | KS | Hutchinson | OH | Marion |
| CA | Covina | LA | Kenner | OH | Massillon |
| CA | Davis | LA | Slidell | OK | Edmond |
| CA | La Habra | MA | Everett | OR | Beaverton |
| CA | La Mirada | MA | Holyoke | PA | York |
| CA | Manhattan Beach | MA | Lynn | RI | Newport |
| CA | Modesto | MA | Melrose | SD | Aberdeen |
| CA | Novato | MA | Newton | TN | Chattanooga |
| CA | Palm Springs | MA | Peabody | TX | Austin |
| CA | Petaluma | MA | Pittsfield | TX | Garland |
| CA | San Jose | MA | Salem | TX | Grand Prairie |
| CA | Seaside | MA | Somerville | TX | Hurst |
| CA | Stockton | MA | Worcester | TX | Killeen |
| CA | Thousand Oaks | MD | Annapolis | TX | Kingsville |
| CA | Tustin | MD | Cumberland | TX | Longview |
| CA | Yorba Linda | ME | Portland | TX | Port Arthur |
| CO | Arvada | MI | Dearborn | TX | San Angelo |
| CO | Longmont | MI | Taylor | TX | Sherman |
| CO | Northglenn | MS | Meridian | TX | Texarkana |
| CT | Norwich | MS | Pascagoula | UT | Layton |
| DE | Newark | MO | Kirkwood | UT | Provo |
| FL | Boynton Beach | MT | Billings | WA | Bellingham |
| FL | Bradenton | MT | Great Falls | WA | Yakima |
| FL | Coral Springs | NC | Kinston | WI | Kenosha |
| FL | Gainesville | ND | Grand Forks | WI | Manitowoc |
| FL | Largo | NE | Lincoln | WI | Oshkosh |
| FL | Lauderhill | NJ | Camden | WI | Racine |
| FL | Miami | NJ | Linden | WV | Parkersburg |
| FL | Orlando | NJ | New Brunswick | WV | Wheeling |
| FL | Tallahassee | NJ | Paterson | | |
| IA | Mason | NJ | Trenton | | |

## Appendix B

# Municipal Elections in the 1980s and 1990s

In the United States we have 19,296 municipal governments, each with an average of approximately 6.5 council members.[1] These 125,000 plus council members must stand for reelection typically every 3.3 years.[2]

## Municipal Elections in the Sample Cities

In most cases four elections were included in the data on the sample cities. I expected that most of the cities would have had their last election in spring 1991, but only 36 cities (31%) have spring, odd number year, municipal elections. The largest group, 42 cities (36%), has fall elections in odd number years. Overall, 40 cities (34%) only have Spring elections, and 57 (48%) have only odd year municipal elections. Twenty-one cities have elections both in even and odd years with all but one in the spring. One cannot make clean statements about the timing of municipal elections in the United States. Data for these cities thus ends in 1992 or 1991 and extends backward for two complete rounds of elections.

Since 34 cities (29%) elect their entire city council each election, for them only two elections constitute two complete rounds. For most of the other cities, the council is divided into two staggers or groupings of council members whose terms overlap. Six cities have three staggers, and one of two commission cities has one of its commissioners elected each year for a five-year term. With the exception of this one commission city, averages are for each of the two most recent rounds of elections, with the most recent being called "recent" and the earlier called "prior."

These complications, unfortunately, fail to exhaust the comparability issues in coding municipal election data. Sixty-six cities (56%) with the city manager form of government have no separately elected executive. In those cities and in the commission cities, the mayor's election was counted as part of the city council. In the 49 (42%) mayor/council cities, the mayor's election was not counted in these analyses. All mayoral elections with the exception of those where the council elects the mayor, are discussed at the end of this appendix.

Nearly half of the cities elect all council members in at-large elections. Such elections can be winner-takes-all elections if by place, which is true in 20 cities.

163

"Top-vote-getter" elections for at-large seats, however, involve some comparability issues. The measure of candidates per seat merely requires dividing the total number of candidates by the total number of seats up for election. Winning margins, however, require the identification of the highest loser, or the candidate that the lowest vote-getter had to defeat to win. The percentage of votes received by the highest loser provided the standard for assessing winning margin for all winners.

Two other institutional factors complicated establishing comparable measures. Many cities (35 or 30%) use runoff elections between the top two vote-getters in the first election, if neither gets above a certain percentage of the vote, generally a majority. Sixteen cities (14%) use either partisan or non-partisan primary elections to limit the general election to only two candidates per seat. In both cases the first election with the most candidates is used to calculate the number of candidates per seat; and the second election provides the winning margins. While 14 cities (12%) use partisan elections, this causes no calculation complications, as they all use primary elections.

Turnout was also a problem in comparability. Many cities had no records of the number of registered voters in prior or even the most recent elections. Cities need only record the number of votes received by each candidate but not the total number of ballots cast or the number of registered voters. While voting age population could be estimated from the Censuses of 1980 and 1990 and is a common measure for estimating turnout, a substantial noncitizen population might exaggerate the potential election turnouts. The 1990 Census gives the percentage of voting aged population that is citizens, but the 1980 Census gave only the noncitizen percentage of the entire population. Assuming that this percentage held for the voting age population as well allows an estimate for the 1980 citizen voting age population. With this estimate for 1980 and the measure for 1990, I estimated the citizen voting age population for all elections as the linear trend.

When cities failed to report the total number of ballots cast in each election, I estimated the number of ballots cast as that for the seat with the most ballots cast. The turnout figures reported are the number of votes cast divided by the citizen voting aged population or CVAP.

Finally, some cities have staggered district elections meaning that the entire electorate does not vote unless there are also at-large seats on the ballot, such as that for mayor. If districts covering only half of the electorate were on the ballot, the number of ballots cast was divided by one half of the citizen voting age population to measure turnout.[3]

# American Municipal Elections in the 1980s and 1990s

In the most recent round of elections in these cities shown in table 1, 69 percent of incumbents ran for reelection and nearly 74 percent won. Overall, nearly 52 percent of council incumbents returned, or viewed from the other perspective, turnover was just over 48 percent. Karnig and Walter (1978) report somewhat higher retention of incumbents of 72 percent running, 78 percent winning, and

44 percent turnover.[4] They note, however, that their values are somewhat higher than those noted by Lee (1963). This would suggest a very modest fluctuation over time. Their assessment, that this turnover is greater than for Congress despite public distrust of that institution, would seem even more apt today. Perhaps we need to reject the model that publicly expressed dissatisfaction augurs poorly for incumbents. At least, it must vary by institutional level from the local to the state and national levels.

In this most recent round, typically, 2.5 candidates sought each seat, and winners defeated their closest opponent by 33 percent. In the prior round the figures are 2.5 candidates per seat and an average winning margin of nearly 32 percent. Neither of these figures has any prior assessment in the research literature to allow a judgment concerning the trend. In these cities, however, little change in candidates per seat or in average winning margin can be noted between rounds of elections.

Turnout of citizens of voting age in these elections averages just over 25 percent with a slight up tick in the most recent round. While this might seem to suggest a downward trend given Lee's 1962 report of 33 percent turnout and Karnig and Walter's 29 percent turnout in 1975, again both used city secretary reports of both ballots and registered voters. Dividing by the number of registered voters, where the data made this possible, shows 35.7 percent voted in the last two waves of elections in these cities. These data suggest that in these cities turnouts increased by 2 percent between rounds of elections. Probably the safest conclusion is that local turnout fluctuates but at a level below even that of even year, state and national offices when the president is not on the ballot. By correcting for disenfranchised noncitizens, the participation measure used here presents local turnout more favorably than would the typical state and national figure where ballots are divided by voting age population with no citizenship correction.

Two measures, both dealing with the electoral success of incumbents, on average varied substantially between this most recent round of municipal elections and the prior round. In the prior round that took place typically in the late 1980s, nearly 6 percent more incumbents who sought reelection won, resulting in much lower turnover. Winning margins also broadened by 1.4 percent. While this is a scalar shift of all cities, many cities are going in the opposite direction.

The last two columns in table 1 show the maximum and minimum figures observed across the two rounds of elections. At least one city across these two rounds saw no incumbent on its city council seeking reelection, while many saw all incumbents seeking reelection. Similarly, voters in one city saw no choice of candidates to fill any seat on their city council, while another had the choice of typically 9 candidates for each seat on the council. Obviously the candidates in the city with no opponents won 100 percent of the vote, but candidates in another city saw on average a winning margin of less than 2 percentage points. Finally, voter turnout shows similar dramatic variations across cities. Virtually, no citizen voting age resident in one city bothered to cast a vote in one city (turnout never exceeded .2 percent). Another, however, saw nearly 63 percent turnout.

*Appendix B*

## Table 1 Elections In the Sample Cities

| Variable | Average for Recent Round | Average for Prior Round | Average Over Two Rounds | Minimum City Over Two Rounds | Maximum City Over Two Rounds |
|---|---|---|---|---|---|
| Incumbents running | 69.0 | 69.4 | 69.2 | 0 | 100 |
| Incumbent winning | 73.9 | 78.9 | 76.0 | 0 | 100 |
| Percent of Incumbents Returned per Round | 51.5 | 56.8 | 54.1 | 0 | 100 |
| Candidates for each seat | 2.52 | 2.50 | 2.51 | 1 | 7.4 |
| Winning margin | 33.1 | 31.7 | 32.4 | 1.7 | 100 |
| Turnout | 25.7 | 25.0 | 25.4 | .2 | 62.8 |

Figure 1 shows some election changes over time across the sample cities. Apart from Incumbents Winning and Average Winning Margins, trends are erratic and flat. Over time, however, incumbents have been winning less often, a decline of 1.6 percentage points each year. However, the winner's margin has been increasing by over one percentage point each year. Perhaps the winning margin is increasing because "good" candidates are increasingly unwilling to challenge the incumbent given the increasing time commitments and lack of pay for the office. We can see, however, that the number of candidates per seat is unchanged. Also incumbents are winning less, which would seem to run counter to any "quality of the challengers" hypothesis. Also incumbents are increasingly loosing, not increasingly quitting.

This stability on average might cause us to expect that individual cities do not vary much over time except for these two trends. This is not the case.

## Consistency in Sample City Elections

Figure 2 shows much variation between rounds of elections in the behavior and success of incumbents in seeking additional terms. While the relationships fall in the expected direction, knowing that one city's incumbents ran, won, and in general returned to office in one round of elections little informs you what to expect in the next round of elections.

Figure 3 shows a different pattern. Cities with narrow winning margins and many candidates per seat in the prior round strongly follow that pattern in the most recent round. Turnout also varies little from one election to the next. The differences noted between figures 2 and 3 suggest that contested elections with narrow winning margins as well as high turnouts are enduring characteristics of some cities, but incumbent success varies greatly among them. Incumbent success may reflect how good a job the public sees incumbents doing, but other measures may reflect institutional patterns.

## Institutional Explanations for Different
## Incumbent Success in Elections

As discussed in chapter 1, the reform movement sought to change American municipal elections by changing institutions. While you will look in vain for present day American cities that allow noncitizens to vote, that do not use state supplied ballots, or that do not require prior voter registration, some of the "reforms" have been less pervasive. The first question is whether cities can be referred to as "reformed" or "unreformed," or even ordered along a continuum of extent of "reform."

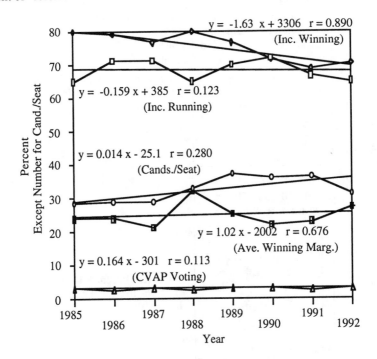

Figure 1 Changes in Incumbents Running and Winning, in Candidates per Seat, in Average Winning Margins, and in Voting Turnout Over Time

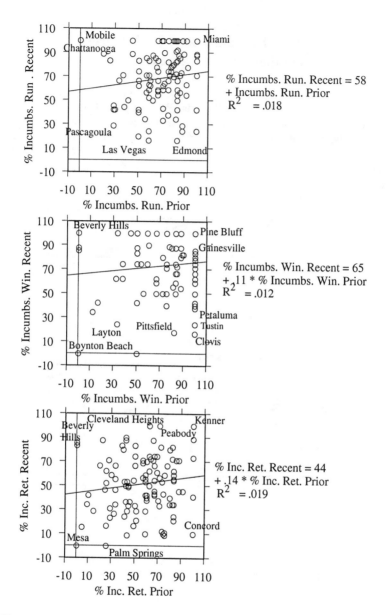

Figure 2 Recent and Prior Round Election Success of Incumbents in Running for Reelection, in Winning, and Overall in Returning to Their Office

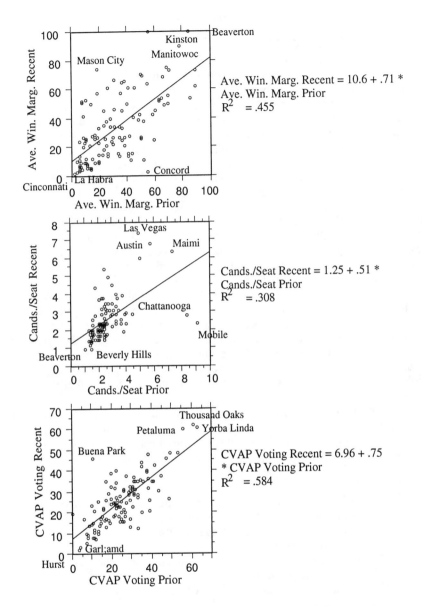

Figure 3 Recent and Prior Round Winning Margins, Candidates per Seat, and
Citizen Voting Age Population Turnout

*Appendix B*

**Searching for Reformed Cities**

Analysis would be easier were institutions in the sample cities to reflect a single dimension, such as "reformed" and "unreformed."[5] Lineberry and Fowler (1967) believed that "reformed" cities followed the prescriptions of the Reform Movement in abandoning the separation between the executive and legislative in the mayor/council form of government, the partisanship evident in partisan elections with Democrats facing Republicans for city offices, the division of the city resulting from districts selecting their own council members, short terms of office putting council members at continual risk of losing an election, and having a large council with all elected in each city election. This all would suggest that reformed and unreformed are a single dimension or factor of city institutions. If this were true, we would merely identify the reformed and unreformed cities. Otherwise we would have to deal with cities that adopted the newer city manager form, but retained partisan elections or short terms of office. The choice is finding where cities fall on a single dimension, such as reform, or considering all facets of institutions independently.

Factor analysis merely assesses how well correlated different measures of interest are with each other. In this case, whether most cities that use the mayor/council form also are partisan, use district elections, have large city council, and elect all council members in the same elections for a short term. If as Lineberry and Fowler argue all are highly intercorrelated, factor analysis would show a single underlying factor or dimension is highly correlated with each. If not, several factors might be needed although fewer than using all variables.

If the resulting factor or factors can be easily understood, we learn that what we assess is not as complicated as it might be and that our analysis is simplified. Factor analysis of the following variables proved unsuccessful in finding such a single dimension, but differences in municipal institutions are not as complicated as they might be.

1. The form of government, whether city manager or mayor/council
2. The number of members on the city council
3. Whether council terms are staggered or not
4. The length of the term of office
5. The percent of the city council selected in district elections
6. The use of runoff elections
7. Whether the city has term limits or not
8. Yearly salary
9. Whether elections are partisan or nonpartisan
10. Whether nonpartisan or partisan primaries are used or not
11. Whether elections are in the spring or the fall.

Four factors have eigenvalues greater than 1.0, but five are orthogonally rotated, giving the results shown in table 2 below. While an oblique rotation was considered, it differed little from the orthogonal solution. These factors explain nearly three-quarters of the variance in these measures. The number of members on the council best defines Factor 1 (labeled the Traditional City Form Factor), but the use of districts, non-staggered elections, and the mayor/council format also proves important for defining this dimension. Clearly this is not a "reformed" or "unreformed" dimension, as the partisan/nonpartisan elections variable is unrelated. The use of partisan elections loads heavily on Factor 2 (given that name), as does the use of primaries. Factor 1 reflects the size of the council and Factor 2 merely captures partisan elections. Factor 3 seems simply the salary paid and is so labeled. Factor 4 seems largely the use of term limits and to a lesser degree length of terms on the council. Finally, Factor 5 captures only the spring or fall timing of municipal elections.

Table 2 Factor Analysis of Municipal Institutions

| Factor Analysis Summary | | Eigenvalues | | |
|---|---|---|---|---|
| | | | Magnitude | Var. Prop. |
| Number of Variables | 11 | | | |
| Number of Cases | 114 | 1 | 2.84 | .26 |
| Number Missing | 4 | 2 | 1.81 | .16 |
| P-Value | <.0001 | 3 | 1.39 | .13 |
| | | 4 | 1.12 | .10 |
| | | 5 | .94 | .09 |

| | Trad. City Form | Partisan Elections | High Salary | More Confidence | Spring Elections |
|---|---|---|---|---|---|
| City Manager or Mayor/Council | .728 | .299 | .075 | .325 | -.158 |
| Number on City Council | .801 | -.039 | -.160 | -.227 | -.107 |
| Staggered Elections | -.752 | .019 | -.075 | -.018 | .218 |
| Percent Districts | .766 | .103 | .127 | .100 | .269 |
| Partisan Elections | .079 | .856 | .110 | .025 | -.074 |
| Primary Elections | .033 | .836 | -.195 | .022 | -.138 |
| Runoff Elections | -.071 | -.078 | .584 | -.110 | .565 |
| Yearly Salary | .109 | -.036 | .845 | -.082 | -.165 |
| Term of Office | -.499 | .072 | .371 | .598 | -.073 |
| Term Limits | -.174 | -.007 | .279 | -.840 | .076 |
| Spring Elections | -.091 | -.193 | -.169 | -.066 | .827 |

To capture the impact of institutions on municipal politics, we cannot merely capture a "reformed" or "unreformed" dimension; there is none. Furthermore, five factors needed to capture conceptually important measures, while capturing much of the variance in these measures, leaves us unable to focus on the institutions that are the focus of lay discussions about city politics. The following analysis therefore focuses on those institutional variables that would seem to have conceptual importance.

## Current Efforts to Reform City Politics

With much encouragement from the federal courts, many cities are moving away from the "reform," at-large selection of council members to the pre-"reform," single member districts. As noted in chapter 1, at-large elections were used to denying minorities their share of representation on the council. Those urging undoing this "reform" see benefits in accurate minority representation. Such issues are discussed in chapter 6, but the consideration here focuses on the impact of using district selection of council members.

Councils ranged in size from 5 to 25, and the average is just under eight. The size of a council might well be expected to influence both council members and the electorate's behavior in elections. Members of a small council might, if the arguments for the differences between the U.S. Senate and House are generalized, hold themselves in higher status and see themselves as more important to their community. If true, they would be more eager to retain their seat, but find others eager to take it. We might well expect salaries to also attract interest in winning and retaining council seats. The population of the city, however, may shape both the number on the council as well as the salaries paid.

I include the population of the city in this analysis although it is unrelated to the number serving on the council.[6] Contrastingly, salary strongly relates to city size, although most cities are small and low salaried, as shown in figure 4. Salaries and small size might well raise the status of council members in the White Plains as shown as a black dot, but this is an outlier.

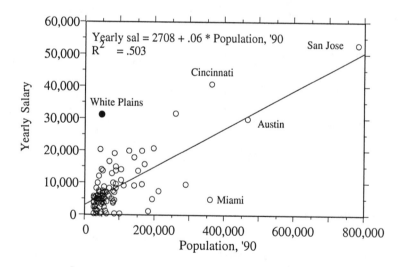

Figure 4 City Population and Yearly Council Salaries

Two other factors would be expected to affect council members' decisions to continue. Regardless of any of these factors, term limits that are found in 12 of these cities could force incumbents out of office. The experience of the city with how long members serve might well set a precedent either encouraging longer service or discouraging it. Similarly, the electorate might treat visible, small size councils differently than large anonymous ones, again depending on the population of the city. Unsatisfactory performance by small, visible councils might be expected to result in more defeats at the polls.

Where responsibility for unfavorable actions is unclear, such as with the checks and balances of the mayor/council form of local government, the public might be unable, even with a small council, to attribute blame for governmental actions. However, when all are council members with identical responsibility, as in the city manager form, blame can be placed on all. Similarly, where elections are staggered, the electorate would have to wait for a second election to "get" all poorly performing representatives. I might hypothesize that staggered elections would affect public involvement in government. Political parties in partisan elections might help focus public sentiments toward the actions taken by the council, even on large councils and in mayor/council cities, and altered the behavior of the electorate.

While there is only faint suggestion that municipal elections in the South differ, the overwhelming importance of the region in explaining state behavior suggests that the norm of elections evident at the state and national levels might also hold at the municipal level. Most state and national offices are of course locally elected.

The following analysis regresses thirteen independent variables on each of the three dependent variables characterizing incumbents in elections in these cities. The first ten derive from my earlier institutional analysis. To these are added three other theoretically justified variables, as discussed above. The independent variables are:

1. The percent of city council selected in district elections
2. The number of members on the city council
3. Whether council terms are staggered
4. The length of the term of office
5. Yearly salary
6. Whether elections are partisan
7. Whether primaries are used
8. The form of government, whether city manager or mayor/council
9. Whether the city has term limits
10. The use of spring elections
11. The average tenure in office of those having completed service
12. The population of the city
13. Whether the city is in the South

## Incumbents Running

Recalling the lack of relationship between cities in which many incumbents ran in the prior and most recent rounds of elections, table 3 presents the results of regression analysis using thirteen independent variables. None proves

*Appendix B*

Table 3 Explaining the Percentage of Incumbents Running in Two Rounds of Elections

|  | Recent | Prior |
|---|---|---|
| Count | 111 | 111 |
| Number Missing | 7 | 7 |
| R Squared | .211 | .298 |
| Adjusted R Squared | .105 | .204 |

| Regression Coefficients | | | | | |
|---|---|---|---|---|---|
| **Recent** | | | **Prior** | | |
| Intercept | 76.4 | † | Intercept | 78.2 | † |
|  | (15.9) |  |  | (13.4) |  |
| Percent District | -.013 |  | Percent District | -.075 |  |
|  | (.064) |  |  | (.054) |  |
| Number on Council | .455 |  | Number on Council | .358 |  |
|  | (.855) |  |  | (.718) |  |
| Staggered Elections | -7.48 |  | Staggered Elections | -.325 |  |
|  | (5.89) |  |  | (4.95) |  |
| Term of Office | -2.92 |  | Term of Office | -7.40 | ** |
|  | (2.85) |  |  | (2.39) |  |
| Yearly Salary | .001 |  | Yearly Salary | .001 |  |
|  | (.000) |  |  | (.000) |  |
| Partisan Elections | -.9.36 |  | Partisan Elections | -.4.62 |  |
|  | (7.41) |  |  | (6.23) |  |
| Primary Elections | 3.02 |  | Primary Elections | .058 |  |
|  | (7.22) |  |  | (6.06) |  |
| Mayor/Council or Manager | 4.36 |  | Mayor/Council or Manager | -1.82 |  |
|  | (5.99) |  |  | (5.03) |  |
| Term Limits | -8.53 |  | Term Limits | -10.7 |  |
|  | (7.61) |  |  | (6.39) |  |
| Spring Elections | -.2.57 |  | Spring Elections | -1.27 |  |
|  | (4.53) |  |  | (3.81) |  |
| Years on Council Completed Terms | .013 |  | Years on Council Completed Terms | 2.77 | *** |
|  | (.943) |  |  | (.792) |  |
| Population, 1990 (1000s) | -.073 |  | Population, 1990 (1000s) | -.033 |  |
|  | (.037) |  |  | (.031) |  |
| South | 2.82 |  | South | -3.39 |  |
|  | (5.41) |  |  | (4.55) |  |

† Regression coefficient (Standard error)

*** $\alpha \leq .001$
** $\alpha \leq .01$
* $\alpha \leq .05$

statistically significant across election rounds. While chapter 3 considers the implications of the lack of relationship between incumbents running across rounds, the relevant finding here is that no institutional difference among the cities contributes to incumbents voluntarily retiring from public office consistently across both rounds of elections. The two that proved statistically significant in the prior round prove unimportant in the most recent round. Institutions have no effect on whether incumbents seek reelection.

## Incumbents Winning

Table 4 shows these independent variables again poorly account for why some city's incumbents win more often. Only cities with traditions of council members serving long tenures prove likely to have high percentages of incumbents winning and then only in the prior round of elections. Notably, institutions little affect whether incumbents run or win.

## Incumbents Returned to Office

Turnover, or viewed from the opposite perspective, how many incumbents return to office, combines the measures of incumbents running and incumbents winning. Given the prior analysis of incumbents running and winning, we might expect that no independent institutional variable would prove important across rounds of elections. This is the case. No institutional variable accounts for the success that incumbents have in these cities over two rounds of elections, perhaps because different cities had successful incumbents in each round.

# Institutional Explanations for Closeness of Elections

In contrast to the success incumbents have, candidates per seat and average winning margin show city elections hold consistent across rounds of elections. The reform movement did little to encourage or discourage interest in running for city council offices. The congressional elections literature, however, would suggest that many will seek an office if it is an "open seat" with the incumbent retiring, thus we might expect open seats, a noninstitutional variable, to shape how many seek office and how narrowly the winner wins. Speculatively, some institutions might encourage or discourage closely contested elections. Since minority controlled district elections are deliberately intended to be uncontested, we might expect institutions to discourage competition. Lacking any extended theory that would include only some institutional variables, all are retained. The mean percentage of incumbents running across the two rounds is also included to assess the impact of open seats. Of course the fewer incumbents running, the more seats are open.

*Appendix B*

Table 4 Regression for Percentage of Incumbents Winning Reelection

|  | Recent | Prior |
|---|---|---|
| Count | 111 | 111 |
| Number Missing | 7 | 7 |
| R Squared | .069 | .255 |
| Adjusted R Squared | - | .155 |

| Regression Coefficients | | | | | |
|---|---|---|---|---|---|
| Recent | | | Prior | | |
| Intercept | 36.6 | † | Intercept | 65.6 | † |
|  | (19.8) | |  | (18.7) | |
| Percent District | .031 | | Percent District | .103 | |
|  | (.080) | |  | (.075) | |
| Number on Council | .786 | | Number on Council | -.477 | |
|  | (1.06) | |  | (1.00) | |
| Staggered Elections | 2.83 | | Staggered Elections | 7.59 | |
|  | (7.32) | |  | (6.90) | |
| Term of Office | 3.75 | | Term of Office | -6.42 | |
|  | (3.54) | |  | (3.34) | |
| Yearly Salary | -.000 | | Yearly Salary | .001 | |
|  | (.001) | |  | (.000) | |
| Partisan Elections | -.1.88 | | Partisan Elections | .808 | |
|  | (9.21) | |  | (8.68) | |
| Primary Elections | .152 | | Primary Elections | -2.12 | |
|  | (8.97) | |  | (8.46) | |
| Mayor/Council or Manager | 5.79 | | Mayor/Council or Manager | -3.49 | |
|  | (7.44) | |  | (7.01) | |
| Term Limits | 6.42 | | Term Limits | -16.1 | |
|  | (9.46) | |  | (8.92) | |
| Spring Elections | -5.12 | | Spring Elections | -.867 | |
|  | (5.63) | |  | (5.31) | |
| Years on Council Completed Terms | .812 | | Years on Council Completed Terms | 4.46 | *** |
|  | (1.17) | |  | (1.11) | |
| Population, 1990 (1000s) | .022 | | Population, 1990 (1000s) | -.029 | |
|  | (.046) | |  | (.044) | |
| South | 11.3 | | South | 2.71 | |
|  | (6.73) | |  | (6.34) | |

† Regression coefficient   *** $\alpha \leq .001$
  (Standard error)   ** $\alpha \leq .01$
   * $\alpha \leq .05$

## Winning Margin of Victory

Table 5 shows that the use of district elections results in larger winning margins or less competitive elections. Each one percent increase in the use of districts results in a .22 increase in winning margin with other factors

Table 5 Regression for Average Winning Margins

| Count | 111 |
|---|---|
| Number Missing | 7 |
| R Squared | .414 |
| Adjusted R Squared | .328 |

| Regression Coefficients | | |
|---|---|---|
| Intercept | -30.0 | † |
| | (17.1) | |
| Percent District | .221 | *** |
| | (.055) | |
| Number on Council | 1.31 | |
| | (.732) | |
| Staggered Elections | 17.1 | ** |
| | (5.062) | |
| Term of Office | .244 | |
| | (2.53) | |
| Yearly Salary | -.000 | |
| | (.000) | |
| Partisan Elections | .006 | |
| | (6.40) | |
| Primary Elections | 7.41 | |
| | (6.17) | |
| Mayor/Council or | 4.72 | |
| Manager | (5.12) | |
| Term Limits | 3.87 | |
| | (6.63) | |
| Spring Elections | -.453 | |
| | (3.88) | |
| Years on Council | .558 | |
| Completed Terms | (.827) | |
| Population, 1990 (1000s) | .002 | |
| | (.033) | |
| South | 13.2 | ** |
| | (4.62) | |
| % Incumbents Running, | .262 | |
| Average | (.135) | |

† Regression coefficient      *** $\alpha \le .001$
(Standard error)      ** $\alpha \le .01$
      * $\alpha \le .05$

controlled. Again somewhat surprisingly, elections for staggered seats differ from those where all seek election at the same time. Those in staggered cities win by wider margins, as do those seeking office in the American South. Given the South's reputation for uncompetitive politics, this may be no surprise. As judged by the percentage of incumbents running for reelection and its strongly positive relationship with winning margins, open seats do make victories narrower. This relationship marginally misses statistical significance with this sample size.

## Candidates Seeking Each Seat

While open seats, measured here as the average percentage of incumbents running across the two rounds of elections, fell just below statistical significance in table 5, not unexpectedly more candidates seek open seats. This is the strongest relationship shown in table 6. Higher salaries for council members also encourage more candidates. Certainly no one would be surprised by these relationships that confirm findings in other arenas. The other strong relationship, however, is surprising. Cities with term limits have fewer candidates seeking office. This is the opposite of the intention of those advocating term limits to keep representatives as less of a class apart from constituents. Two dynamics may explain this relationship. Either prospective candidates are reticent to run for an office that would force them out after the limit, or cities with term limits have an election climate that finds few interested in local politics. Open seats, here assessed as fewer incumbents running, encourage more candidates to run and marginally narrower winning margins.

# A Closer Look at the Role of District
# Rather Than At-Large Elections

Because at-large elections encompass diverse interests across the community, we might expect that divisions based on these interests would be resolved at the ballot box, as candidates championing each view sought election to council office with the intention of passing their preferred policy. The defeat of candidates with opposing views would also be a goal. More homogeneous districts, by contrast, could unify behind a single candidate reflecting their preferences, resulting in little competition. Competition might be more evident in at-large elections. Alternatively, district-based elections may bring out uncompromising candidates driven by personal confidence that their position is just. Others, realizing that such candidates cannot gain the support of other council members, whose votes are needed to pass policy, might seek to deny them public office. District selection might be more competitive.

Thus far, cities using district selection more have shown only increases in winning margins. On this measure, at-large seats prove more competitive. While preceding tables include many controls to deal with difference across cities, the 48 cities that have a mix of district and at-large councils afford an opportunity to assess the impact on elections of the method for selecting council members within the same cities. Table 7 compares the measures of competition between at-large and district seats both for all cities (the top portion of the table) and for cities with both types of council members (the bottom of the table). Among all cities, district-based council members win with a margin of 46.3 percent, but at-large members by a narrower 24.2 percent. Among cities with both at-large and district selected council members, we can see that the disparity

Table 6 Regression for Candidates per Seat

| Count | 111 |
|---|---|
| Number Missing | 7 |
| R Squared | .424 |
| Adjusted R Squared | .340 |

| Regression Coefficients | | |
|---|---|---|
| Intercept | 3.52 | † |
| | (.757) | |
| Percent District | .-.001 | |
| | (.002) | |
| Number on Council | -.037 | |
| | (.032) | |
| Staggered Elections | -.231 | |
| | (.223) | |
| Term of Office | .139 | |
| | (.112) | |
| Yearly Salary | .000 | * |
| | (.000) | |
| Partisan Elections | .088 | |
| | (.283) | |
| Primary Elections | .088 | |
| | (.273) | |
| Mayor/Council or | -.240 | |
| Manager | (.226) | |
| Term Limits | -.696 | * |
| | (.293) | |
| Spring Elections | .078 | |
| | (.171) | |
| Years on Council | -.019 | |
| Completed Terms | (.037) | |
| Population, 1990 (1000s) | .002 | |
| | (.001) | |
| South | .256 | |
| | (.204) | |
| % Incumbents Running, | -.016 | ** |
| Average | (.006) | |

† Regression coefficient    *** $\alpha \leq .001$
  (Standard error)      ** $\alpha \leq .01$
                    * $\alpha \leq .05$

holds. Again at-large members win more narrowly, 25.6 percent versus 44.7 percent. Consistently, within cities with both selection processes, the overall pattern from the random sample cities holds. District selected council members experience less competition as shown by wider winning margins and fewer opponents. Running for reelection and winning show only slight differences, but consistently incumbents from districts run and win more often.

*Appendix B*

Table 7 The Impact of Selection Basis on Elections in Mixed and All Cities

| For All Cities | | | | | | | |
|---|---|---|---|---|---|---|---|
| Incumbents Running | | Incumbents Winning | | Winning Margin | | Candidates/Seat | |
| At-Large | District | At-Large | District | At-Large | District | At-Large | District |
| 69.2 | 70.6 | 76.3 | 80.7 | 24.2 | 46.3 | 2.68 | 2.26 |

| For Cities With Both At-Large and District | | | | | | | |
|---|---|---|---|---|---|---|---|
| Incumbents Running | | Incumbents Winning | | Winning Margin | | Candidates/Seat | |
| At-Large | District | At-Large | District | At-Large | District | At-Large | District |
| 70.2 | 71.0 | 80.1 | 82.1 | 25.6 | 44.7 | 2.60 | 2.19 |

Even within the same cities, at-large incumbents are more likely to run for reelection, but they are less likely to win. At-large contests attract more candidates for each seat up for election, and their margins of victory are narrower. At-large seats would seem more competitive even within the same cities; and as noted in all cities, the use of districts weakens competition, as measured by winning margins. No other impact of selection basis was statistically significant.

In the mixed cities, at-large seats seem viewed as more desirable. In coding these data, I saw many council members who switched to the at-large seats from the district seats. Perhaps the opportunity to claim to represent the entire city, rather than just some of it, attracts candidates or proves invaluable in the debate over policy. Perhaps also the route to higher office leads through at-large council seats.

If this hypothesis were true, we might expect that serving at-large as mayor in a city manager form city would be more attractive than even other at-large seats. But in all cities with the city manager format and electing their mayor at-large, mayors prove less likely than either at-large or district council members to run for reelection (60.2%) and less likely to win (75.6%). The office of mayor in such circumstances does attract more candidates (3.2 candidates per seat), but winning margins are not as narrow as those for all at-large council members (34.2%). As compared to other at-large council members in the city manager format, mayors face more opponents in elections but win by wider margins. They also run less and win less. It is attractive but risky to seek to be the council member designated "mayor" in the city manager form cities.

I have no information on the motives and thoughts of candidates for public office that would give me insight into why at-large seats are sought. *Clearly, however, the main impact of the move to more district-based selection of city council members is to broaden winning margins—to reduce competition.*

Table 8 Regression of Institutional Factors on Turnout

| Count | 114 |
|-------|-----|
| Number Missing | 4 |
| R Squared | .302 |
| Adjusted R Squared | .234 |

| Regression Coefficients | | |
|-------------------------|--------|-----|
| Intercept | 27.1 | † |
| | (7.09) | |
| Percent District | -.061 | * |
| | (.031) | |
| Number on Council | .519 | |
| | (.380) | |
| Staggered Elections | -7.88 | ** |
| | (2.76) | |
| Term of Office | 1.54 | |
| | (1.33) | |
| Yearly Salary | .000 | |
| | (.000) | |
| Partisan Elections | .542 | |
| | (3.43) | |
| Primary Elections | -2.06 | |
| | (3.44) | |
| Mayor/Council or Manager | .932 | |
| | (2.80) | |
| Term Limits | -3.86 | |
| | (3.45) | |
| Spring Elections | -.7.21 | *** |
| | (2.06) | |

† Regression coefficient     $*** \alpha \le .001$
(Standard error)     $** \alpha \le .01$
       $* \alpha \le .05$

# Accounting for Turnout

Generically, three sets of variables might well explain why the electorate in some cities votes more. These are: institutional factors; demographic factors; and the nature of the elections, such as the number of candidates vying for each seat. The institutional factors considered in table 8 are those considered in previous analyses. Most could be conceived as the basis of expecting greater turnout; thus partisan elections with their structuring of the debate might encourage greater turnout; or cities using district elections might be expected to turn out because they have a representative of their local area.

Despite much speculation about what affects turnout, the findings are meager. Both the use of staggered elections and spring elections discourage turnout. Also consistent with the earlier finding of fewer candidates seeking district seats and wider winning margins, district elections attract less voter attention and interest.

### Timing of Municipal Elections

Figure 4 shows that not only do fall elections have higher turnout, the highest turnout is in fall elections in even number years, especially when municipal elections coincide with state and national elections. When the use of municipal elections coincide with state and national elections, which is true of only 8 cities (7%), the adjusted R Square rises to .310 with such cities having nearly 14 percentage points higher turnout.

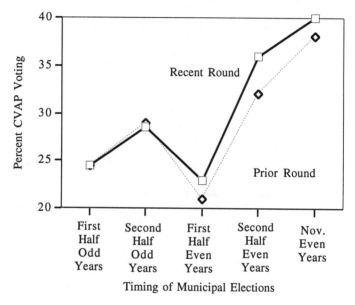

Timing of Municipal Elections

Figure 4 Turnout of Citizens of Voting Age by Timing of
Municipal Elections

## Demographic Explanations for Closeness of Elections

Demographic factors derive mainly from survey research focusing on presidential and congressional contests. Here they are aggregate characteristics of cities rather than individual attributes, meaning that we need to be careful to avoid the ecological fallacy. Turnout might be higher in larger cities by the logic of Karnig and Walter as mentioned in chapter 1, namely that the office in such cities is more important, resulting in greater interest by the electorate. Cities with much population change might find many newcomers unregistered and thus not voting. Alternatively, newcomers may chafe at the traditional politics of their new city and turnout to change things.

Table 9 Regression of Demographic Factors on Turnout

| Count | 115 |
|---|---|
| Number Missing | 3 |
| R Squared | .320 |
| Adjusted R Squared | .254 |

| Regression Coefficients | | |
|---|---|---|
| Intercept | 4.12 | † |
|  | (19.2) | |
| Population of City, 1990 | .000 | |
| (1000s) | (.000) | |
| Population Change, | .009 | |
| 1980-1992 | (.042) | |
| Percent Hispanic | -.063 | |
|  | (.114) | |
| Percent African-American | .007 | |
|  | (.086) | |
| Median Age, 1990 | .497 | |
|  | (.373) | |
| Percent HS or over | -.248 | |
|  | (.207) | |
| Median Family Income, | .281 | * |
| 1989 ($1000s) | (1.36) | |
| South | -10.2 | *** |
|  | (2.66) | |
| Heterogeneity of Age | .333 | |
|  | (.509) | |
| Heterogeneity of Income | .427 | * |
| ($1000s) | (.192) | |

† Regression coefficient     *** $\alpha \le .001$
  (Standard error)            ** $\alpha \le .01$
                              * $\alpha \le .05$

Minorities typically vote less; thus we might expect that cities with high minority populations would vote less. Similarly, youthful voters typically vote less, while those with more education and higher incomes turn out more, either out of civic duty or self-interest. Thus cities with older, more educated, and wealthier populations might vote more. The South has long had low turnouts both in individual reports and in aggregate measures in state and national contests. We might well expect this to also hold for city council contests. Finally, more heterogeneous publics might be expected to vote more to protect their portion of the public from threats of the "others." Obviously, this is entirely an aggregate phenomenon.

Table 9, assessing the role of demography on turnout, shows three

*Appendix B*

statistically significant variables. Southerners vote less in municipal contests, even with income and minority percentages controlled. Additionally, higher median family income as well as economically heterogeneous cities vote more, presumably to protect their personal interests with class-based politics perhaps dividing the candidates.

Notably, two characteristics of cities unexpectedly cause lower turnout in municipal elections, confirming Luttbeg's (1987) earlier Texas local election study. Contrary to the voting literature, better-educated cities vote less, not more, in municipal elections. Hispanic cities also tend to vote less in municipal contests. Neither achieves statistical significance, however. While this study

Table 10 Regression of Election Characteristics on Turnout

| Count | 118 |
|---|---|
| Number Missing | 0 |
| R Squared | .129 |
| Adjusted R Squared | .090 |

| **Regression Coefficients** | | |
|---|---|---|
| Intercept | 19.6 | † |
| | (10.4) | |
| % Incumbent Running | .233 | |
| Average | (.154) | |
| % Incumbent Winning | .007 | |
| Average | (.115) | |
| Winning Margin Average | -.150 | ** |
| | (.052) | |
| Candidates/Seat Average | -1.16 | |
| | (1.08) | |
| % Incumbents Returning | -.059 | |
| Average | (.188) | |
| † Regression coefficient | *** $\alpha \le .001$ | |
| (Standard error) | ** $\alpha \le .01$ | |
| | * $\alpha \le .05$ | |

includes no turnout data on associated school elections, Luttbeg (1987) suggests that both better-educated and Hispanic cities turn out more heavily for school elections. Perhaps those decisions more concern them.

Table 10 considers the impact on turnout of my five captured characteristics of competition in municipal elections. Only average Winning Margin proves statistically significant. Closely contested elections probably encourage both turnout and narrower winning margins. Notably, open seats discourage turnout, although this is not statistically significant. The sign is positive indicating that as more incumbents run for reelection, turnout increases rather than decreases as the congressional literature might cause us to expect. Also the sign on candidates per seat is opposite of what we might expect. When more candidates are on the ballot, turnout is lower. *At least in municipal elections, voter turnout poorly relates to characteristics of competition for elective offices.*

Finally, table 11 considers selected variables from all classes of variables expected to influence turnout. Additionally, two variables, whether the municipal elections are in the spring as opposed to in the fall and whether the municipal election coincides with state and national elections, have been added. Both variables proved important in accounting for why turnout was lower in some cities. Again only eight cities use municipal elections that coincide with other elections, but they prove unusually high in turnout.

The lower turnout of the South and the higher turnout of wealthier cities are not unexpected. Surprisingly with the other factors controlled, cities with staggered elections have lower turnout. Certainly, it is understandable that an electorate would be put off by seeing only half or a third of all representatives on the ballot. It is also possible that local media discount such elections, as the entire council cannot be evaluated. All of this awaits further research to provide solid answers. Introducing the percentage of seats selected by districts does not affect the impact of staggered elections, thus the mere separation of the council into overlapping terms, meaning that the electorate must partially deal with their representatives in each election, discourages turnout.

Finally, election timing proves important, as *spring elections discourage turnout.* However, since November of even number year elections sharply increase turnout and leave spring elections still important, I can only say there must be distractions during the spring that keeps people from voting. Finally, the relationship with the South declines but remains statistically significant with the introduction of the spring election variable. Spring elections are common in but not exclusive to the South.

## Some Additional Considerations

Bledsoe (1993) stresses the importance of leadership in community governance. While he does not argue that mere tenure in office improves leadership, he clearly sees short tenure as discouraging leadership. Good leaders have to have time to learn the craft. Several factors contribute to longer tenure in his estimation. These include higher salaries, partisan elections, and at-large elections.[7] Table 12 assesses the importance of these variables in the sample cities with the additional controls for winning margin and percentage of incumbents returned to office.

Only partisan elections much affect tenure in office, as assessed by those having completed their term; and it fails to achieve statistical significance. Cities that retain incumbents for long tenures are also those returning incumbents to office at high rates. Perhaps they are satisfied with the jobs being done by incumbents. An alternative explanation that such tenure comes from no competition seems unwarranted because winning margins poorly relates to tenure in office. My explanation of Bledsoe's analysis thus far is limited to suggesting that some cities are patient with their council members, allowing them to become leaders. However, higher salaries and the use of districts for council selection fail to improve tenure in office.

*Appendix B*

Table 11 Regression of Selected Variables and Voter Turnout

| Count | 115 |
|---|---|
| Number Missing | 3 |
| R Squared | .489 |
| Adjusted R Squared | .451 |

**Regression Coefficients**

| | | |
|---|---|---|
| Intercept | 22.0 | † |
| | (4.74) | |
| Winning Margin Average | -.076 | |
| | (.045) | |
| Median Family Income, | .194 | * |
| 1989 ($1000s) | (.079) | |
| South | -.5.39 | * |
| | (2.11) | |
| Heterogeneity of Income | .302 | * |
| ($1000s) | (.147) | |
| Percent Districts | .012 | |
| | (.026) | |
| Staggered Elections | -9.20 | *** |
| | (2.00) | |
| Spring Elections | -4.29 | * |
| | (1.81) | |
| Election Date Same as | 12.0 | *** |
| State and Federal | (3.50) | |

† Regression coefficient     *** α ≤ .001
  (Standard error)        ** α ≤ .01
                             * α ≤ .05

# Conclusion

Since the presumed success of the "reform" movement, Americans optimistically change institutions to deal with social problems. Presently, the courts, in particular the federal courts, optimistically order changes to improve minority representation that entails abandoning at-large elections and gerrymandering single member districts to assure minority success in winning those districts. Sample cities prove to have varied experience in their elections. Only some institutions shape winning margins and turnout, and often the impact is not as intended. Shorter terms, for example, encourage incumbents to seek reelection. Moreover, the institutions that shape elections are mainly those considered to have no impact.

Table 12 Accounting for Tenure in Office

| Count | 116 |
|---|---|
| Number Missing | 2 |
| R Squared | .159 |
| Adjusted R Squared | .121 |

### Regression Coefficients

| | | |
|---|---|---|
| Intercept | 4.51 | † |
| | (.699) | |
| Yearly Salary | .000 | |
| | (.000) | |
| Partisan Elections | 1.21 | |
| | (.646) | |
| Percent District | -.005 | |
| | (.006) | |
| % Incumbent Running | .047 | *** |
| Average | (.012) | |
| Winning Margin Average | .003 | |
| | (.012) | |

† Regression coefficient      *** $\alpha \le .001$
 (Standard error)             ** $\alpha \le .01$
                               * $\alpha \le .05$

Table 13 shows the simple relationships shown in the more thorough analysis with controls. District rather than at-large elections widen winning margins (51.2% versus 23.5%), not only in minority districts. With term limits, fewer incumbents run (55.6% versus 70.9%) and fewer candidates seek each seat on the council. All other institutional factors that impact on elections are unanticipated. Cities with longer terms of office have fewer incumbents running and more turnover, and city manager form cities have less turnover on their councils. The use of overlapping or staggered terms unanticipatedly widens winning margins (a very slight pattern in table 13) and lowers turnout (22.8% versus 31.7%). The most surprising institutional impact is the substantially lower turnouts shown in cities with spring rather than fall elections (20.8% versus 30.1%). While much higher turnouts when municipal elections coincide with state and national elections seem entirely plausible, spring elections continue to discourage turnout, even with this controlled.

*Appendix B*

## Table 13 Bivariate Summary of Findings

| Winning Margin Average | District or At-Large Selection | |
|---|---|---|
| | 100 Percent Districts | 100 Percent At-Large |
| All Cities | | |
| 118 | 14 | 56 |
| 32.4% | 51.2% | 23.5% |

| Incumbents Running | Term Limits | |
|---|---|---|
| | With Term Limits | Without Term Limits |
| All Cities | | |
| 118 | 12 | 106 |
| 69.4% | 55.6% | 70.9% |

| Incumbents Running | Term of Office | |
|---|---|---|
| | 2 or 3 Year Term | 4 Year Term |
| All Cities | | |
| 118 | 39 | 78 |
| 69.4% | 74.1% | 66.6% |

| Average Turnover 1983-92 | Format of Government | |
|---|---|---|
| All Cities | Mayor/Council | City Manager |
| 118 | 66 | 49 |
| 14.1% | 15.6% | 12.4% |

| Winning Margin Average | Staggered Elections | |
|---|---|---|
| All Cities | No | Yes |
| 118 | 34 | 84 |
| 32.4% | 32.1% | 32.6% |

| Turnout | Staggered Elections | |
|---|---|---|
| All Cities | No | Yes |
| 118 | 34 | 84 |
| 25.4% | 31.7% | 22.8% |

| Turnout | Election Timing | |
|---|---|---|
| All Cities | Spring | Fall |
| 118 | 60 | 58 |
| 25.4% | 20.8% | 30.1% |

# Notes

1. U.S. Department of Commerce, *Statistical Abstract of the United States 1993* (Washington: U.S. Government Printing Office, 1994), 291; and Heywood T. Sanders, "The Government of American Cities: Continuity and Change in Structure," *The Municipal Year Book 1982* (Washington: International City Management Association, 1982), 182.

2. Sanders, 183. Averaged by author.

3. One Washington city voted to move, presumably not under court order, to district elections, but in the first election under the new plan, police had to be called to remove voters who insisted that they had the right to vote for their representatives. Voters voted to return to at-large elections before the next councilmanic election.

4. Albert K. Karnig and B. Oliver Walter, "Municipal Elections: Registration, Incumbent Success, and Voter Participation," *Municipal Year Book 1977* (Washington: International City Management Association, 1978), 66.

5. Robert L. Lineberry and Edmund P. Fowler, "Reformism and Public Policies in American Cities," *American Political Science Review* (September 1967): 701-716.

6. Number on Council = 7.759 + 1.317E-6 * Population, '90 $R^2$= 1.364E-3. An increase of 100,000 in population even were the relationship strong would add 1.3 seats.

7. Timothy Bledsoe, *Careers in City Politics: The Case for Urban Democracy* (Pittsburgh: University of Pittsburgh Press, 1993), 67-70, 92, and 120.

# Appendix C

# Questionnaire on Episodes of Competition

City _____     Who Asked? _____

## Questionnaire on Episodes of Competition

I have been studying municipal elections in 120 randomly chosen American cities and have discovered several instances or episodes where all or most incumbents seeking reelection lost. I have received a small grant from Texas A&M University to inquire about what happened in these instances. I hope I can get your help in completing this questionnaire, as one of these instances happened in your city. I have presented three ways in which you might respond. First, I have asked what happened; second, I have inquired about what was involved; and third, I have presented several scenarios, asking you to select that closest to what you think happened. Since I am in your debt to become informed, please answer however you wish. Finally, what impact did this election have? Thanks.

In the election of 1991:
    John Doe defeated the incumbent, Mary Alice, getting 70 percent of the vote.
    Richard Allen defeated the incumbent, Joe Smith, getting 55 percent of the vote.
    Bob Green defeated the incumbent, Ho Who, getting 60 percent of the vote.

1.  What factors do you think explain what happened in the election?

    _____
    _____
    _____
    _____
    _____
    _____
    _____
    _____
    _____
    _____

_____
_____

2.  In some instances, all incumbents up for election were involved in some
    questionable actions. Was that true? _____
    _____
    _____
    _____
    _____
    _____
    _____

In some instances, changes in the format of elections, such as going to
districts, may account for what happens. Is that true here? _____
_____
_____
_____
_____
_____
_____

In some instances, all happened to have been long time members of the
council, and challengers convinced voters that it was "time for a change."
Is that true here? _____
_____
_____
_____
_____
_____
_____

In some instances, a vote by the council upset a vocal minority in the city,
with that minority then successfully challenging the incumbents. Did that
happen here? _____
_____
_____
_____
_____
_____
_____

In some instances, a vote by the council upset voters so that they decided to
"throw the rascals out." Did that happen here? _____
_____
_____
_____

3.  Please check the scenario that best applies
    ___ 1.  Three council members benefited from the city council's decision to not increase city employees retirement package. These council members hired many city employees and resented the expense of buying out their retirement. When they came up for reelection, challengers pointed out this impropriety and found the voters to be receptive.
    ___ 2.  When the city moved to district rather than at-large seats, minority groups used this change to support minority candidates who defeated the incumbents.
    ___ 3.  Three council members were first elected in 1982. They had served well but were growing stale and disinterested. Young challengers charged that the incumbents were out of touch and won.
    ___ 4.  Given a change in public interest what was happening locally, the long serving incumbents faced many "single issue" challengers and lost.
    ___ 5.  Several eager for higher office candidates decided that a good starting point was to run for the city council. They surprised the incumbents.
    ___ 6.  The incumbents irritated a major employer who sought challengers who were more responsive to the city's need to economically develop. These challengers enjoyed the financial support of this employer and won.
    ___ 7.  Those opposed to the incumbent council members strong support for attracting more business to the community because it made the city less pleasant to live in and threatened the environment, voted for environmentally concerned challengers who won.
    ___ 8.  The city manager decided that sewer development needs on the westside of the city were most pressing. When the incumbents up for reelection supported that decision, the voters in other sections expressed their dissatisfaction with both the manager and council by electing the challengers.

4.  What impact did this election have in your city? _____

# References

Abney, Glenn F., and John D. Hutcheson, Jr. 1981. "Race, Representation, and Trust: Changes in Attitudes After the Election of a Black Mayor." *Public Opinion Quarterly* 45 (spring): 91-101.

Adrian, Charles R. 1988. "Forms of City Government in American History." *Municipal Year Book 1988.* Washington: International City Management Association, 3-12.

Adrian, Charles R., and Oliver Williams. 1959. "The Insulation of Local Politics Under the Nonpartisan Ballot." *American Political Science Review* (December): 1052-63.

Advisory Commission on Intergovernmental Relation. 1981. *Measuring Local Government Discretionary Authority.* Washington: U.S. Government Printing Office.

Agger, Robert E., Daniel Goldrich, and Bert E. Swanson. 1964. *The Rulers and the Ruled: Political Power and Impotence in American Communities.* New York: Wiley.

Alozie, Nicholas O., and Lynne I. Manganaro. 1993. "Women's Council Representation: Measurement Implications for Public Policy." *Political Research Quarterly* (June): 383-98.

Bahl, R. W. 1969. *Metropolitan City Expenditures: A Comparative Analysis.* Lexington: University of Kentucky Press.

Banfield, Edward C. 1961. *Political Influence.* New York: The Free Press of Glencoe.

Barber, James David. 1965. *The Lawmakers: Recruitment and Adaptation to Legislative Life.* New Haven: Yale University Press.

Berry, Jeffrey M., Kent E. Portney, and Ken Thomson. 1993. *The Rebirth of Urban Democracy.* Washington: Brookings.

Bledsoe, Timothy. 1993. *Careers in City Politics: The Case for Urban Democracy.* Pittsburgh: University of Pittsburgh Press.

Bledsoe, Timothy, and Susan Welch. 1987. "Patterns of Political Party Activity Among U.S. Cities." *Urban Affairs Quarterly* (December): 249-69

Bobo, Lawrence, and Franklin D. Gilliam, Jr. 1990. "Race, Sociopolitical Participation, and Black Empowerment." *American Political Science Review* 84 (June): 377-93.

Browning, Rufus P., Dale Rogers Marshall, and David H. Tabb. 1984. *Protest Is Not Enough.* Berkeley: University of California Press.

———. eds. 1990. *Racial Politics in American Cities.* New York: Longman.

Bullock, Charles S., and Susan MacManus. 1987. "The Impact of Staggered Terms on Minority Representation." *Journal of Politics* (May): 543-52.

———.1990. "Structural Features of Municipalities and the Incidence of Hispanic Councilmembers." *Social Science Quarterly* (fall): 75-89.

Bureau of Census. 1995. *City/County Data Book, 1994.* Washington: U.S. Government Printing Office.

Cameron, David R. 1978. "The Expansion of the Public Economy: A Comparative Analysis." *American Political Science Review* (December): 1243-61.

Campbell, Donald, and Joe Feagin. 1975. "Black Politics in the South: A Descriptive Analysis." *Journal of Politics* (February): 12-59

Cassel, Carol. 1985. "Social Background Characteristics of Nonpartisan City Council Members: A Research Note." *Western Political Quarterly* (September): 495-501.

Christensen, Terry. 1995. *Local Politics: Governing at the Grassroots.* Belmont, Calif.:Wadsworth.

Clark, Terry N., ed. 1968. *Community Structure and Decision-Making: Comparative Analyses.* San Francisco: Chandler.

———. 1974. *Comparative Community Politics.* New York: Wiley.

Clark, Terry N., and Lorna C. Ferguson. 1983. *City Money.* New York: Columbia University Press.

Cole, Leonard. 1976. *Blacks in Power.* Princeton: Princeton University Press.

Cole, Richard. 1975. "Citizen Participation in Municipal Politics." *American Journal of Political Science* (November): 761-82.

Cottrell, Charles, and Arnold Fleischman. 1979. "The Change from At-Large to District Representation and Political Participation of Minority Groups in Fort Worth and San Antonio, Texas." *Urban Affairs Quarterly* 10 (September): 17-39.

Cox, Gary W., and Samuel Kernell. 1991. *The Politics of Divided Government.* Boulder, Colo.: Westview.

Dahl, Robert A. 1961. *Who Governs?* New Haven, Conn.: Yale University Press.

Darcy, Robert, Susan Welch, and Janet Clark. 1987. *Women, Elections, and Representation.* New York: Longman.

Davidson, Chandler, and George Korbel. 1981. "At Large Elections and Minority Group Representation: A Re-Examination of Historical and Contemporary Evidence." *Journal of Politics* 43 (November): 982-1005.

Dawson, Richard E., and James A. Robinson. 1963. "Inter-Party Competition, Economic Variables, and Welfare Policies in the American States." *Journal of Politics* (May): 265-89.

Downs, Anthony. 1957. *An Economic Theory of Democracy.* New York: Harper & Row.

Dye, Thomas R. 1980. "Taxing, Spending and Economic Growth in the American States." *Journal of Politics* 42 (winter): 1085–1107.

———.1966. *Politics, Economics, and the Public: Policy Outcomes in the American States.* Chicago: Rand McNally.

———.1965. "State Legislative Politics." In *Politics in the American States: A Comparative Analysis,* Herbert Jacob and Kenneth N. Vines, eds. Boston: Little, Brown, 151-206

Eldersveld, Samuel. 1964. *Political Parties: A Behavioral Analysis.* Chicago: Rand McNally.

———.1982. *Political Parties in American Society.* New York: Basic Books.

Engstrom, Richard, and Michael McDonald. 1981. "The Election of Women to City Councils: Clarifying the Impact of Electoral Arrangements on the Seats/Population Relationship." *American Political Science Review* (February): 344-54

——.1982. "The Underrepresentation of Blacks on City Councils." *Journal of Politics* 44 (November): 1088-1105.

——.1986. "The Effect of At-Large Versus District Elections on Racial Representation in U.S. Municipalities." In *Electoral Laws and their Political Consequences,* Bernard Grofman and Arend Lijphart, eds. New York: Agathon Press.

Erikson, Robert S., Norman R. Luttbeg, and Kent L. Tedin. 1980. *American Public Opinion: Its Origins, Content, and Impact.* 2nd ed. New York: Wiley.

Eulau, Heinz, and Kenneth Prewitt. 1973. *Labyrinths of Democracy.* Indianapolis: Bobbs-Merrill.

Ferman, Barbara. 1985. *Governing the Ungovernable City: Political Skill, Leadership, and the Modern Mayor.* Philadelphia: Temple University Press.

Fiorina, Morris P. 1992. *Divided Government.* New York: MacMillan.

Gelb, Joyce. 1970. "Blacks, Blocs and Ballots." *Polity* 3 (fall): 45-69.

Gottdiener, Mark. 1987. *The Decline of Urban Politics.* Newbury Park, Calif.: Sage Publications.

Hall, Grace, and Alan Saltzstein. 1975. "Equal Employment in Urban Governments: The Potential Problem of Interminority Competition." *Public Personnel Management* (November/December): 386-93

Hawley, Willis D., and Frederick M. Wirt, eds. 1968. *The Search for Community Power.* Englewood Cliffs, N.J.: Prentice-Hall.

——.1973. *Nonpartisn Elections and the Case for Party Politics.* New York: Wiley.

Heilig, Peggy, and Robert Mundt. 1984. *Your Voice at City Hall.* Albany, N.Y.: State University of New York Press.

Hofferbert, Richard I. 1966. "The Relation Between Public Policy and Some Structural and Environmental Variables in the American States." *American Political Science Review* (March): 73-82.

Howell, Susan E., and Deborah Fagen. 1988. "Race and Trust in Government: Testing the Political Reality Model." *Public Opinion Quarterly* 52 (fall): 343-50

Hunter, Floyd. 1953. *Community Power Structure.* Chapel Hill: The University of North Carolina Press.

International City/County Management Association. 1993. *The Municipal Year Book.* Washington: International City/County Management Association, 15-16.

Jacobson, Gary C. 1983. *Strategy and Choice in Congressional Elections.* 2nd ed. New Haven, Conn.: Yale University Press.

Joint Center for Political Studies. 1983-1993. *National Rosters of Black Elected Officials.* Washington: Joint Center for Political Studies.

Jones, Clinton. 1976. "The Impact of Local Election Systems on Black Political Representation." *Urban Affairs Quarterly* 11 (March): 345-54.

Kantor, Paul, and Stephen David. 1988. *The Dependent City*. Glenview, Ill.: Scott, Foresman.

Karnig, Albert K. 1976. "Black Representation City Councils: The Impact of District Elections and Socioeconomic Factors." *Urban Affairs Quarterly* 12 (December): 223-42.

Karnig, Albert K., and B. Oliver Walter. 1976. "Election of Women to City Councils." *Social Science Quarterly* (March): 605-13.

———.1978. "Municipal Elections: Registration, Incumbent Success, and Voter Participation." *Municipal Year Book 1977*. Washington: International City Management Association.

Karnig, Albert K., and Susan Welch. 1979. "Sex and Ethnic Differences in Municipal Representation." *Social Science Quarterly* (December): 465-81.

———.1981. *Black Representation and Urban Policy*. Chicago: University of Chicago Press.

———.1982. "Electoral Structure and Black Representation on City Councils." *Social Science Quarterly* (March): 99-114.

Kerr, Brinck, and Kenneth R. Mladenka. 1994. "Does Politics Matter? A Time-Series Analysis of Minority Employment Patterns." *American Journal of Political Science* (November): 918-43.

Key, V. O., Jr. 1949. *Southern Politics*. New York: Knopf.

———.1956. *American State Politics: An Introduction*. New York: Knopf.

King, Gary, and Andrew Gelman. 1991. "Systemic Consequences of Incumbency Advantages in U.S. House Elections." *American Journal of Political Science* 35 (February): 110-38.

Kramer, J. 1971. "The Election of Blacks to City Councils: A 1970 Status Report and Prolegomenon." *Journal of Black Studies* (June): 443-76

Lee, Eugene C. 1960. *The Politics of Nonpartisanship*. Berkeley: University of California Press.

———.1963. "City Elections: A Statistical Profile." In *The Municipal Year Book 1963*. Chicago: International City Managers' Association, 74-84.

Liebert, Roland J. 1974. "Municipal Functions, Structure, and Expenditures." *Social Science Quarterly* (March): 765-83.

Lineberry, Robert L., and Edmund P. Fowler. 1967. "Reformism and Public Policies in American Cities." *American Political Science Review* (September): 701-16.

Lowery, David, and William D. Berry. 1983. "The Growth of Government in the United States: An Empirical Assessment of Competing Explanations." *American Journal of Political Science* (November): 665-94.

Luttbeg, Norman R. 1987. "Multiple Indicators of the Electoral Context of Democratic-Responsiveness in Local Government." A paper presented at the annual meetings of the Midwest Political Science Association, Chicago.

Luttbeg, Norman R. 1988. "The Role of Newspapers in Local Election Coverage and in Political Advertising." *Journalism Quarterly* (Winter).

——.1992. *Comparing the States and Communities: Politics, Government, and Policy in the United States.* New York: HarperCollins.

——.1995. "District Versus At-Large City Council Seats: Not Again; But Wait, What About Competition?" A paper presented at the annual meetings of the Midwest Political Science Association, Chicago.

——.1998. *Comparing the States and Communities: Politics, Government, and Policy in the United States.* 3rd ed. Dubuque, Iowa: Eddie Bowers.

MacManus, Susan. 1978. "City Council Election Procedures and Minority Representation." *Social Science Quarterly* 59 (June): 153-61.

——.1979. "At Large Elections and Minority Representation: An Adversarial Critique." *Social Science Quarterly* 60 (November): 338-40.

Massialas, Byron G. 1969. *Education and the Political System.* Reading, Mass.: Addison-Wesley.

Mayhew, David R. 1986. *Placing Parties in American Politics.* Princeton, N.J.: Princeton University Press.

Molotch, Harvey. 1976. "The City as a Growth Machine." *American Journal of Sociology* (November): 309-31.

Morgan, David, and John Pelissero. 1980. "Urban Policy: Does Political Structure Matter?" *American Political Science Review* 74 (December): 999-1006.

Morlan, Robert L. 1984. "Municipal vs. National Election Voter Turnout: Europe and the United States." *Political Science Quarterly* (fall): 457-70.

National League of Cities. 1983-1992. *Directory of City Policy Officials.* Washington: National League of Cities.

Peterson, Paul E. 1981. *City Limits.* Chicago: University of Chicago Press.

Polinard, Jerry, Robert Wrinkle, and Tomas Longoria, Jr. 1991. "The Impact of District Elections on the Mexican-American Community: The Electoral Perspective." *Social Science Quarterly* (September): 608-14.

Presthus, Robert. 1964. *Men At the Top.* New York: Oxford University Press.

Prewitt, Kenneth. 1970. *The Recruitment of Political Leaders: A Study of Citizen-Politicians.* Indianapolis: Bobbs-Merrill.

Prewitt, Kenneth, and Heinz Eulau. 1969. "Political Matrix and Political Representation: Prolegomenon to a New Departure from an Old Problem." *American Political Science Review* (November): 427-43.

Ranney, Austin. 1965. "Parties in State Politics." In *Politics in the American States: A Comparative Analysis,* Herbert Jacob and Kenneth N. Vines, eds. Boston: Little, Brown, 61-99.

Robinson, Theodore, and Thomas Dye. 1978. "Reformism and Representation on City Councils." *Social Science Quarterly* 59 (June): 133-41.

Rogers, Chester, and Harold Arman. 1971. "Nonpartisanship and Election to City Office." *Social Science Quarterly* (March): 941-45.

Rush, David. 1993. *Cities Without Suburbs.* Washington: Woodrow Wilson

Center Press.

Sanders, Heywood T. 1982. "The Government of American Cities: Continuity and Change in Structure." In *The Municipal Yearbook 1982*. Washington: International City Management Association.

Schlesinger, Joseph A. 1966. "A Two-Dimensional Scheme for Classifying the States According to Degree of Inter-Party Competition." *American Political Science Review* (November): 1120-28.

————.1966. *Ambition and Politics*. Chicago: Rand McNally.

Schneider, Mark. 1989. *The Competitive City: The Political Economy of Suburbia*. Pittsburgh: University of Pittsburgh Press.

Shaffer, Stephen D., and George A. Chressanthis. 1991. "Accountability and U.S. Senate Elections." *Western Politics Quarterly* 44 (September): 625-39

Sharkansky, Ira, and Richard I. Hofferbert. 1971. "Dimensions of State Policy." In *Politics in the American States,* 2nd ed., Herbert Jacob and Kenneth N. Vines, eds. Boston: Little, Brown, 315-53.

Shefter, Martin. 1989. *Political Crisis / Fiscal Crisis: The Collapse and Revival of New York City*. New York: Basic Books.

Sigelman, Lee. 1976. "The Curious Case of Women in State and Local Government." *Social Science Quarterly* (June): 34-47.

Stone, Clarence. 1989. *Regime Politics: Governing Atlanta 1946-1988*. Lawrence, Ks.: University Press of Kansas.

————.1990. "The Politics of Urban Restructuring: A Review Essay." *Western Political Quarterly* (March): 219-31.

Svara, James H. 1977. "Unwrapping Institutional Packages in Municipal Government." *Journal of Politics* 39 (January): 166-75.

————.1990. *Official Leadership in the City: Patterns of Conflict and Cooperation*. New York: Oxford University Press.

————.1991. *A Survey of America's City Councils: Continuity and Change*. Washington: National League of Cities.

Taebel, Delbert. 1978. "Minority Representation on City Councils: The Impact of Structure on Blacks and Hispanics." *Social Science Quarterly* 12 (June): 142-52.

Tiebout, Charles. 1956. "A Pure Theory of Local Expenditures." *Journal of Political Economy* (December): 416-24.

Tucker, Harvey J. 1982. "It's About Time: The Use of Time in Cross-Sectional State Policy Research." *American Journal of Political Science* (February): 176-196.

Tucker, Harvey J., and Ronald E. Weber. 1992. "Electoral Change in U.S. States: System Versus Constituency Competition." In *State Legislative Careers,* Gary Moncrief and Joel Thompson, eds. Ann Arbor: University of Michigan Press.

Tucker, Harvey J., and L. Harmon Zeigler. 1980. *Professionals Versus the Public: Attitudes, Communication, and Response in School Districts*. New York: Longman.

Vidich, Arthur J., and Joseph Bensman. 1960. *Small Town in Mass Society*. Garden City, N.J.: Anchor Books.

Weicher, J. C. 1970. "Determinants of Central City Expenditures: Some Over-Looked Factors and Problems." *National Tax Journal* : 379-96.

Welch, Susan. 1990. "The Impact of At-Large Elections on the Representation of Blacks and Hispanics." *Journal of Politics* 52 (November), 1050-76.

Welch, Susan, and Timothy Bledsoe. 1988. *Urban Reform and its Consequences: A Study in Representation.* Chicago: University of Chicago Press.

Welch, Susan, and Albert Karnig. 1979. "Correlates of Female Office Holding in City Politics." *Journal of Politics* (May): 478-91.

Williams, Oliver P., Harold Herman, Charles S. Liebman, and Thomas R. Dye. 1965. *Suburban Differences and Metropolitan Policies: A Philadelphia Story.* Philadelphia: University of Pennsylvania Press.

Wirt, Frederick M. 1974. *Power in the City.* Berkeley: University of California Press.

Yates, Douglas. 1977. *The Ungovernable City.* Cambridge, Mass.: MIT Press.

# Index

# About the Author

Norman Luttbeg received his Ph.D. from Michigan State University. He has authored and co-authored many works, including *Public Opinion and Public Policy: Models of Political Linkage*; *American Public Opinion: Its Origins, Content and Impact*; *Trends in American Electoral Behavior*; and *American Electoral Behavior: 1952-1992*. All unfortunately depend on public surveys by the National Election Studies. Professor Luttbeg's more recent research centers on representation questions using actual votes and actions with states and cities as the units of analysis. He would hope to see a better functioning democracy for his four grandchildren.

Norman Luttbeg is currently professor of political science at Texas A&M University, having previously taught at SUNY-Stony Brook, Florida State University, Temple University, and Southern Illinois University.